THE KOP

Also by Stephen F Kelly in Virgin Books
SHANKLY: IT'S MORE IMPORTANT THAN THAT
GÉRARD HOULLIER: THE BIOGRAPHY

THE KOP

Liverpool's Twelfth Man

Stephen F Kelly

This edition published in 2008 in Great Britain by
Virgin Books Ltd
Thames Wharf Studios
Rainville Road
London
W6 9HA

First published in Great Britain in 1993 by Mandarin Paperbacks

A catalogue record for this book is available from the British Library.

ISBN 978-07535-1808-3

The paper used in this book is a natural, recyclable product made from
wood grown in sustainable forests. The manufacturing process conforms
to the regulations of the country of origin.

Typeset by TW Typesetting, Plymouth, Devon
Printed and bound in Great Britain by CPI Bookmarque, Croydon

CONTENTS

This book is dedicated to Scallies,
Scouser Tommies and Kopites
wherever they may be.

ACKNOWLEDGEMENTS

Since this book was first published in 1993, shortly before the Old Kop was pulled down, a number of those people I interviewed and included in the original edition have died. After careful consideration, I have decided to leave their interviews as they were and have also left their description as it was in the original publication. I trust that their families and friends will understand.

Although some of the comments and observations about the Old Kop are now outdated, they nonetheless provide a picture of what it was like to be a fan standing on the Kop prior to its being seated.

For this new edition, which includes an updating chapter taking account of the New Kop, a number of others now need to also be acknowledged for the part they have played in the updating of this book. First, may I thank all the new interviewees. These include Alex Finlason, Joe Murray, John Williams, Harry Leather, Wayne Gordon, Andrew Cashin, Roger Webster, Steve Morgan, Gill Holroyd, Graham Shaw, Harry Leather, William Mcintyre, Gareth Roberts, John Doyle and Dave Woods.

I would also like to thank various Liverpool fan websites, especially Koptalk and You'll Never Walk Alone, as well as Neil Toothill of architects Atherden Fuller Leng for providing detailed information on the design and construction of the new Kop. Eddie Barford and Tony Hall of the *Liverpool Daily Post and Echo* were helpful in the supply of photographs, as was Steve Hale.

My thanks must also go to my agent John Pawsey and to my editor Stuart Evers of Virgin Books, himself a Liverpool fan who has stood and sat on the Kop. My love and gratitude, as ever, goes to my family, Judith, Nicholas and Emma – all of whom can count themselves as genuine Kopites – for their continued support over the years.

During the course of writing this book I have interviewed more than a hundred people, most of them ordinary Kopites. I can honestly say that interviewing every one of them was a delight. I spent many enjoyable hours over pints of beer or cups of tea just nattering about the Kop and the fortunes of Liverpool Football Club. Each was a credit to the club and to the city of Liverpool. So, my first vote of thanks must go to all those who so willingly made time available to talk with me. Most, though not all, have made it into the pages of this book. In one or two instances I have changed the name of the person to protect their identity.

In alphabetical order they are: John Aldridge, Jeff Anderson, Steve Anderson, Phil Aspinall, Bob Azurdia, Geoffrey Banfield, Michael Banfield, Robert Banfield, Gordon Banks, Eric Barnsley, Brian Bird, Billy Butler, Steve Cain, James Catling, John Chadwick, Dave Clay, Ray Clemence, George Courtney, John Cull, Eric Doig, Stanley Doig, Wendy Doig, George Edwards, Leslie Edwards, David Fairclough, John Frank, Jim Gardiner, Harry Gough, Mick Graham Bob Greaves, Jim Hartley, Jim Hesketh, Emlyn Hughes, John Jeffrey, Pat Jennings, Judith Jones, Tony Jones, Paul Kelly, Alan Kennedy, John Kennedy, Andrei Kissilev, Brian Labone, Denis Law, Mark Lawrenson, Harry Leather, Bob Lyons, Eileen McAuley, Duncan McKenzie, Tommy McKinlay, Yvonne McLeod, John Mapson, Gerry Marsden, Joe Martin, Neil Midgeley, Charlie Mitten, Denis Mooney, Sydney Moss, who sadly died shortly after our interview, Rob Noble, Billy O'Donnell, Hugh O'Neill, Ron Pawsey, Jack Payne, Richard Pedder, Keith Richards, Ted Robbins, Sandy Ross, Ian St John, Jeff Scott, Ian Sergeant, Steve Shakeshaft, George Shannon, Sheila Spears, Ray Spiller, John Stile, Albert Stubbins, Bernard Swift, Rogan Taylor,

Andrew Thomas, Ian Thomson, Phil Thompson, Louise Tovey, Bob Tweedale, The Rev Jackie Waterman, Barry Wilford, John Williams, Billy Wilson, Harry Wilson, Linda Winrow, Lennie Woods.

There are also a number of organisations and other individuals to whom I owe a special gratitude. They are Irene Anderson for hoarding copies of her son's *Kop* magazine for 25 years, knowing that one day they would come in useful, Phil Aspinall for collecting many of his songs together, John Doig for his hospitality, Bill Gilson of the architects Atherden Fuller, the editors and publishers of *Kop* magazine wherever they may be, the very efficient and friendly staff of the microfilm department of Liverpool Central Library, the Liverpool City Council surveyors department and in particular Norman Whibbley, the *Liverpool Daily Post and Echo*, especially Steve Shakeshaft, Liverpool Football Club, the Liverpool Supporters Club, and in particular Ted Morris and Richard Pedder, who steered me in the direction of many elderly supporters, the Manchester Central Library, Roger Hughes of Radio Merseyside, the Merseyside Police Force and especially Inspector Bernard Swift for allowing me to spend a Saturday watching a game from the police control room, the St John Ambulance Brigade and Hugh O'Neill, the fanzine *Through The Wind And Rain*, Ivor Rolands for his song collection and the Association of Football Statisticians.

I must also acknowledge the generosity of a number of publishers in allowing me to include extracts from the following in order to supplement the oral history: from *The Liverpool Football Book* (Stanley Paul, 1970) on pages 62, 69 and 75, by respectively Stan Kelly, Derek Hodgson and Bob Paisley; from *Shankly* (Arthur Barker, 1976) on pages 71 and 149; from *Kevin Keegan* (Arthur Barker, 1977) on page 86; from Craig Johnston's autobiography *Walk Alone* (Collins, Australia, 1989) on page 84; from Geoffrey Green's *Great Moments in Sport* (Pelham Books, 1972) on page 140; from Brian James's

Journey to Wembley (Marshall Cavendish, 1977) on page 219; and from a piece by myself in the *Kingswood Book of Football* (Kingswood Press, 1992) on page 177. And I must also thank Steve Hale for his kindness in allowing me to reproduce photographs in this book.

I owe a debt of thanks to Billy Wilson, not only for his lengthy reminiscences but also for carrying out a number of interviews on my behalf. Mention should also be made of my editor, Tony Pocock, who has so enthusiastically encouraged this project and given much advice, and my agent, John Pawsey, who has always been happy to chat over problems. Finally, a special 'thank you' to three special Kopites, my wife Judith and children Nicholas and Emma.

Stephen F Kelly
1993 and 2005

INTRODUCTION

Even when empty and glimpsed in the dazzle of a summer's day it is an awesome prospect. But gleamed through the haze of the floodlights and the swirling cigarette smoke of a misty European evening, it is a truly breathtaking sight. There was a time on the old Kop when 25,000 bawling, chanting, dancing, cavorting fans, could be seen tumbling one way and then crashing another in a rough old sea of a crowd. And the noise, the sheer noise of it all, was almost enough to lift the roof off.

Now that the capacity is just 12,000 seated fans it might not be quite the same, but on European evenings, especially those of the 2004–05 season when Liverpool stormed triumphantly towards European Cup glory, it can be every bit as passionate, noisy and dramatic.

This is the Anfield Kop, renowned throughout the world of football. If not the largest single stand in British football, it is surely the most exhilarating, the most intimidating, the most frightening. Little wonder visiting teams have taken the field with terror in their eyes, no surprise opposing goalkeepers have been seen to shake. The former Liverpool manager Bill Shankly claimed it was Liverpool's twelfth man and worth a goal start; few would disagree with him.

It was, and still is, to the Liverpool fan a cathedral, a place of worship, and after Hillsborough, a shrine. The building itself was always impressive, its roof a mighty steel frame hanging dauntingly over the heads of 25,000 spectators, held up by just a handful of stanchions. The steps, and there were precisely one hundred of them, seemed to stretch upwards forever. Even from the outside it looked dramatic, angles here, angles there thrusting out over the Walton Breck Road, cream-painted pillars, fancy red bricks and even windows. Today, it is not perhaps as awesome as it once was. Rather it is streamlined, modern and utilitarian. And with no stanchions, pillars, and with 12,409 seats it is a comfortable stand affording a splendid view of the game.

But despite all the changes, it is the people who have made the Kop the envy of world football, those who have stood or sat on it over the years, sometimes crushed together in a frenzy of excitement or jumping up as a corner swings into the penalty area. Without them the Kop is simply a spectacular piece of civil engineering. With them it is something else, a community, a congregation, a culture.

In the South African province of Natal, some miles inland from Durban and close to Ladysmith, there is a small hill known locally as Spion Kop. The South Africans sometimes even spell it Spionekop or Speonkop and usually pronounce it 'Spee-on Kop'. The name would almost certainly never have travelled much beyond Durban and would unquestionably never have become part of football's vocabulary had it not been for a fearful battle that took place there on 24 January 1900. The Battle of Spion Kop, seen for just a day or so as a 'famous victory', to quote the *Manchester Guardian*, soon went down in history as the most mismanaged battle of the entire Boer War and one of the most disastrous in the history of the British military. It was a scandal that was conveniently swept under the carpet.

The British had rightly spotted the Boers' position on Spion Kop, yet there was never any strategic reason why they should attack them. When asked why he had ordered the assault on Spion Kop, General Buller answered like some Alpinist climber, 'because it is there'. He was then asked what they should do when it was captured. Buller considered for a moment then replied 'Stay there'. The seeds for disaster had been sown. But the most appalling mistake was the military's lack of geographical knowledge. No balloon had been sent up to examine the Kop, nor were any local guides consulted. It was to prove the most calamitous mistake of all.

At 7.30 p.m. on 23 January, the assault began. Over 1,500 men – mainly from the Lancashire Fusiliers, the Royal Lancasters and the South Lancashires – began the steady march towards the foothills of Spion Kop. No machine guns were taken; the order was simply 'fixed bayonets'. At 11 p.m. they reached the foothills and slowly began to climb through the mist and drizzle. Early the next morning they encountered their first Boers and after a brief skirmish the Boers fled. The army, believing that they had taken Spion Kop, sent three cheers to the men below and began to dig in. The trenches they dug were to become their graves. As dawn broke and the mist cleared they realised with horror that beyond Spion Kop lay the further and higher ridges of Aloe Knoll and Twin Peaks where the Boers waited peering down their gun sights. The British army was stranded. They had dug themselves into a death trap. In the torrid heat of the next day, without food, water and running out of ammunition, the brave lads of Lancashire fought heroically until the generals back at camp began to realise their error and called for a withdrawal. By then the damage had been done: 383 British soldiers were dead, over a thousand had been wounded and 303 were missing, presumed held prisoner. The Boers suffered between 350 and 800 fatalities. Although the death toll was to pale into insignificance compared to the later losses in the First World War, at the time it seemed – and indeed was – an appalling loss of life. The brief celebrations of the press soon gave way to horror as more accurate telegrams reached Fleet Street. The nation was appalled and the Battle of Spion Kop was to remain in British memories for some years.

Six years later, as Liverpool clinched their second league championship, the directors of the club – led by its redoubtable chairman John Houlding and secretary John

McKenna – decided that Liverpool FC – and its ever growing number of supporters – was deserving of a more stately home. It was therefore decided to reconstruct Anfield with a variety of new facilities, including a new terracing at the Walton Breck Road end of the ground to replace the simple terracing and stand that already existed behind the goal. In late May work began on constructing a high banking with wooden steps. Crash barriers were also erected – though there were surprisingly few. It was a grand scheme and more than enough to impress the papers. 'Liverpool, having provided themselves with an up-to-date enclosure, now possess a home worthy of their title as league champions,' commented the most famous sports newspaper in the country, *The Athletic News*, adding that 'when completed, the Liverpool ground will be equal to anything in the country both as regards size, convenience and equipment.'

The new stadium was designed by that noted architect of football grounds Archibald Leitch and erected by Messrs E. F. Blakeley and Company of Vauxhall Ironworks, Liverpool. The *Liverpool Echo* was also full of praise and reproduced a sketch by Leitch detailing the finished product. 'People who have not been permitted to view the ground except from the top of passing tramcars,' commented the *Echo* 'have marvelled and expressed astonishment seeing the rise of the Oakfield Road embankment.' Of course, strictly speaking, it was not in Oakfield Road at all but in the Walton Breck Road. The terrace was said to have 132 steps – though in 1993 the author counted only 100 – and it was reckoned there was space for 20,000 spectators, bringing the overall capacity of Anfield up to 60,000. The pitch was also raised by five feet and a paddock constructed all around the ground.

As the 1906/07 season kicked off, the Kop took its place in football mythology. Elsewhere in Liverpool the TUC was about to begin its annual conference at St George's Hall, while George Lashwood and the Vaudeville Beau Brummel, Leo Stormont, were playing at the

Empire. Further afield, Yorkshire were taking on the MCC in one of the concluding games of the cricket season and there were riots in St Petersburg. But back in Liverpool the city was basking in a heatwave that had struck the nation. All week temperatures had hovered in the high eighties and on Saturday 1 September 1906, as the new football season began, the temperature in Liverpool hit a staggering 124 degrees. All over the country games were halted as players collapsed and there was some doubt around Anfield that the game would even kick off. But kick off they did, even if the referee was so concerned that the half time interval had to be extended while the players recovered. Rarely, if ever, can Anfield or the Kop have basked in such a heat. Nobody made any mention of what it must have been like on the crowded Kop that day, but just over 30,000 turned up for the occasion, a useful increase on the kind of gate Anfield had been pulling the previous season. It was even more impressive considering the opponents that day were the distinctly unglamorous Stoke City, who would spend the season propping up the rest of the division. The Kop must have sizzled.

Within twenty minutes of the kick off, the Kop experienced its first explosion of noise as Joe Hewitt swept Liverpool into the lead. Unfortunately, that goal did not usher in another successful season. Though they were the defending champions who could boast players of the calibre of Sam Hardy, Alex Raisbeck, Sam Raybould and Jack Cox – some of the greatest names in the club's history – they would eventually lose almost as many encounters at home as they won, and finish the season in fifteenth spot.

But what to name the new terracing? Nobody gave it much thought at first, but it soon became clear that the Walton Breck Bank was something of a mouthful. Then Ernest Jones, the sports editor of the *Liverpool Daily Post and Echo* came up with the novel idea of calling it Spion Kop. The phrase had apparently been used some time before to describe the terracing at Woolwich Arsenal's ground but had never stuck. Perhaps Ernest Jones had read it somewhere, perhaps it was coincidence. Whatever the explanation, his idea was seized upon and before the season was out the name Spion Kop came to take on a new meaning.

Also erected a short time later on the corner of the Kop with the Kemlyn Road was the topmast of the ship *The Great Eastern*, one of the first iron ships in the world. Launched in 1860 *The Great Eastern* had been broken up in Rock Ferry and shortly after the completion of the Kop, the topmast was floated across the Mersey and hauled up Everton Valley by a team of four horses to be erected as a flagpost. It still stands today on what is now commonly known as flagpost corner.

The Kop, like most football crowds, is a social barometer. Once the preserve of the working man, it always reflected the fortunes of working class life and culture. At the turn of the century, as the sport began to take root, it was given a timely boost by the reduction in the working week on the docks to five and a half days, freeing Saturday afternoon for the pursuit of trivial pastimes: and what could be better than a few pints and a visit to Anfield with your work mates? In the twenties and thirties when soccer emerged out of the Edwardian era as the nation's number one sport it was here that the dockers came, direct from their Saturday morning shift. And there they were; flat hats, mufflers, trilbies, even the occasional bowler and of course cigarettes, they all seemed to smoke, and those long, hollow faces. Even in those days they were swaying, not deliberately, just moving gently under the sheer weight of the crowd.

For the next twenty years the Kop remained much as it was. Since its construction it had been open to the elements. The driving wind that swept in from the west, up the Mersey and across Stanley Park hardly made it the most popular venue for watching football. On wet days it could be as miserable and raw as the Mersey Bar itself – though on a summer's day the view across Stanley Park was said to be spectacular. Even club secretary John McKenna could appreciate that you had to be either desperately poor or deeply fanatical to pay to sit on the Kop on a wet Saturday afternoon. There was only one solution and in 1928, flush with money, the board authorised the building of a roof to protect the entire Kop. A cover was constructed that turned the ordinary cinder banking into a cathedral of sound. Mr J. Watson Cabre was the architect contracted to draw up the plans and as soon as the season drew to a close, work began in earnest to complete the job in time for the start of the new season.

'The covering of the Spion Kop,' wrote *The Athletic News* 'has been linked to the two main stands. This gives protection to over 37,000 spectators behind the goal, bringing the total covered accommodation for the ground up to 60,000.' The grandstand was also extended to hold an additional 600 seats and the Kemlyn Road stand capacity was increased by 200 spectators. There was probably no other stadium in the country where so many supporters were sheltered – at the time it was estimated that Anfield would be able to hold as many as 70,000 spectators. However its maximum capacity to this day remains the 61,905 who watched the fourth round cup game against Wolves in February 1952. Somewhere along the line someone had got their sums wrong. It is doubtful that the Kop could ever have held 37,000 – between twenty-five and twenty-seven thousand would be a more accurate guess – which would have made the maximum capacity nearer 60,000.

On 25 August 1928 the new Kop was formally opened by John McKenna, president of the Football League and a former secretary, director and chairman of the club. There could be no more appropriate person. Spectators were urged to be in their place on the Kop by 2.45 p.m. and precisely five minutes later McKenna and a party of distinguished guests walked through the players' tunnel and across the pitch towards the Kop where they dutifully unfurled a commemorative flag.

* * *

No sooner had the flag been hoisted than the Kop had the chance to test its new acoustics. The visitors were Bury, a fair side in those days, and they were one-nil down within the first minute, or 50 seconds to be precise – debut boy Billy Millar heading in Dick Edmed's corner. On the half hour Albert Whitehurst added a second and Millar struck another with twenty minutes remaining. It was a grand and portentous start for the new Spion Kop, though Billy Millar managed only two more games before he left the club.

After the match there was further speechmaking in the boardroom. McKenna was presented with a gold cigar holder to commemorate the occasion. 'We cannot live in the past,' he proceeded to tell the guests, 'but I think the past should be an inspiration for the present. Now that the spectators are assured of their places under more comfortable conditions, I would like to give a word of advice to the directors, that is to stay their hands in the direction of further improving the ground and devote their finances, energy and intelligence to creating a team worthy of the splendid surroundings.'

There was clearly a division on the board with some directors already drawing up plans to tear down the Kemlyn Road stand and build a new double decker stand in its place. But John McKenna's wise counsel held, though perhaps for a trifle too long, and there would be few further ground improvements for another forty years.

Liverpool at that time was a very different city than it had been in 1906. Unemployment was creeping upwards, poverty was on the rise and the music halls were giving way to a new vogue – the picture house. The fortunes of Liverpool Football Club were not much richer either. After picking up two championships at the beginning of the 1920s the side had slunk into complacency. Lady Luck had taken up residence across Stanley Park where Dixie Dean had just fired in 60 league goals in one season for Everton. But there were still a few players worth paying to see each Saturday afternoon at Anfield, especially

Elisha Scott, Parson Jackson and Gordon Hodgson, all favourites of the newly roofed Kopites.

The new roof also opened up the possibilities for other sporting activities and during the 1930s Anfield became a regular home for boxing. At least one world title fight – Nelson Tarleton against Freddie Miller – was held there along with numerous British and Empire championships. Professional tennis was also staged, with Fred Perry and Bill Tilden thrilling a rapturous audience. The Liverpool marathon concluded its city run with a final lap around Anfield and of course Anfield continued as a venue for the occasional international match – particularly those involving Ireland and England – as well as hosting the odd FA Cup semi-final.

By the time War broke out, the Kop had taken its place in history. Players from the thirties talked of its partisanship, its mighty roar and intimidating atmosphere. But sadly the team had never been able to capitalise on its enthusiasm. All that, however, was about to change. As peace returned so Liverpool stormed to the top of the division to clinch their fifth league title, a young Billy Liddell and a tough little half back by the name of Bob Paisley becoming the toast of the Kop. Even during the dark days of second division football in the 1950s, the Kop was a revelation. Always hopeful, always loyal, always heaving – even when the opposition was lowly – it was a crowd that deserved better – much better. The club needed someone to galvanise the support and to turn its energy into an additional force. Shankly and the Kop would produce the synergy that would propel Liverpool to success. The best was about to happen.

During the early 1960s the Kop came into its own as the city of Liverpool became the focus of a new pop culture. The Kop was almost a pop group of its own. Each week it was packed with a swaying, singing, Cavern-stomping mob. It was an odd collection. Twenty-five thousand, mostly male, revellers getting together to live out their teenage fantasies. It was a throng of so many missed opportunities, forgotten dreams, if-only-I-had-a guitar-stories. You may not have made it to the Cavern or the Iron Door but at least you were there on the Kop. If you couldn't be a footballer or performer at the London Palladium on a Sunday night, then you could be part of the Kop. Anyone on Merseyside could pretend they were an idol and when Liverpool played at home everyone standing on the Kop became pop stars for the afternoon. You can still picture them: boys with bushy Beatle hairstyles, men in black-framed Buddy Holly glasses, lads with scarves, duffle coats, polo necked pullovers, old men with toothless smiles, open necked shirts and every one of them singing, no matter what their age, no matter what their inhibitions.

Football and pop music were the escape from the ghetto; the route to fame and fortune. During those days almost anyone with a guitar, a set of drums, a mouth organ or some maracas could climb aboard the make-it-rich bandwagon. They knew all the words, especially of the Liverpool hits – 'She Loves You', 'Anyone Who Had A Heart', 'Yellow Submarine'. If ever there was a public display of popular culture this was it. Tens of thousands of cheery voices singing 'She Loves You'. And what's more they would all go 'Yeah, Yeah' and then add 'And with a love like that you know you should be glad *wuuuuuw*.' They even adopted one of their own pop groups' songs, 'You'll Never Walk Alone,' as their anthem and began to adapt the lyrics of other songs. 'When the Reds Go Marching In', 'You've Not Seen Nothing Like The Mighty Emlyn', 'We All Live On A Red And White Kop.' Here were 25,000 Paul McCartneys, John Lennons, Gerry Marsdens, George Harrisons, Billy J Kramers. Even Cilla and Ringo were not forgotten.

Liverpool was a city of hope once more. Jobs became more plentiful after Ford opened a plant at Halewoods and the docks were still bustling despite beginning their sad decline. And if you couldn't get a job you could always go to Frank Hessy's and buy a guitar on the never-never. And, of course, we had Bill Shankly. It wasn't long before everyone was imitating us. The Stretford Enders chanted, The North Bank sang and Roker Park roared to 'The Blaydon Races'. But they were never as witty, never as inventive, never as committed as us Scousers. And as Liverpool travelled across Europe with their fanatical following in tow, so the Europeans adopted our fanfares. Even today they sing 'You'll Never Walk Alone' in Milan.

So how did all the singing start? I remember at the time pondering this question and someone gave me an answer which, thirty years later, still seems to be as good an explanation as any. My friend's theory was that it was a combination of boredom and the Beatles. Boredom, because Liverpool's success meant that everyone would be on the Kop in their place hours before kick off, the Beatles because they were the soundtrack to Liverpool life. To while away the time you read the programme but there was little else to do. And the size of the crowd meant that you were stuck in your place, unable to move. Then of course the public address system would be churning out the latest chart hits. Inevitably the Mersey groups always figured prominently and everyone knew the words. They would no doubt have been singing the songs in their heads, so it became just a short step to then start singing them out loud. It only needed to happen once.

Of course, It wasn't the first time anyone had sung at a football ground. There had been a tradition of community singing at Anfield going back to at least the post-war years, but that was usually organised – although the anarchic element on the Kop were always likely to strike up a different number to the one the band was playing. Community singing at Wembley was also a national tradition; every football fan knew that after waving your song sheets to the TV cameras, you joined in the Cup Final hymn 'Abide with Me'. Then of course there was Cardiff Arms Park where crowd singing had been elevated to an art form and the battle hymns of 'Land of my

Fathers' and 'Bread of Heaven' were always likely to bring a tear to the eye and inspire the Welsh three quarter line to even greater glory. But the Kop singing was different. It was unorganised. There was no choir master, no conductor, and the songs were the popular favourites of the time.

Groups of supporters would meet on a Saturday lunchtime in local pubs to plan the afternoon's entertainment. The Albert next door to the Kop was a regular haunt and rehearsal hall for the Kop choir and there were at least another half dozen pubs dotted around the city where the same ritual took place. Even today, if you go in prior to kick off you will be greeted with a cacophony of singing. There is even evidence of song sheets being handed out to the unofficial choir behind the Kop goal, while away trips were an ideal opportunity to invent new lyrics or new songs. The singing, Shankly and the sheer noise of the Kop were more than enough to propel Liverpool towards league, FA Cup and European glory.

In the seventies the Kop visibly changed. European football had arrived in force and the fans saw new horizons, met new supporters and learned new lessons. They had travelled to Rome, Munich, Lisbon and St Etienne and from there they brought back both souvenirs and continental habits. A new culture was born. Suddenly banners, chequered flags and flares were the vogue. They even reflected the city's sense of humour. 'Joey [Jones] ate the frogs' legs, made the Swiss roll and now he's munching Gladbach,' read one of the wittiest banners of all. It was a small progression from the raised red and white scarves that had accompanied the singing of 'You'll Never Walk Alone'. But it was the first time it had been seen on English grounds. And always it was accompanied by the noise.

But the terraces of the seventies were not always so fun loving and friendly. While the rest of the football world seemed to be engaging in hand to hand fighting, the Kop remained, as it always was, a safe haven. There were those, however, who sought a little more excitement and transferred their allegiance to the Anfield Road End where they could confront visiting supporters more easily. But on the Kop there was never any danger that war would spill over onto their territory. No visiting army would ever contemplate invading the Kop.

Then in the eighties a severe spell of football gout struck. Fat with success and over-indulged, the Kop became tired, lethargic, complacent even. Years of unrivalled success had taken their toll. It seemed they didn't need to sing any more, or, as Bill Shankly once so famously put it, 'suck the ball into the net'. It just went in automatically. The opposition arrived fully expecting to be defeated, running up the white flag even before they had appeared on the pitch. The Kop simply waited, silently, in anticipation. There were exceptions: if the visitors swept into a surprising lead, temporarily stinging the pride of players and Kopites alike, the Kop would arouse itself and bellow until the natural order was restored. But there was no doubt the atmosphere had changed.

The roots of this complacency probably stemmed from the 1978–79 season when Liverpool conceded just four league goals at Anfield. Furthermore, in the whole of the 1970s Liverpool lost just thirteen league games at Anfield. Some supporters must have stood on the Kop for years without seeing their favourites lose. In this kind of climate, it's hardly surprising that complacency crept in. I once witnessed Liverpool win 6-0 but the Kop were still complaining about missed chances. It was also a new generation who had taken their places on the Kop, the sons of the fathers who roared against Inter Milan and Celtic. But this generation had never known anything but success, never out of the top two, never a bare shelf in the trophy room. The 1950s seemed light years away. 'Liverpool in the second division once and beaten by a non-league side ? Ger away, when was dat ?' They still remembered Shankly but many had never even seen him.

Nor were they all Liverpudlians. They came from further afield, attracted by the winning glamour and the glitz of being associated with Liverpool. The coaches rolled in from the Midlands, Yorkshire and Wales; the trains shepherded fans down from north of the border; while the planes came from Belfast, Dublin, Norway and Denmark. By 1990 it was estimated that Liverpool were drawing two thirds of their support from outside the city. Times were changing. People had shifted from the city centre to the outlying areas of Knowsley, St Helens, the Wirral, Warrington and Southport where housing and jobs were more plentiful. They were the same areas where the players lived and with it the culture was beginning to change. There was still wit but it was less pronounced, there was still enthusiasm but it was less passionate. The allegiance was to the team, not the city. Yet the trophies kept on coming. They sang their hearts out at Wembley (many times), Paris and in Rome, though it was never quite the same as it was first time round.

Then there was Heysel. Many a stalwart called a halt to their enthusiasms, ashamedly pushing a scarf and red hat to the bottom of a drawer. For a while it seemed disrespectful to sing and cheer. The silence at the first game after the disaster was frightening. And when Liverpool scored, the Kop didn't know what exactly to do. After a second's pause they roared and the recuperation was under way. That year saw them beat Everton in a Wembley Cup final to win the double – and in doing so they achieved the ultimate. It could only go downhill from there on, whispered the fanatics. But worse was to follow on a warm April day in Sheffield when many Kopites lost their lives supporting the team they loved. The popular culture of the terraces was now at an end.

The 1980s closed with Hillsborough and turned the Kop into a national shrine, a symbol for mourning. Thousands – from Princes to paupers, supporters and those who knew nothing of football – came and paid their respects. In the mild spring breeze the thunderous roar of the Kop was replaced by the crinkling sound of cellophane that wrapped so many bouquets. And the smell of cigarettes gave way to the lingering fragrance of flowers.

Half the pitch was strewn in flowers, the Kop was awash with scarves, rosettes, bobble hats and other mementoes, a parting gift from the living to their comrades of the Kop. It wasn't the first time the Kop had been a shrine. For years the ashes of the dead had been scattered on its terracing or buried in caskets behind the goal. They bury sailors at sea, why not football fans where their hearts lie? In Liverpool football is a way of life. But nobody had ever expected a tragedy quite like Hillsborough. It would leave its scars on all associated with Liverpool Football Club.

Everyone at Anfield had always been mindful of a possible accident. The disaster at Ibrox on the infamous stairway thirteen where 66 soccer fans had died, was a warning to everyone. Fearing a similar tragedy, the club decided to rebuild the outside stairway to the Kop. It had been similar to the one at Ibrox, dropping dramatically from the roof to the Walton Breck Road below. Anyone who remembers carefully edging their feet on to it as the great crowd surged out of the Kop will testify to its danger. In that struggling mob it was quite common to be swept along, feet off the ground, and through the exit gates before your feet found dry land again. That there was never an accident was more by luck than judgement. The Safety of Sports Ground Act 1975 also brought a new wave of crush barriers as well as the new stairwell.

Then during the summer of 1987 further work was carried out in strengthening the crush barriers. A total of 750 iron rods were to be piled into the ground as part of the operation but on 6 July as they piled rod 572 into one of the concrete steps the rod suddenly disappeared. The workmen gazed down to see a gaping hole. A shaft plunged downwards to a huge hole measuring some twenty feet by fifteen feet. A sewer at the bottom of the hole had collapsed causing the downpour. The shaft had originally stretched from the sewer to a manhole cover on the Kop but as the sewer collapsed so too did the shaft.

The sewer had been built in 1860, long before a football ground had stood there. Quite how long it had been like that was anyone's guess, although when it had last been inspected four years previously there was no sign of collapse. Experts reckoned it was probably the piledriving for the new barriers which had caused the damage but there was only flimsy evidence to back their claim. Just four inches of concrete and a crumbling layer of ash were all that came between the Kop and a major disaster. The problem was rectified in record time, though Anfield was forced to postpone the debut of new signings John Barnes and Peter Beardsley.

It's impossible to forget your first encounter with the Kop of those days. For many it was a case of paying five shillings at those old wooden doors where a million Kopites had passed before, then beginning the steep hike up the old stairway. Programme in one hand, a soaking pie in the other, you neared the top with a sense of expectation. And yet outside on the steps there was rarely any hint of noise beyond. It was not until you finally breeched that last step and gazed down before you that your heart suddenly missed its beat. This vast wave of sound, rising into the formidable echoing roof of the Kop. It was like opening the door into some Hieronymus Bosch picture. All calm, orderly and sane on one side but clamour, despair and pandemonium on the other.

I never ceased to be excited by that moment, the anticipation, the uproar. For years I would take visiting friends and force them to briefly close their eyes as they climbed those last few steps until they reached the pinnacle and could then gaze down on the scene below. After the stairwell had been constructed a slight sense of the dramatic disappeared but it was still there in some degree, still the same echoing chamber, the same thunderous noise, rumbling everywhere, and the shrill sound of singing. The chanting rising from the belly of the Kop,

LIV-ER-POOL, LIV-ER-POOL, then the raising of red and white scarves and the slow, almost mournful, drone of 'You'll Never Walk Alone', followed by a deafening roar as Liverpool appear through the tunnel and raced towards the Kop.

Like an ocean, the Kop's waves rose and then crashed. In one corner people tumbling, in the centre the crowd stumbling back to its original position, in another spot the fans spilling downwards while elsewhere the side to side swaying and toppling as they pushed to find some breathing space. It was a mass of bodies and faces that had been transformed into something else, a human sea, everyone grappling for their lives. Men could have drowned in that sea.

If the Kop had not existed, television would have created it. The two were made for each other: the ultimate combination of sight, sound and spontaneity. The visual impact was dramatic and the Kop's fame quickly spread around the world. They came from far and wide to try and understand the phenomenon. The first ever *Match of the Day* was broadcast from Anfield and back in the early 1960s Panorama produced a memorable film about the 'fun loving' Kop. Some of the finest wordsmiths tried to recapture the atmosphere. They wrote about it everywhere and over the years the Kop has spawned more than a few publications of its own. In the 1960s there was a newspaper actually called *Kop*, which was published in Bootle and is a rich vein of material for the soccer historian. Published fortnightly, it was a lively and attractive paper with the usual catalogue of player portraits, letters, match reports and analysis. There was even a Miss Kop. The publishers claimed a readership of 70,000 with subscribers dotted around the world and, judging by the letters page, it was certainly reaching exiled Kopites as far afield as Australia, America, South Africa and even one in the South Pole. It was essentially a reverential publication, and although there was occasional criticism it was met with a barrage of complaints from 'loyal Kopites' the following week. But it will always be remembered for its numerous reports of budgies and parrots that could sing 'You'll Never Walk Alone' or chant St John's name.

In the 1980s the Kop spawned another magazine, this time less precious, and a forerunner to the fanzine. *The End* caught the mood of the times, combining music with the culture of the terraces. Its originators later went on to greater fame with the pop group The Farm (who in 1995 recorded the official Everton song for the FA Cup!). The 1980s and the 1990s saw the emergence of more fanzines including *Through The Wind and Rain*, one of the most successful and readable of them all. In Norway the 4,000 strong supporters club had a glossy magazine of its own, titled inevitably, *Kopite*, while today there is yet another publication called *The Kop* and one of the most successful websites is known as Koptalk. Another is called Red and White Kop. Scarves, banners, flags, magazines, websites; the Kop is an industry of its own.

But in 1990 came the most dramatic change of all. Lord Justice Taylor published his final report into the Hillsborough disaster, which recommended that first division grounds should become all seater stadia. There was of course an outcry. Many on the Kop argued that there had never been an accident at Anfield, that the Kop was perfectly safe and by seating it its unique atmosphere would be destroyed. There was a general feeling that had Shankly been alive he would have been the first to lie down in front of the bulldozers, but the then manager Graeme Souness said little. Like others, mindful of the Hillsborough disaster, he shrugged his shoulders and admitted that seating the Kop was inevitable. And after what had happened most Kopites felt incumbent to accept Lord Justice Taylor's recommendations out of respect for the 96 who had died. But it was not a popular decision. Couldn't there still be some 'safe' areas allotted for standing was one argument. It will only lead to higher prices was another. But there was no backing down. At least make us as proud of our new Kop as we were of the old, was the one sentiment everyone concurred with. The club agreed that they would build a totally new stand and not simply put seats on the terraces as many others clubs planned. And so as the 1993/94 season drew to an end plans for a new Kop were unveiled.

The final game in front of the old Kop took place on Saturday 30 April 1994 with Norwich City as the visitors. Before the game, past players came to pay their respects. Albert Stubbins, who had banged in many a goal in front of the Kop in those grim post war years, Roy Evans, a part of most Kop triumphs as player, coach and manager, John Toshack, another regular marksman, plus the likes of Ian Callaghan, Steve Heighway, Tommy Smith, Billy Liddell, Emlyn Hughes, Phil Thompson, Ron Yeats, Ian St John as well as Nessie Shankly and Jessie Paisley – widows of the two greatest managers the club had ever had – were all present. The Kop celebrated, sang its repertoire, and when the game ended simply refused to go home. The players paraded in front of them, returned to their dressing room, but still the fans would not go. There were tears, and one or two fans, one dressed in his desert Scouser Tommy outfit, invaded the pitch. But the police were lenient. Eventually everyone drifted out, but it had been a full hour since the game had finished in glorious sunshine. Sadly Norwich had failed to read the script and won 1-0. Maybe the occasion had just been a little too much for the players. Nobody really cared though.

In recent years as new safety measures had been introduced with a reduction in numbers and increased barriers, the capacity of the Kop had already fallen to 17,000. Now it would fall even further, to around 10,000. That of course would mean reduced revenue, and as everyone suspected prices went up to compensate. The new Kop would cost £10 million, revenue the club could barely afford, and that in itself meant changes in the boardroom with David Moores coming in as a director and rich benefactor.

The club had been very insistent in its talks with the Manchester-based sports stadia architects, Atherden Fuller Leng, that they wanted the new Kop to maintain an atmosphere and acoustics similar to the old Kop. The club also wanted the new Kop Grandstand, as it was to be called, to visually fit in with the Centenary Stand which the same architects had designed some years earlier. The only other notable problem was that the planners had restricted the height of the new grandstand to be no higher than the ridge of the old Kop.

It was a tall order, but in the end the architects came up with a design that seemed to fit the bill. There would be 76 rows, providing seating for 12,390 fans. There would also be 21 turnstiles to enable fast entry and exit from the ground with drinks kiosks, food outlets, toilets, programme stands and so forth in the concourse area. The corners of the ground at the Kop end were also filled in at the same time in order to maximise seating. It was the biggest single tier structure of its kind in Britain. The cost of building the stand and the concourse areas was approximately £7 million with further money later spent on designing the museum and shop. The American burger outlet McDonalds came on board the project a little later to help finance the payment in exchange for an outlet. The job of completing the work was given to the builders Alfred McAlpine.

Days after the final match, the bulldozers moved into the Walton Breck Road and began to tear down the Kop brick by brick, terrace by terrace, until the whole end had been flattened. It was a difficult job and there was a tight schedule. The new Kop had to be ready for occupancy for the first home game of the new season. Throughout that warm summer the painstaking work of building the new Kop went on.

Ready for the start of the season, as planned, the new Kop Grandstand was greeted by cautious praise. Everyone agreed that in many ways it was better than the old Kop. For a start there were toilets, more than enough for the

12,000 fans. And there were food and drink counters where you didn't have to fight to get served. The view was also better; there were no stanchions so everyone had a perfect, clear view. And of course, there was no shoving and swaying every time the ball came anywhere near the Kop goal. Some have argued that the atmosphere isn't quite the same but then there are half the number as used to stand on the old Kop. And anyhow, the Kop in the eighties was much less noisy than in its glory years of the sixties and seventies.

Most fans were agreed that it was something to be proud of, as good a stand as any in the country – although the presence of a McDonalds at the back of the Kop did not go down so well with many fans. But there was a magnificent new souvenir shop and a museum, something the club had needed for years. The club's administrators also later moved their offices into the Kop.

Since then, the Kop has played host to the 1996 European Football championships as well as a number of international matches, plus the odd pop concert. Memories of the old Kop and what it used to be like are distant. A whole new generation of football fans has grown up sitting in the Kop with no recollections whatsoever of what it was like standing.

Yet, if anyone thought the Kop could not be as noisy as it used to be, there have been recent occasions – on great European nights especially – when the atmosphere at Anfield has excelled those memorable nights of Inter Milan and St Etienne. The Roma game, for instance, when Gerard Houllier returned to Anfield following his heart operation, was as emotional as any. And the Barcelona and Celtic games will go down among the greats. And then of course there is the 2004/2005 season when Liverpool marched majestically towards a memorable Champions league triumph. That season, the games against Olympiakos, Bayer Leverkeusen, Juventus and finally Chelsea – in as dramatic a night as any Anfield has witnessed – put an end to suggestions that the Kop and

Anfield had lost its voice and reputation as Liverpool's twelfth man. It was still there.

Those then are the bare details. What follows is the story of the Kop told by those who have stood and sat on it over the years, those who have faced it, those who have played in front of it, those who have earned their living through it. It is a story, not just of a steel and concrete structure, but of people and a community. The Kop is about their reminiscences, memories, wit and songs. It is told entirely in their words. It is their community just as it is indeed Liverpool's twelfth man.

The Opening Match At Anfield.

One

THE STORY OF THE KOP

A Poor Scouser Tommy

THE LIVERPOOL FOOTBALL ECHO
First ever edition, Saturday 16 November 1889

At each side are large covered stands, behind each goal are other stands, holding nearly 4,000 each; and taking all the stands together, about 12,000 people have a good view of the game from them; while another 6,000 have the same free standing room on the ground. Notwithstanding this, the spectators at times are almost inconveniently crowded, and gates of nearly 20,000 are not altogether unknown. The total receipts last year were £4,000; but of this sum at least £45 was expended every week for paying the professional players.

ATHLETIC TIMES
1889

Phew! How the dense mass of spectators rolled in to the high-pitched tune of 18,000 or 20,000. Some walked, some ran, some drove. Vehicles of all sorts were requisitioned. Broad cloth and fustian elbowed each other in their haste to get a good view, and jarvies were tipped to urge their horses on at top speed.

I was lucky to strike a waggonette in Lime Street the first time of asking and thus saved the cost of a hansom. My enthusiastic fellow-occupants in the not over-spruce turnout, to the number of nearly three dozen, yelled and shouted for Everton the whole of the journey.

Nearing Anfield, the thoroughfares leading to the enclosure were lined with hurrying crowds which, as load after load of people bound on the same errand overtook them, increased their pace determined to get the best place.

It was about five minutes past one when the gates were opened, at which time about two or three thousand persons were waiting admission. Before half past one several thousand persons had settled in their places; at two o'clock the cheaper stands were crowded; and half an hour later – minutes before the advertised kick-off – it seemed impossible to pack another head away anywhere on the ground.

Even a proportion of the space reserved for the unusually large number of pressmen present was taken up by certain 'dead-heads', who once in couldn't be got out. This occasioned the reporters considerable inconvenience and annoyance and is a matter which should be taken notice of by the Everton executive.

The crowd, a well-ordered one by the way, included a large contingent from Bootle as well as other clubs in the district, while Preston supplied a brigade of its own, one train from the 'proud city' bringing between 500 and 600 partisans.

During the wait for the start speculation ran high as to the possible result of the tussle. Sanguine Evertonians professed themselves certain that the local champions would win, but the majority were in expectation of a draw or, perhaps, a 2–1 or 3–2 victory for North End.

Just before time, Mr J.H. Houlding headed a party of gentlemen across the ground, a banner and a print shirt being fluttered from a couple of house windows opposite as he did so. Mr Houlding acknowledged the applause with which he was received by raising his hat.

At 2:40 the Everton men raced on to the field and were warmly welcomed by a now thoroughly wound-up crowd. A minute or two later North End followed, their reception being most enthusiastic, Jack Ross in particular getting a hearty cheer from every side.

George Farmer had a similar hearty greeting and cries of 'Now Georgie', 'Play up George', stimulated the arrival of Mr F.T. Norris, referee. The coin was tossed and North End, winning, placed their backs to the sun, Everton defending the Anfield Road goal.

The scene and hush on the ground when Geary kicked off was one of the most impressive I have experienced on a football field. Suppressed excitement was written on every face. Even the great number of ladies present betrayed much agitation and interest.

THE LIVERPOOL ECHO
Saturday 25 August 1906

The ground has now been completely walled in with fancy brick setting, with large exit gates on the four sides as well as numerous entrances. Therefore, there will be no difficulty in either entering or leaving the enclosure. The directors' aim has been to provide as compact and comfortable a ground as possible in which every person, no matter what position he may visit, will have a full view of the game. The pitch has been raised 5 ft with a paddock all round. Roofed-in stand accommodation will be plentiful, and at one end, as seen in the sketch, will be an elevated terrace consisting of 132 tiers of steps which will afford space for something like 20,000 spectators. The entire scheme is modelled on a new departure from what football grounds are generally supposed to be, and when completed it will provide ample space for about 60,000 visitors. The stands, of which only two are erected at present, are built on massive brick foundations and are as safe as skill and good workmanship can make them, and ample provision for the comfort of players in the way of bath and recreation rooms has been attended to.

The ground has been in the hands of a gang of workmen for the past three months, but another season at least must elapse before it is perfected and the full ambition of the directors becomes a reality. The main features of those connected with the new erection have been compactness, comfort, and an uninterrupted view of the field of play.

The constructional steel work for the grandstand has been supplied and erected by Messrs. E.F. Blakeley and Co. of Vauxhall Ironworks, Liverpool, who also erected the big grandstand for the Everton Club at Goodison Park.

STANLEY DOIG
Kopite

My father was the Liverpool goalkeeper, Ted Doig, who signed for the club in 1904. Before that, he had played with Arbroath in Scotland and then had been the goalkeeper of the famous Sunderland 'Team of All the Talents'. He was one of the greatest goalkeepers of all time and was in the Scottish side on the day of the Ibrox disaster in 1902. In his first season at Anfield, Liverpool won the second-division title and the following year they won the championship.

I remember seeing my father against St Helens Recs in a Lancashire Combination game at Anfield. It was the first time I had ever seen him play, and Liverpool won 5–2. It was the 1907–08 season, and at the end of that season he was sacked. We got a postcard one Sunday morning and it simply said, 'Your services are no longer required.' He flew into a rage. 'Why this?' he shouted. I'll never forget. He tore everything off the table. We scampered upstairs, frightened.

Anyhow, he then joined St Helens Recs and, by jove, who should they go and draw in the Lancashire Cup but Liverpool at Anfield. Sam Hardy was in goal that day for Liverpool; he'd taken over from father. Well, St Helens won 5–2, reversing the scoreline of the previous season. Father played the game of his life that day. And, at the end of the match, he stood on the great rollers that they had for rolling the pitch, alongside the Kemlyn Road stand, and announced to the crowd that he had just played his last game. He was forty-two years old.

The Kop didn't have a roof on in those days. It was a big mound, like a giant wall. It had been built when I was about six, just before I first went there. There were all these steps going up from Oakfield Road with about six double gates to get in. And you climbed all these steps, and there it was below you. It was impressive even in those days. There were rails on it just as there are today, but not as many. Everyone used to stand there in their flat hats and mufflers. I had a bowler, and it had a red ribbon on it with the club crest which my father had given me. The ribbon had been on a straw boater which was given to him when the club visited Paris in about 1904. When Liverpool scored, everyone used to throw their hats into the air. Sometimes you wouldn't get your own hat back and you'd have to make do with someone else's.

I can remember getting swept out of the ground by the crowd, carried along with my feet off the ground. It was terrifying. I was only a youngster. The crowds weren't as big then, either. They hadn't all that long since split with Everton and they still did not have a large following. It cost sixpence to get in, but sometimes they didn't even get enough money to pay the players' wages. My father was earning £3 15s a week playing football for Liverpool. There were also little betting syndicates on the Kop, and sometimes a lot of money changed hands, you know, betting on the result or who was going to score. These were the days before the bookmakers' shops, and betting at football was very popular. I don't know where they got the money from.

Ted Doig was the first great goalkeeper that Liverpool ever had. Given that the Kop was built in 1906, he was probably the first Liverpool goalkeeper to play in front of the Kop. He loved it, and the Kop certainly loved him. His speciality was in punching the ball, and he could punch it out and find any man in his own half. He could punch the ball more than fifty yards to the half-way line. He used to practise by tying a ball to a band and then tying it to the bar of the goalposts, sometimes down on the Kop goal. Then he would punch it while holding a 14 lb dumb-bell in each hand. The ball would come shooting back at him from all angles. Sometimes he would put the dumb-bell on the floor, often quite near the goalpost, punch the ball, race to pick up the dumb-bell and then punch the ball again. He'd been a boxer as well, so he had quite a punch. They used to do a lot of their training on the Anfield pitch, running around the track or up and down the Kop. They had these rollers, three massive ones they were, and they used to have to push them up and down the pitch to build up their strength.

LESLIE EDWARDS
Former journalist, Liverpool Daily Post and Echo

It was my father, Ernest Edwards, who christened the Kop. He suggested the name Spion Kop. He had come to Liverpool from Birmingham to become sports editor of the *Liverpool Daily Post and Echo* in 1902. Three years later they built the Kop, and he suggested that they name it after the hill in South Africa where so many young Liverpool lads had lost their lives in the Boer War. During the early days of the century, football reporters used to take a bag of pigeons with them, and they released messages on tissue paper at the intervals and at the end of the match.

I followed in my father's footsteps on the *Daily Post and Echo* and began reporting on Liverpool in 1922. That was the season they won the championship. Spectators did not have much protection from the rain and the weather in those days. The Kop was just a mound, completely open to the elements. When it rained, everybody got soaked. Practically every fan in those days wore a flat cap or a trilby. Nobody ever encroached on the field of play, and there was never trouble outside the ground nor on the trains or trams.

I think the Kop was even more humorous in the 1920s and 30s. They didn't chant the obscenities which they do today. The swaying was even more frightening then than it is now. Of course, there were fewer barriers, so the sway was much greater.

Players were paid £8 a week with a £2 bonus for a win and £1 for a draw. If they were with the club for five years they qualified for a benefit of £650. In the summer, they existed on £6 or £7 a week. The players were the very model of propriety. They were non-smokers and non-drinkers, wore bowlers and trilbies and sported watch-chains, just like the directors.

Anfield in the early days had no dressing-room facilities, and players changed at the Sandon pub and walked across to the ground. Many Kop fans will be unaware of the fact that the flagpole down behind the Kop is one of the topmasts of the *Great Eastern* iron ship. It was broken up on the banks of the Mersey, over on the Birkenhead/Rock Ferry side at a ship-breaker's yard. And the mast was floated over to the Liverpool pierhead. It was put on wagons and pulled through the streets of Liverpool and up Everton Valley by a team of eight horses. And it still stands there today.

Anfield has had many famous visitors in its day, but I especially recall the visit of King George V and Queen Mary back in 1921. They had come to Liverpool for the Grand National, which used to be run on a Friday in those days. Anyhow, the next day they came to Anfield to watch the FA Cup semi-final between Wolverhampton Wanderers and Cardiff City.

There was a lot of trouble with the IRA even in those days and, with this being Liverpool, the police decided to take no chances and, once everyone was in the ground, the gates were locked. I had to leave the ground at one point and when I came to get back in, all the gates were shut. I tried getting into the Kop even, but all the gates were tightly locked. The King and Queen might not have been

9

on the Kop that day, but many famous people have stood on the Kop. I remember Bud Flanagan writing to my father once and telling him that he had once stood on the Kop. I don't suppose many people know that.

THE MEN FROM ANFIELD'S SPION KOP
(Sung to the tune of 'The Shores of Tripoli')

We are the men from Anfield's Spion Kop,
Our team is Liverpool FC.
We like to sing and shout,
Because we know,
We'll cheer our team to victory,
For it's a great team you'll agree,
And we'll go down in history.
We've won the cup, been champions too,
And today we'll murder you.
We're the Liverpool FC.

And if you care to go to any ground
You will always hear our songs.
To see our team, we'll travel anywhere,
If it's Europe we'll be there.
For we know our team will
FIGHT, FIGHT, FIGHT It's gonna be a
     glorious
SIGHT, SIGHT, SIGHT

We all agree it's gonna be
Another glorious victory
For the Liverpool FC.

BILLY O'DONNELL
Kopite

I'm 82 years old now and I started going to Anfield when I was 12 or 13. It would be about 1922. That's seventy years of going to see Liverpool play. In those days I used to go at three-quarter time, that was when they opened the big gates at the back of the Kop and we could all get in free. They were hard times and nobody had much money and there would always be a crowd of us waiting for the Kop gates to open, mostly kids. As soon as they opened, we would all rush in and on to the Kop hoping to see a late goal.

I always seemed to get there when there was a corner. Those were the days when the Kop didn't have a roof, it was just open terrace. It was always cold and very windy. We all wore caps in those days in case it rained. And if you were standing down at the bottom of the Kop you needed to wear wellingtons. Not just because of the rain pouring down the Kop but because of the toilet problem. You see, when you're stuck in the middle of the Kop and you've had a few pints before the match you have to get rid of it somehow. Well, you can't go to the toilet, cos if you do you'll never get back and you certainly wouldn't find your mates again. So everybody used to just do it there. They would bring a *Liverpool Echo* with them, roll it up and wee into it so that it didn't splash everybody!

You had a great view from the Kop, and if you were near the back you could see all over Liverpool. The steps weren't concrete either like they are today. They were cinder and had wood running alongside the upright of the step. I'm also pretty sure that the crush barriers were made of wood. Of course, there weren't as many then as there are now.

My Saturday routine was to have my dinner and then go for a few pints before the game with some of my mates. Then we'd all walk up to Anfield or maybe even catch the tram; it was only 1d. We always went on the Kop; it was the cheapest and cost one shilling, and we always went in the same spot. Week after week we'd be there. We knew all the blokes around us. We used to have a sweepstake for the first goal as well. Everybody put a shilling in, and you drew a piece of paper out of a hat. There were ten pieces of paper, each had a number on for the ten forwards from the two sides. So you'd have Liverpool 7, 8, 9, 10 and 11 and then, say, Wolves 7, 8, 9, 10 and 11. And if your number and team scored the first goal you pocketed the ten shillings. Little sweepstakes like that were going on all over the Kop. Then, after the match, we'd all go off and have another pint and a natter about the game. There was never any aggro. It was a great day out.

I used to look forward to Arsenal coming to Anfield. They were a fine team. Alex James, with his shorts almost down to his ankles. But what a player. Then there was Blackpool who, in the 1940s and 50s had Stanley Matthews and Stan Mortensen. West Ham were another side I liked because they wanted to play good football. My other favourite was Newcastle. They had a little inside-forward, a Scot called Hughie Gallagher. He was only small, flat nose, but by jove he could play. Elisha Scott hated him. I think there was a period when he always seemed to score against Scott. He got a hat-trick once. They were a great side. They would bring a lot of supporters with them and they would all come on the Kop with their black and white stripes.

When the teams came out they used to run up to the Kop end. Elisha Scott, the goalkeeper, would get a great cheer. The two full-backs would stand in the goal alongside him during the kick-in, knocking the ball out with their elbows to the forwards to practise their shooting. One of the defenders was Jimmy Jackson. He was a parson, ordained by the church. He was known as 'Parson' Jackson. He couldn't hit a dead ball for the life of him, but he was a good stopper.

Well, Elisha Scott used to shout and swear at him throughout the game. Scott was always one for organising his defence, and he'd curse them if they didn't get it right. All the time he'd be effing and blinding at Jackson, calling him every name under the sun, and Jackson would be wagging his finger at him, going 'tut, tut'. The Kop would be in uproar at this because we could hear every word.

Teams would have five forwards in those days, all attacking. And when the ball went back down their end, the forwards stayed where they were, in the opposition half, they didn't go running back to help out like they do now. Goals could be scored so quickly. It only took a few touches from the kick-off. Out to the wing, past the half-back, round the full-back, square the ball, and there was the centre-forward or inside-right to knock it in. It was so simple. I sometimes wonder what would happen if a team played five forwards today.

Outside the Kop there would be blokes walking around selling things like sweets. They would be selling bargains, throwing this, that and the other into a bag, shouting, 'Who'll give me such and such for this bag of chocolates', and then he'd throw an extra bar in. People would crowd around him. It was a bit like being down the market. There was another bloke who used to sell ice-cream. He used to shout: 'As cold as ice, as sweet as honey.' There were never any policemen to be seen. There was never any bother.

You used to get good crowds even at the reserve games in those days as well, 14,000 or 15,000 would go. I once went to see Liverpool schoolboys play Stockport school-boys. Stockport had a lad named Brennan. 'Boy' Brennan, they called him. They said he was supposed to be the best player in the world for his age. He was so big, he was like a man. Anyhow, 45,000 turned up for this match. Liverpool won. Boy Brennan didn't do much good and he never made it in league football either. But can you imagine, 45,000 for a schoolboy match? You don't even get that for a Premier League match now.

I love football. I wish I'd been good enough to play for Liverpool. It would have been a dream come true. These days I have to confess I no longer go on the Kop. I'm getting a bit old, so I go in the Paddock where I can sit down. Up to a couple of years back I was still going on the Kop. But what a shame it will be to see the Kop seated. I thought it would come, I've been saying so for a few years. It will be the end of an era. All those generations, fathers and sons reared on the Kop, standing behind the barriers, cheering Liverpool on. It won't be the same.

HARRY WILSON
Kopite

The first game I saw at Anfield was in 1927. I'd be about 18 years old then. I never missed a home match or a reserve match after that until about 1945 or 1946, when I got a job and could not get to go to games. I always went on the Kop and, when I started going, the Kop did not have a roof. It was just open to the elements, and by jove, it was cold. The wind used to rip across Anfield. You had to put an overcoat, scarf and gloves on in the winter, it was that cold. It still had the same steps and the barriers, though.

At the back of the Kop was a wall about six feet high, but you could see over it and look down on the Walton Breck Road and towards Everton Valley. You got a spectacular view from the top. Looking the other way you could see all the way across Anfield and Stanley Park and down to Goodison. But, of course, it was even windier up at the back on the top. Behind the Kop was a grass mound which dropped down to road level, and there were the stairs, about twelve feet wide, which climbed right up to the top of the Kop. They pulled those down after the 1971 Ibrox disaster and built that new stairway. Those stairs were a bit dangerous, but I never saw an accident there.

In those days, the crowds were not as great. I suppose there would be between 20,000 and 30,000. The Paddock and the Anfield Road End were always packed, but not usually the Kop, except on a derby day. I can remember when they put the roof on. The atmosphere without the roof was nowhere near as good as it was when the roof went on in 1928. It made a big difference. We didn't get wet any more. We thought it was the finest thing that had ever happened. It was out of this world, no wind ripping across Anfield at us. There was a boys' pen as well, up in the corner of the Kop. That was always packed. You should have heard the language that came from it – you couldn't print it.

Every Saturday me and my mate would go to the match. We'd meet at our house at about one o'clock and walk to the ground. I had a red and white rosette with the name Liverpool emblazoned across it. I wore it for every game and still had it up until a year or so ago, when it got thrown away. Nobody wore scarves or had flags and banners in those days. When we got to the ground we'd buy a programme for 3d, or if we couldn't afford it we'd ask someone if we could have a look at theirs. People didn't mind sharing.

There was no singing in those days, I can tell you that. But there was lots of chanting. We used to chant the names of the players. When Harry Chambers, our centre-forward, scored we'd all chant, 'Cham-bers, Cham-bers'. He was one of our favourites. And then there was Elisha Scott, the greatest goalkeeper of them all. We called him 'Lisha'. He was idolised by the Kop. They would shout, 'Lisha, Lisha'. When the players came out on to the pitch they would run down to the Kop end just as they do now, and Lisha would wave to us. He also used to give us a wave when he left the pitch. He was the great favourite. It was a great crowd on the Kop. We had so much fun.

The opposition fans would be there as well, but there were never any problems. We would joke with them, and if Liverpool scored or beat them we would just say, 'Bad luck.' They would cheer for their side during the game as much as we cheered. The derby games, of course, were the best. Most of the Evertonians would go down the Anfield Road End, but you used to get a few on the Kop. That was the only time there was ever any bother but it wasn't really much. They just used to take the mickey. They used to give us a lot of stick. They used to call Chambers 'Toilet' and they'd shout it at him. Then they used to tell

Dick Forshaw to go to Southport, and they called Wadsworth 'Wandsworth'. 'Go to Wandsworth,' they'd yell at him. And Elisha Scott was called 'The Baker' because of Scott's bakery. We used to have names for their players as well. It was like a festival, all fun.

It was a very working-class crowd on the Kop, mainly dockers and the like. The toffs were in the Paddock and the stands. We called them 'the mob' or 'the toffs'. It wasn't nasty or anything. The Anfield Road End was also full of working-class men. Before the game started, men would walk around the pitch carrying billboards advertising things like Ovaltine or cocoa and especially the boxing contests at the stadium, which were very popular in those days.

JACK PAYNE
Kopite

I went to my first match at Anfield in 1929. I would be about eight years old then. My uncle took me, and it was a Liverpool/Everton derby game. It was a special occasion, so I got all dressed up, best suit, polished shoes, cap and so on. I was going with my uncle, see, so I had to be smartly dressed. He took me on the Kop. It was amazing. I didn't know much about football. All we did was throw a couple of coats down on the ground in the park for goalposts, or play in the jigger [alley] with the walls as goalposts. But being on the Kop was wonderful. The atmosphere was incredible. After that I started going to every game.

We lived in Bootle at the time, but I used to walk to Anfield, a little toddler, running across the fields. There were fields in those days, and I could take a short cut. It took me about half an hour or so. I used to go for three-quarter time, when they opened the gates at the back of the Kop and we got in for nothing. Of course, I didn't wear a suit then. Then I got a paper round and I could afford to pay and go to the whole game.

At first, I went in the Boys' Pen. In those days, it was on the Kemlyn Road. You paid to go in, however, in the Anfield Road, at the corner with the Kemlyn Road. The Boys' Pen was shaped like a triangle, with the long side running from the corner-post to the half-way line. And it was right along the touchline. You had a great spec, probably the best in the ground, and at half-time all the men used to come and jump in. After the war they moved it on to the Kop.

There used to be some characters at Anfield. I always remember this old chap. He had grey hair, big bushy eyebrows, and he wore a white jacket. He had a wicker tray with leather straps which he wore around his neck, and on the tray he sold home-made biscuits. They were about the size of a digestive biscuit but made of treacle. They were delicious, and for a penny he'd give you half a dozen or so which he would wrap up very cleverly in a cone of paper. I can still taste them. He was really funny, this man. At the time, Gordon Hodgson was our star player. And this bloke used to walk around the running track shouting, 'Hodgson's choice, Hodgson's choice!' The next week he'd be up at Goodison shouting, 'Dixie's choice, Dixie's choice!'

There used to be a band as well, usually a local one. They would play before the game and at half-time, marching around the pitch. They were led by a man with a mace, and as he marched towards the Kop he would hurl his mace high into the sky and catch it as it came down. When he caught it, the Kop would give out a loud cheer. The Kop used to sing along as well. They were mainly popular tunes they played, and one of the Kop favourites was, 'Oh yes, we have no bananas'. Lots of people on the Kop used to have rattles as well with the team colours tied to them. If you stood by one of them you could be deafened, they were so noisy. They would be classed as an offensive weapon now. You never see them today.

If I was going to the game with my mates we would go and have a pint beforehand, then off to the ground, always going in the Kop. We'd buy a programme, and after we'd all read it we'd start chatting to the opposition supporters. There was no segregation. We'd introduce them to our sweep as well. We never had disputes with the sweep. Sometimes, if we weren't certain who had scored, we would take the general opinion and pay out on that. But there was never any fights or anything like that.

BOB TWEEDALE
Kopite

Back in the old days, you could walk from the Anfield Road down to the Kop. There were no barriers to stop you. The Kemlyn Road had a paddock, so at half-time, if Liverpool had been kicking towards the Anfield Road, everyone would start making their way out of the Anfield Road down the Kemlyn Road paddock and into the Kop. Of course, that meant there were even more people in the Kop for the second half. And, with twenty minutes to go, they would also open the gates of the Kop. But people never left. It just meant that a few hundred more poured into the ground free of charge.

BILLY O'DONNELL
Kopite

You used to get a lot of tram drivers going on the Kop in the old days. You could spot them a mile off. They had red, weather-beaten faces. You see, the trams were open at the front where the driver was sitting, and they used to get the full force of the wind, rain and sun in their faces. They also used to wear these big oilskin coats and had their tram-driver hats on with the badge on it. They would drive the trams up to Anfield and, if it was near kick-off time, they would leave them there because there wouldn't be time to take the tram back into town or wherever and get back before the end of the game. So they would just be left standing in the Walton Breck Road. The drivers would go into the Kop and watch the game, then come out ten minutes before the end to get them ready to take everybody home.

Lots of other people used to go to the game on their bicycles. You could lock the bikes up in someone's yard. All those little houses around the ground used to let you put your bike in their yard. They would charge you 6d a time, give you a ticket, and all the bikes would be locked up together. The trouble was that if you came out early you couldn't get your bike until everyone else had arrived.

HARRY GOUGH
Kopite

There was a chap who would walk around the ground with a blackboard with the team changes chalked on the board. Those were the days before tannoy systems, and this was the only way of telling everyone about the line-ups. I remember there was also a man with a sandwich-board, and he would walk around the pitch as well. The sandwich-board told you what fights were on at the Liverpool stadium that week. They used to have boxing at Anfield as well, but I never saw any of it. It was during the 1930s, and I was too young, though I do remember minding a man's motor bike and side-car for a couple of pence the night Nelson Tarleton fought there.

But I did see some tennis at Anfield. Boards had been laid down in the centre circle and a net put up. There were some big stars there that night. Fred Perry played, as well as the American Big Bill Tilden and, I think, Elsworth Vines. Howard Marshall was the commentator. It must have been during the late 1930s. The spectators either sat in the stands or stood on the Kop, just like it was a football match. But I don't recall that all that many came. Tennis isn't really a Liverpool game. You don't see much of it in this city. And then, some time before Shankly arrived, the Harlem Globetrotters came. So we've seen a bit of everything from the Kop.

JACK PAYNE
Kopite

When I was a kid in the 1930s, I used to go to Anfield during the summer holidays, after the players had come back for training. I'd go and watch them, spend the best part of the day there. They used to train where the car park now is, at the back of the Main Stand. They would be there practising their ball control and doing exercises. And you could also see them running around Stanley Park. Everton would be there as well. The players used to talk to you in those days. They would stop and have a chat, give you their autograph. You would regularly see them around the area. They were a part of the community. Today they live miles away in the suburbs in expensive houses and don't have any time for the fans.

ALBERT STUBBINS
Liverpool player, 1946–53

It was a wonderful experience just to play at Anfield, particularly when you were playing towards the Kop. If you were losing, say, 0–1 and you were playing into the Kop in the second half, it was worth a goal. The enthusiasm, the wave of sound that came out of there was terrific. It will be a sad loss when it's seated or pulled down or whatever they finally do with it. Even in the post-war years, the attendances were tremendous. It meant that the Kop was bursting every week. There was never a spare space anywhere. For a Liverpool/Everton game we'd have a 50,000-plus crowd.

We always had our pre-match kick-ins down at the Kop end, like they do today. The energy that crowd could put into it was amazing. We would thrive on it. I've never really experienced anything like it. I was used to the noise of a big crowd as I had been at Newcastle before Liverpool. I've been lucky to have played my career in front of the two best crowds anywhere – Liverpool and

Newcastle. To a visiting player it must have been intimidating. But I never played for the away side at Anfield. I only ever played there for Liverpool.

There wasn't any organised chanting in those days; that came later with Shankly. There was some singing but it was usually drowned out by the vast noise. The Liverpool fans, even then, were very witty. You could catch the occasional comment if things suddenly went quiet. Mind you, the average Liverpudlian is a very witty man. The thing that always struck me about the Kop was that it was always moving. Swaying one way, then the other. Aye, they were happy memories.

BOB TWEEDALE
Kopite

I started going on the Kop during the Second World War. I saw lots of wartime games. You often didn't know who was going to be playing. Sometimes there was a team sheet, but often as not there was none. And if there was one it would have on it A.N. Other. I've loved every minute, and fifty years on I'm still going on the Kop every game.

I've always likened it to a giant heart beating. You can feel the pulse of it, the vibration. For the big games during the 1960s, particularly the European matches, you had to get there really early. Sometimes it meant bunking off from work early.

O COME ALL YE FAITHFUL
(Traditional carol)

O come, all ye faithful,
joyful and triumphant,
O come ye, O come ye,
To Anfield.
Come and behold them,
They're the cream of Europe.

21

O come, let us adore them,
O come, let us adore them,
O come, let us adore them,
Liverpool.

HARRY WILSON
Kopite

The war didn't make much difference to me, I still went to Anfield. But there weren't the crowds, probably 20,000 at the very most, and usually only around 10,000 or so. Everybody was scared of going out to public places like that. You didn't know if the bombs were going to drop. Nothing like that ever did happen, though. The bombs came at night, not on a Saturday afternoon. There was no tannoy at Anfield, and I don't ever remember an air-raid siren. It was always a problem knowing who would be in the team as there were so many guest players. The changes from the programme would be chalked on a board by where the players come out. Sometimes we got a few unexpected stars playing for us.

SHEILA SPIERS
National Secretary, Football Supporters' Association

My father was the publican at the Sandon Hotel in Oakfield Road. It was, of course, a very famous landmark in the history of the club. It used to be owned by John Houlding, the man who started both Liverpool and Everton Football Clubs, and for some years it was where the players used to change before the game. That was in the 1880s and 1890s. We took over the pub in 1948 and stayed there until 1959. I vividly remember that there used to be a picture done in tiles on one of the walls of the pub. It was of Sandy Young, the Everton centre-forward at the turn of the century. I saw it recently at Goodison where it has been removed to. It was the first time I had seen it for years. It brought back some nice memories. I used to see it every day once. There used to be lots of photographs of the Liverpool teams on the walls as well, but I don't know what happened to them.

Everyone who came to the pub seemed to be a football supporter. We used to have an old barman who was so bigoted he wouldn't even go to Goodison for the derby matches. On match-days, the atmosphere in the pub was incredible. It would be busy from about 11 a.m. onwards, and between 1 p.m. and 2 p.m. it would be absolutely packed. In those days before floodlights, the games used to start at two o'clock. I was 11 at the time we took over the pub, and I was completely fascinated by it all, the noise, the people, the horses, the policemen. I just wanted to know what was going on. I was always a very sporty person, so it was inevitable that I became interested. I used to go down to the ground at three-quarter time and I would run up and down the steps at the back of the Kop. Then, occasionally, I'd pluck up a bit of courage and go inside the Kop and chase up and down a few steps there if there was any room. The men standing there would tell me to bugger off and go back home.

It was a totally male-dominated area in those days. But I wanted to be part of it. It was all so fascinating. I told my dad, and he said, 'Why don't you go and see the reserves?' So I did. I went in the stand then. Then I decided I wanted to see a big match, so my dad said I could if I went in the Boys' Pen, which used to be on the top corner of the Kop. It was the 1949–50 season. We almost won the league that season and, of course, we reached the Cup final.

The Kop was pretty staid in those days. There was no singing and not much chanting. They just cheered. But, in the Boys' Pen, we made a lot of noise and we jumped around a great deal. I was the only girl there, but the boys accepted me. There was nobody saying, 'What's a girl like you doing here?' They just accepted it. Kids are like that. I was there all by myself. There was never any problem, and the Sandon was just a stone's throw from the ground.

After that I started going in the stands with my dad, and I have to confess I've never been on the Kop since, just that one season in the Boys' Pen – or should it be the Boys' and Girls' pen?

ERIC BARNSLEY
Kopite

During the old days, they used to have midweek matches in the afternoon. Those were the days before floodlights, but you still got good crowds. Liverpool always had their games on a Wednesday afternoon, when the shopkeepers had a half-day. When Liverpool or Everton were at home in midweek, the docks used to come to a standstill. There'd be nobody there, they'd all be up at Anfield. You had to think up good excuses, though. You had a bad back or a sore throat, they were the best, though some people came up with the most amazing tales. Of course, in those days they had casual labour in the docks, so it was fairly easy. You just didn't show up in a morning. Lots of blokes would leave home, pretending to their wives that they were going down the docks to work, and they just wouldn't sign on. They'd hang around somewhere all morning until it was time to go to the match. Then they'd wander home at five o'clock, telling the wife they'd done a day's work. She'd never know any different. Of course, they didn't get paid but somehow they'd manage to cover it up at the end of the week.

The other thing was that, during the winter, the games used to finish up in near pitch-blackness. You still had a 3 o'clock, or often 3:15 p.m. kick-off. So by 4 o'clock it was getting pretty dark. And when you were standing on the Kop half the time you couldn't make out what was going on down the other end of the pitch, it was so dark. When the floodlights came it caused a social revolution. Everybody had to work a full week, there were no midweek afternoon games any more, and suddenly we started going to football in the evening. It was an amazing change. The employers loved it. But, privately, I think the dockers quite enjoyed having the occasional Wednesday afternoon off. It broke the week up nicely.

JOE MARTIN
Kopite

The first time I ever heard singing on the Kop was in the 1950s, when Arthur Kagan came. He was the man who used to conduct the community singing at Wembley for the Cup finals. Well, they brought him to Anfield one Saturday, and there was a band as well. He was there to try and organise some community singing. It was a game against Blackpool. Blackpool always used to attract a big crowd because of Matthews and Mortensen.

Well, that day the band started playing and Kagan began conducting, but the Kop being the Kop started singing a different song. Every time the band struck up, the Kop sang, 'Oh yes, we have no bananas, we have no bananas today.' It was dead funny. There he was trying to organise us. But as anyone will tell you in this city, you can't organise the Kop. It has a mind of its own. Kagan got so frustrated he gave up. They also had a duck there that day. It was painted orange, the colours of Blackpool, and they paraded it around the pitch before kick-off.

WE SHALL NOT BE MOVED
(Sung to the tune of the same name)

We shall not,
We shall not be moved.
We shall not,
We shall not be moved,
Just like the team,
That's gonna win the Football League,
We shall not be moved.

Two

COMRADESHIP

I am a Liverpudlian, I Come from the Spion Kop

JOHN WILLIAMS
*Kopite and researcher at the Sir Norman Chester Centre
for Football Research, Leicester University*

In the 1960s, the Kop became a cultural focal point. It
was about the young people of the city and about their
music. Football and music became intertwined. It also had
a global perspective, in that the whole world was looking
at Liverpool. For the first time ever, pop culture and
football culture came together. That was very important
and has had repercussions ever since. But, at the same
time, you cannot judge the Kop as some homogenous
group. It isn't. It is broken up into various constituent
parts. There are the youngsters who like to go down at the
bottom by the pitch; then there are the singers who want
to stand in the middle; and there are also the more
respectable types who stand at the sides. There are those
who want to dance up and down, and there are those who
are fashionable. There are all these different groups all
over the Kop.

Another thing is that the Kop is desperately important
to many people who no longer live in the centre of the
city. As the city has changed, new towns such as Kirkby
and Netherley have sprung up, and there are now more
exiled scousers working and living away from home than
ever. For them, the Kop is the place where they come to
re-establish themselves, to regather and to celebrate the

fact that they come from Liverpool. It's very important to them. It's a kind of coming home, back to their grassroots.

The other thing that has to be remembered is that the Kop is a very safe place. Any trouble that there has been has always been down the Anfield Road End. It has never stemmed from the Kop, and you would be hard put to ever find any incidents of violence on the Kop. People feel very comfortable there and even take their children on the Kop. We did some research shortly after the Heysel disaster, talking to young people about their experiences of football. The interesting thing was that a number of kids, particularly girls, said that the Kop was like a family. The young girls often went there with their uncles or some close relation and always felt safe. It was only elsewhere that there was trouble. So the Kop had this reputation of being calm, safe and dignified.

Of course, that didn't suit everybody. Some of the young lads wanted a bit of excitement and, in the 1970s, they forsook the Kop and went down the Anfield Road End. As I've said, there was never any trouble on the Kop. It may have been a tradition for visiting supporters to come along and take the home supporters' end, but that was impossible at Anfield. The Kop, like the Holte End or the Stretford End, was just too big with too many supporters, so they never even tried to take it. Hence all the violence took place elsewhere.

It's also interesting how different the Kop is today from what it was, say, ten years and more ago. I can remember going to the Ajax game with 25,000 on the Kop, and they were passing bodies overhead. Today, especially after Hillsborough, we wouldn't even contemplate that kind of a crowd. It strikes me that people must have been far more concerned about each other in those days, that they helped protect one another, you know, older men looking after the kids or the elderly. You wouldn't get that today, there is no longer that sense of cohesion. It may be the same terracing, but there isn't the same caring.

One of the problems about seating the Kop which people tend to forget is how groups regather for each game. Go to the same spot any week and you will find the same faces, the same groups of people. People don't have to make arrangements or go to the game together, they just meet at the same spot on the Kop, week in, week out. And there are those coming from a distance who meet up for the one occasion. There is an informality. You may not go for six weeks, but the next time you do go you know some of your pals, the more regulars, will probably be there at their usual spot. Seating could destroy that, especially if you have to sit in the same seat week after week.

RICHARD PEDDER
Kopite

The wonderful thing about the Kop is that it is a community. In fact, it's more than that. It's a whole number of small communities. It's groups of people who all know each other. You're never alone on the Kop. You can go to the same spot each game and you always see the same people. You might not even know their names but you're on speaking terms with them, you're pals with them. You ask how they are, you chat to them and so on.

But once the Kop is seated, that comradeship will disappear. There won't be the same groups. You won't be able to go where you want and you won't be able to have a block booking of seats so that all your pals can be with you. At Goodison, they've tried to accommodate this problem by not numbering the seats so that you can sit anywhere. But it doesn't really work because you can't save half a dozen seats for your pals if you happen to be early. It's first come, first served. That's what we shall all miss about standing on the Kop – the ability to stand wherever you want and with whomever you want. The comradeship will never be the same.

JOHNNY KENNEDY
Radio City DJ

When they talk about seating the Kop they really shouldn't be talking about seating the Kop, they should be talking about destroying the Kop. They obviously don't use that kind of emotive language, but that's what they are doing. Once they put seats into the Kop there will be no Kop. The Kop at Anfield will cease to exist. The Kop and standing are synonymous. Maybe you can have a seated Kop at some other ground because it's not the proper Kop, but at Anfield you're not seating the Kop, you're destroying the Kop. The club will argue that the Taylor Report has made it a necessity. Personally, I don't go along with that. I think the club are happy to have the Kop seated for financial reasons. It won't be the Kop any more. You can call it what you like, but the day they seat the Kop is the day the Kop ceases to exist.

The great thing about being on the Kop in the great days, and it still applies to some degree today – a few weeks ago, Graeme Souness felt that it was an important factor – in the great days of the Kop, you really felt as though it was the next best thing to playing for them. We all wanted to play for them but, of course, that privilege is given only to a very few, people like Phil Thompson, who graduate from the Kop to the pitch, but such a small percentage make it. But it was the next best thing to playing, and there is no doubt about it that you could play your part in influencing a game. No doubt about that.

The great night against Inter Milan on 4 May 1965 was real psychological warfare, apart from walking around the ground with the cup before the game, which was the great Shankly masterstroke. But the crowd themselves that night, and particularly the Kop, played a great part in the victory. OK, Liverpool were already on a high, but the support they got from the crowd that night really swept them along, and it definitely intimidated the Italians. We won 3–1 that night, and anyone who was there will tell you 5–0 would have been a fairer reflection of the superiority of Liverpool. So you felt that you were taking part in the game.

PHIL THOMPSON
Liverpool player, 1971–85

I had the distinction of standing in the Kop for years. I first started going to Anfield when I was about 12 or 13. This fella used to take my brother and me. We'd go in the Anfield Road End or the Paddock. But we'd always be looking at the Kop, saying we'd be up there one day with them. My mum was a bit concerned and didn't want us to go in the Kop.

Anyrate, my brother was a bit older than me so he started taking me in the Boys' Pen up in the Kop. My mum didn't know. We'd pay our 1s. 6d to go in the Boys' Pen, and then we'd climb over at the top corner and sneak into the Kop with the steward usually chasing us. Later we started going in the Kop properly. My brother was working and he would give me 50p a week to mind a spot for him on the Kop. I used to be there about 1:30 p.m., but he worked on a Saturday morning so he didn't arrive until 2 p.m., but I'd be there keeping his place. I'd have to push people away to keep this spot by the barrier. We were stood right behind the goal, in the middle, but a bit down so that we were just above the crossbar. It was a prime position, the heart of the Kop. I was only about 14 or 15 and I wasn't very big. I didn't see much, but that hardly mattered. It was just being there that counted.

A few years later, I was playing for the reserves. I'd be turning out for the reserves on a Tuesday night, and then I'd be in the Kop on the Wednesday with my brother. I'd be there chanting the names of the players that I was working with and playing football with every day. I made my debut when I was 18, and after that people started recognising me. It got a bit embarrassing being in the Kop and being recognised, so I stopped and, of course, not long after that I was playing all the time.

There was never any problem being in the Kop. There would be these huge crowds, 25,000 or 27,000, but nobody ever got that hurt. People fainted, and we'd pass the bodies over us. It was a regular occurrence. 'Man coming down,' someone would shout, and we'd all put our hands above our heads and take the weight of the body, passing it down towards the front. It would never be tolerated these days, and I suppose looking back we were lucky there was never a serious accident.

I used to go out of the Kop via the steps in the corner and I'd cut down to the left, and I always remember I used to love just letting the crowd carry me through the main gate. The crowd was just swept along, and I used to deliberately take my feet off the ground to see how far I would be carried. Every match I used to do that. It was a great feeling just being swept along without your feet on the ground.

It's hard to describe what the Kop means to you. To come from being on the Kop to playing in front of it was just amazing. You get such a buzz. I was one of them, and here I was. Every match I used to run down the Kop end and wave to my brother. He'd still be standing in the same spot. People say to me, how could you possibly spot your brother in all that crowd? But I knew precisely where to look.

Without a shadow of a doubt, it gives the team a great buzz. It's frightening, all those people. And there's no doubt that it swayed referees when there were twenty-odd thousand demanding a penalty, especially in those European games. Coming down the Kop end and hearing them chant your name is incredible. It's a great feeling. But it's not what it used to be, hasn't been for some years really. It's socially different now.

There was a time when at least 20,000 of those on the Kop went there to sing as well as watch the game, but now there's only about four or five thousand who want to sing and chant. It's not the same, and once it's seated it will be even less so. It's a shame, but it's got to happen.

Liverpool of all clubs, especially after Hillsborough, cannot say no.

JOHN ALDRIDGE
Liverpool player, 1987–89

That final game for me was very emotional. I knew it was my last game for Liverpool. I was set to sign for Real Sociedad, the Spanish club, the next day. I didn't really want to go, I didn't want to leave Liverpool Football Club, and I didn't want to leave the city of Liverpool. But I could see that my chances of playing were fairly limited. The match was against Crystal Palace, and I was on the bench. Liverpool were well ahead when we got a penalty. Kenny asked me if I wanted to go on and take it. I didn't need much prompting. I was on and put the ball in the back of the net. We won 9–0 that night. After the game I went up to the Kop. I was in tears. I threw my jersey to them and then I thought, 'I might as well start with a new pair of boots,' so I pulled my boots off and threw them into the Kop as well. It was very emotional for me.

I can still remember the first time I went to Anfield. I went with my Uncle Tommy. I was about 10 years old then, and he took me in the Paddock. Then, later, I started going by myself and went in the Boys' Pen. My dad wouldn't let me go on the Kop proper. Eventually, he relented but told me to stay at the sides and not go in the middle. Then I was going with mates, and as I got older I was there in the middle of the Kop with the true Kopites. The first time I ever played in front of the Kop was for Oxford United in a league match in March 1986. I had done a piece with Tony Gubba for *Grandstand*, and it went out that lunchtime. I was telling him how wonderful Liverpool Football Club was, and how I used to stand on the Kop as a lad. Anyhow, when we came down the Kop end for the second half, the Kop gave me a tremendous reception. 'Aldridge is a Kopite,' they were all chanting. It was great. Unfortunately, we got beat 0–6. Rush and Molby got a couple each.

I can't remember much about the first time I pulled on a Liverpool shirt at Anfield, as I first came on as a sub. But I do vividly recall the first full game I played. That was against Southampton, and we won 1–0 and I scored. It was a great start, and the Kop gave me a wonderful welcome.

I had a great relationship with the Kop. I never went in the stands at Anfield until I was a player, it was always the Kop for me. I was a local lad and had done well. I was one of them. I had done what they all dream of doing, of going from the Kop to pull on a Liverpool shirt and score goals in front of the Kop.

THE REDS ARE COMING UP THE HILL

(Sung to the tune of 'Tramp, Tramp, Tramp, the Boys are Marching')

Oh, the Reds are coming up the hill, boys,
Oh, the Reds are coming up the hill, boys.
They all laugh at us,
They all mock at us,
They all say our days are numbered.
But born to be a scouser,
Victorious are we.
If you want to win the cup,
Then you'd better hurry up,
We're the Liverpool FC.

JOHNNY KENNEDY
Radio City DJ

The first time I ever went on the Kop is easy for me to remember, because I was only a very small boy, before I started school. I'd be about 4. My uncle took me on the Kop to see Liverpool play Everton, not in a league match but in a Liverpool Senior Cup game, and I was so small he put me on his shoulders. And the thing that I can remember is that everybody was very nice to me and very friendly, like they always are to a kid. After that it was difficult to get in the Kop. As a kid you had to go in the Boys' Pen, you couldn't actually roam free in the Kop. But I mean, when I was old enough I started going in and I never wanted to go anywhere else, and although I've got a season ticket now I still go on the Kop.

I never bother buying a ticket for any of the cup games, I always go on the Kop. I enjoy the game far more from the Kop, it's a different experience. There is nothing like the Kop, and I've had some incredible times there watching Liverpool, some marvellous wins, nights like St Etienne, Inter Milan. But there have been other wonderful games as well, defeats even. I remember when they got beat by Swansea in 1964 in what must be the most one-sided game in the history of football; Liverpool were on top throughout, but they still got beat. As a kid, of course, Billy Liddell stands out particularly as the hero of the Kop.

But it hasn't always been about great occasions for me. One of the best days I ever had in the Kop was when I was a kid, when Louis Bimpson got four in forty-five minutes in a game for Liverpool against Burnley, and all at the Kop end. That was an incredible day because Louis, who was a great player, was a one-hundred-percenter, and he gave everything for Liverpool, and the crowd loved him. He could stand on the ball, and they'd forgive him because they knew he was doing everything he could to get the ball in the net. That was the day it all came right for Louis, and he got four against Burnley. The Kop was like a carnival, so thrilled for him.

I also remember one particular time I was in. I used to go with a mate of mine called Georgie Jones, and I don't remember who we were playing, but it was during Alfie Arrowsmith's golden period. But the longest spell he had in the team was when St John was in hospital, and Alfie had a long run, and I'm sure we won the championship. It was in the days before the modern crush barriers were installed and, when Liverpool attacked the Kop end, the Kop used to surge forward and it was quite normal to sway thirty yards. It sounds horrendous now, but you could go thirty yards down the Kop and then all come back together. But, this particular day, I remember Liverpool were attacking and Alf Arrowsmith scored. The Kop went berserk, you see, and they all swayed forward and I went with them, but for some reason I got detached on my own. I went flying through the air on my own, and when I came back I hit the back of one group, and they all surged back and I came back with them, but minus one of my shoes.

Now that wouldn't necessarily have been that bad, except that I vividly remember these shoes. It was in the era of winkle-pickers. Don't ask me what I was doing wearing winkle-pickers in the Kop, but I was. Anyrate, I came back minus a shoe. Well, Georgie Jones, actually, for some reason, hadn't swayed forward and he saw me disappearing like on a tidal wave and suddenly thrown off and flying along on my own and suddenly coming back minus a shoe. And, of course, when he realised, I was saying, I've lost me shoe, where's me shoe?' But there was nothing I could do about it, cos the sea had closed over and one shoe was thirty yards down.

I waited until the end of the game to look for my shoe but I never found it. I think to this day there is somebody who's got that left winkle-picker of mine. And I want it back! They were great days. We went to a pub called The King Harry down Rockfield Road, on the cobbles with one shoe missing and, of course, all the lads were laughing. In the course of a game, a shoe could get kicked a long way. I think somebody picked it up for a laugh, or maybe he had a one-legged uncle or something like that.

I travelled once from Birmingham. I was doing a week at a club called the 'Dolce Vita', right in the centre of Birmingham near the Bull Ring. And Liverpool were playing Leeds United. I don't think it was a Saturday; I've got a feeling it was a holiday game. I drove all the way back and, in those days, I didn't have a season ticket. So there I was queuing at this gate to get on to the Kop, and it was in the days when Liverpool and Leeds was the fixture of the entire Football League season. And I was the very last one left outside when they locked the gates. There was a rumour going that they were going to lock the gates any minute now, and I'm getting nearer and nearer to the gate, and I was the very last one. And they closed that narrow wooden door, slammed it in my face, and that was that. I never got in after coming all that way from Birmingham.

In some ways, the Kop is a reflection of the city of Liverpool, especially with its humour. And also in its great loyalty. I stood on the Kop for a very long time, and there are people who have stood on the Kop their entire lives watching Liverpool and would never go anywhere else. To be a Kopite meant something. You would say it with pride. Like in an army, some men were proud to be private soldiers and not NCOs or officers. The Kop is a real army. I'm a Kopite, I'm a real supporter, and I'm sure that feeling still applies today, which is why it is particularly sad that the Kop is now threatened – it's almost bizarre, really – by Liverpool Football Club itself. But there is no doubt about it that there have been games which the Kop have won – as far as any crowd can ever win any game – won by inspiring Liverpool and at the same time demoralising the opposition.

I know some players say they rarely hear the crowd. I don't know about that, and anyhow it's not the same with all players, but no matter how intense your concentration is I don't believe players don't hear the crowd. They definitely do hear the crowd, certainly at Anfield. I mean, you'll see players occasionally react to the crowd at Anfield, to something specific which the crowd have chanted. Crowds can influence games.

Also players have left clubs because of the crowd. That hasn't very often happened at Liverpool, but I would suggest that it happened in the case of Jimmy Melia. They were unkind to Melia. And I also think it influenced the club's decision about a potential signing. There was a time when Liverpool were seriously considering signing Peter Barnes. The Kop did not like this idea at all and they started chanting, 'If you hate Peter Barnes clap your hands', and the whole Kop chanted it. It was never mentioned again.

The relationship with Kevin Keegan turned sour because the Kop felt that Keegan wasn't trying in his last season. It's as simple as that. He would no doubt say that he was trying, but that wasn't the impression given in that season. And it was reinforced by his great performance in the European Cup final of 1977, people saying that he was performing on the European stage there but, in the run-of-the-mill matches during the season, he wasn't trying. But, yeah, they still won the league. It's also difficult to imagine any man getting away with that under Bob Paisley.

Crowds can be fickle. I think Keegan today is not as popular in retrospect as he should be. It's partly because of that last season but more so, I think, because since he left Liverpool, although he's never ever hidden his great admiration of Bill Shankly, too often he has compared Liverpool – the Kop, that is – unfavourably with other clubs, particularly Newcastle, and some of his comments haven't gone down too well. Also we thought that if he ever came back he would come to us and, of course, he didn't. So, in a sense, they don't regard him as a red through and through, although he was a great player, no question of that.

STEVE ANDERSON
Kopite

I shall never forget the first time I ever went on the Kop, though for all the wrong reasons. I used to go in the Paddock with my dad, and I kept on going on to him about letting me go in the Kop on my own. I was only nine at the time. All my pals were going in so, of course, I wanted to go. Well, eventually he relented and said that I could go in the Boys' Pen. Liverpool were playing Chelsea that day. It was September 1967. Liverpool had just signed Tony Hateley from Chelsea. I remember Liverpool won 3-1, and Hateley scored a couple.

Anyhow, my mum knitted me a new scarf especially for the occasion. It was a beautiful red scarf and had all the players' names carefully knitted on to it: Lawler, Byrne, Yeats, Hunt, St John, and so on. Well, of course, it got nicked, didn't it? There were 53,000 there that day, and in the crush not only did my scarf disappear, but my programme and my special Liverpool pen.

I was distraught. Anyhow, I went up to this copper and told him that somebody had nicked my scarf and he said, ' 'Ere are, lad, 'ave this one, it's just been nicked off somebody else.' I took it, but it wasn't as good as my mum's. I was terrified of going back home. All I can remember all the way home was having to face my mum. I was so frightened. It was the first time I'd worn it. But, of course, my mum took my side when I got home.

PAUL KELLY
Kopite

I think you can almost trace a decline in the Kop back to 1978. A large group split off then and went down to the Anfield Road End. They were looking for a bit more excitement and did everything that was the very opposite of the Kop. They were vocal, but they were not of the 'We are the famous Kopites' variety. They didn't wear scarves or anything like that. They didn't want to be identifiable, but they finished up wearing the uniform they didn't want to wear because they were identifiable by the very fact that they didn't wear scarves or badges. They just stood out. Why did they do it? I suppose it was because it was easier for their brand of hooliganism. But they did cause a change. A huge chunk – and there must have been a thousand of them – disappeared from the Kop.

The Kop is not what it used to be. Much of the fun has disappeared. For instance, there was this bloke who would run on the pitch every week and kick the ball into the back of the net. The police knew how to handle it. They'd let him kick the ball into the goal and then they'd throw him back on to the Kop. It was all very friendly. But if you went on the pitch now you'd be arrested and charged. That's not the police's fault, it's just the way the game has changed. The policing at Anfield is very good but it's got rid of a lot of the fun. Oddly enough, they don't seem to bother about the drug-taking that goes on. Go on the Kop for any night game, and the smell of dope is heavy in the air. People are puffing away, but the police don't bother. I suppose they're after the big dealers, not the occasional smoker.

The other thing about the Kop is that it's not a good view. You can't judge offside, although everybody on the Kop will swear blind that someone was offside. It is a very different perspective. But at least you can see the game these days. When the Kop had a higher capacity you hardly saw the match at all, you were just pushing and struggling to stay on your feet. But there is no doubt that the Kop is witty. Some people say it's witty at all grounds, but it's not. When I was working in Oxford I used to go and watch Oxford United regularly. I'd stand behind the goal, and they were shooting up the league at the time, but there was never the wit that you get at Anfield. There's a bloke stands behind me on the Kop, and every game at some point he shouts, 'Get Heighway on!' He must have been shouting that for twenty years now.

Perhaps we've all grown up a bit, especially after Hillsborough. I used to go just for the atmosphere, to shout and sing, but now I go to watch the football. Shanks said, 'Football is not a matter of life and death, it's much more than that.' Well, it is important when the game is being played, but you have to realise that there are other things in life. There is more to life than just football. The club has changed as well. It's more and more of a business, the fans are becoming alienated. They haven't had a full house this season. It's expensive, there's television, and then next season the Kop will have been seated.

HARRY LEATHER
Kopite

I've never felt in any kind of danger in the Kop. It's a very safe place, apart from the swaying. But there has never been any danger from hooliganism. I can honestly say that, in the thirty years I have been going to Anfield, I have only ever seen trouble on the Kop once, and that was in a derby game against Everton.

What happened then was that, as usual, all the Liverpool and Everton fans were mixed on the Kop, and there was a sudden flying of fists. It was probably one brother hitting another over some disputed foul, and nothing more than that. Anyhow, it was all over within a second and peace was quickly restored, and that is the only occasion when I have seen violence on the Kop. I suppose the Kop is just so big and packed that even the hardest visiting supporters steer clear. Come to think of it, I have rarely seen violence inside Anfield at all. What violence there has been has always taken place down the other end in the Anfield Road, where the visiting supporters are. There would be the occasional flurry down there, but it never seemed to amount to very much.

Problems with hooliganism have always been outside the ground, and I know for a fact that there have been running battles in the streets around Anfield after a game. But never inside the ground, and especially not on the Kop. I don't doubt, however, that some Kopites liked to mix it when they went to away games. There was always more scope for fighting at other grounds.

I think the biggest problem was always thieving. It's ironic that Liverpool now has this terrible name for violence after Heysel, when the truth is that there have been so few problems at Anfield. The Kopites of old prided themselves on their good humour and generosity, though I have to say that I detected a changing persona during the 1980s, when there were many accents from outside Liverpool taking up residence on the Kop. They were Liverpool supporters, but they weren't scousers and they didn't have the traditions.

BILLY WILSON
Kopite

The late 1970s and the early 1980s were the period of the 'style wars', although I know from listening to older fans that the whole of the 1970s was a decade when Liverpool fans tried to assert their superiority by dressing sharply.

As I was more into indie (Ian McCulloch of Echo and the Bunnymen always gave the Kop a plug in the music press) I wasn't really a participant, but this is what I vaguely remember. Sports gear was the essential ingredient, preferably exotic continental brands. It has been said that most of it was 'lifted' from unsuspecting shops on the Continent at away European ties. So they'd be kitted out in continental anoraks/training tops/cycling tops/sports coats. Then the trainers had to be the correct type to be cool. At the time, Nike weren't as widely available as they are now – they were just making inroads into the UK market and were quite desirable items. I also saw quite a few Adidas suede trainers. 'Kicker' shoes were also rather popular in the early 1980s, and The Fall wrote a song about football aggro called 'Kicker Conspiracy'.

There was a phase in the early 1980s when jeans were cut up both seams to fit them over trainers or Kickers. This made the jeans, which were usually a size or two too long, flare out over the trainers and scuff along the ground. The conclusion to this fashion move was that, in the 1984–85 season, semi-flares were sported on the Kop. There were unwritten rules about how flared they could be, just enough to cover the laces but not the whole shoe.

I actually bought a pair, but it marked you out at away games as a Liverpool fan.

To return to the late 1970s/early 1980s, I recall wedge haircuts as being essential for any cool Liverpool fan. After the Italian games in 1984 and 1985, a lot of Italian banners, tops and hats were sported on the Kop. Roma and Juventus were, quite naturally, well represented. Just as an aside, I saw quite a lot of hats with 'Munich '58' scribbled on them prior to Heysel in 1985.

In the early 1980s, pullovers were also fashion items, with the two most popular types being a plain-coloured V-neck, sometimes brightly coloured, usually Pringle, and Pringle's other popular model, a chequered golfing jumper, which cost a packet – so I think it's fair to say a few of them were lifted, considering half of Liverpool was on the dole at the time.

As well as jeans, cords were also a popular fashion item. These came in a variety of colours and thickness of cord. I'm sure that there was a subtle difference between being trendy and being gauche. There was a phase when brightly coloured jumbo cords were 'in', then it changed to neutral colours; beige, olive, and so on.

Around this time, there was also a phase of wearing chequered shirts with your low-key cords. The 1984 season also saw the bobble-hat phenomenon. These were usually one half Liverpool, one half Celtic or Rangers, although the more dedicated would have one side Liverpool, one side Austria Vienna or something. The bobble was cut off the hat to make it square like a ski-hat. There was a lot of continental-style beanie/cricket hats being sported at this time, some with 'Munich '58' written on them like I said. Around 1987, there was an outbreak of Barbour-type coats on the Kop, but that seems to have dropped off a bit.

I would say that the Kop drops something when they see that other clubs' supporters have copied their ideas, whether it be clothes, banners or whatever. Throughout this whole time, late 1970s to mid-1980s, Liverpool fans wore their various styles as a uniform, so that other clubs would know just who they were dealing with. The other thing is that Liverpool supporters feel they created this whole 'new-mod' scene, and laughed off counter-claims from London and Manchester.

It's interesting to note that, during the inflatables craze of 1988, Liverpool fans didn't take any part, and it's debatable whether this is because they didn't think of it first or because they thought it was uncool. The craze was started by Man. City, and it strikes me as something the Kop of a different era might have enjoyed.

JEFF SCOTT
Kopite

I started in the Boys' Pen in 1958. I did my apprenticeship there for two years. I remember them throwing things from the Boys' Pen when you could walk around from the Paddock. They'd be throwing coins and spitting at the away supporters. They came in for some stick in those days, but there wasn't that many of them.

Then in 1960, when I was 11 or 12, I moved to the Kop. I got in there dead early on one of my first visits to the Kop. I'd been playing football at school in the morning, and I'd gone straight to Anfield and on to the Kop. I'd gone right to the front and, because I was small and the first step was low down, my chin was resting on the rough concrete wall. So I'd been there for hours and then, just before kick-off, all the drunks came in from the pub. Some of them started barging me out of the way, so I said, 'Stop pushing, I've been here since it opened.' And one of them says, 'What, you've been here since 1892,' and pushed me out of the way. I thought, 'Sarcastic git!'

ANDREW THOMAS
Kopite

It was my first visit to Anfield. I remember I was very excited at the prospect of going on the Kop. I had seen it so often on television. It was actually smaller than I had imagined it to be; it didn't seem to go back as much. But the sound was so powerful, so dramatic, and it was especially good-humoured.

I can't remember too much about the game now, though I do recall that Liverpool won. But my abiding memory of the Kop that day were two small boys who can't have been more than 10 years old. They were sitting on a crush barrier at the end of the game waiting for everybody to go, and were asking each other the most detailed and testing questions about the club's history and players. They were coming up with questions and answers that showed that they had learnt the entire history. They clearly knew the reference books off by heart. Had they put as much endeavour into their school work they would have been well on course for university. They were really that good.

BILLY WILSON
Kopite

There was a cracking atmosphere the day we played Queen's Park Rangers in the autumn of the great 1987–88 season. QPR were actually top of the league when they came to Liverpool, and John Barnes scored one of the best goals ever seen at Anfield. What made it even better was that it was scored at the Kop end. After that goal, the Kop was feeling so benign – I'm sure critics would say arrogant – that they cheered every time QPR got the ball.

At one point, however, Rangers got the ball in a dangerous position on the right-hand side and, as they got nearer to the Liverpool goal, the Kop continued cheering their moves. It may have started as irony but, as QPR got even closer, it was as if the Kop was supporting them. Having started the cheering, it was interesting to see how far they would have continued it, even to the extent of a goal. Some of the Kopites started worrying and shouting, 'Shut up, shut up', and the mood became really heavy between the two groups – one cheering QPR and one booing them. Fortunately, the QPR move broke down, and I've never encountered that situation since.

DAVE CLAY
Kopite

From the age of 13 until the 1970s, I regularly went to all the home and away games. I'm 41 now and I still go, though not as often as I used to as I play football myself on a Saturday. But I do go to all the night games. I used to stand right in the middle of the Kop and I was fairly well known on account of going to so many of the away games.

When I was about 12 or 13 I accepted the fact that there were not too many black players so that, when any black players came to Anfield with the visiting sides, I was really made up. I remember Leeds United coming to Anfield prior to the FA Cup final in 1965, and Albert Johanneson was playing for them. The crowd were all shouting 'Coco Pops', and 'Go back to Africa'. Now that really affected me. It was my first encounter with racism of that kind. My dad was from Africa, even though I had been born in Liverpool. It was really traumatic.

It was also bad at Goodison during the 1966 World Cup finals, the attitude to Brazil and Portugal was disgusting. But that was Everton. I've never liked Goodison. I got into my only fight there. It was when Mike Trebilcock was playing for Everton. It was against Liverpool, and Trebilcock was getting some terrible abuse down the Park End, where all the Liverpool supporters were standing. There was racial chanting, and they were spitting at him. I had a fight over it, and they were saying to me, 'We're not getting at you, you're a scouser, you're all right!' They just didn't seem to understand.

There were two or three of us from our school went on the Kop. There was me who was black and two Chinese guys. A lot of the racism was not from the people around us, but you react at your own risk. I never had any personal abuse, it was always directed at black players, and I would never show outwardly how I felt. I was disgusted, but I loved Liverpool so much that I was still determined to go.

As I got older, of course, I got a lot more conscious of it. I had had trials myself, and although I knew that I was an excellent footballer I wasn't successful. But there were others who were white and not as good as me who were taken on. I felt that I didn't make it because I was black. Other blacks were also having the same problem. So I began to look at things a bit more critically. There were no blacks on the turnstiles, no blacks selling programmes, no black players and so on. Other clubs were signing black players, but not Liverpool. Why?

Whereas once I used to really look forward to seeing black players on the visiting side, I slowly began to dread it. I knew the kind of reception they were going to get. I wondered about going to the games but I did cos, as I say, I really love Liverpool. I did have a break in the late 1970s, but that wasn't a conscious decision, it was just that there were other things to do.

Then, when John Barnes signed, I started to go again more regularly. It was interesting to see the effect of Liverpool having to come to terms with a black player. In terms of race relations in the city, the signing of John Barnes was a turning-point. Suddenly, young black kids wanted Liverpool kits. I gave a talk one day at the Bronte youth club, and the kids there were saying that John Barnes wasn't really black. They suddenly didn't notice his colour. They just didn't want to acknowledge that he was black. I knew the kind of problems a black player faces at Anfield. I knew Howie Gayle and his family and I was under no illusions. The thing that didn't occur to me for a while was that the players might also be racist. I'd just assumed that it was the fans.

I've been in the Kop a few times recently, and it's funny because they get the black players mixed up, particularly

Michael Thomas and Mark Walters. You know, it's the they-all-look-the-same attitude. I'm always having to tell them, 'No, that's Michael Thomas, not Mark Walters, he isn't playing.'

I'm made up that the club has now taken the issue on board. There was a very bad response at first from the club and the supporters. There was graffiti on the walls outside the Kop, and we had to petition the club to get it cleaned up. They didn't seem to be interested. But things are better now. There's not that much racist chanting on the Kop these days, and it's certainly not as bad as it was when 20,000 were chanting 'Coco Pops'. And whereas there weren't many black supporters a few years ago, there's quite a lot now. I see loads of people I know.

I guess the racism is not as overt now, it's more subtle. It hasn't taken away the racism, but you have to say that Kenny Dalglish did a brave thing in bringing John Barnes here. Had it been anyone else, who might have been a failure, then it would have been terrible. But Barnes is so good that he has been able to pave the way for others like Walters and Thomas. But I dread to think what might have happened had Mark Walters been the first black player to sign for Liverpool.

BILLY WILSON
Kopite

While waiting to go into the Kop for the European Cup semi-final against Zurich on 20 April 1977 I had a slightly worrying experience. I was 13, and had just started going to Anfield after coming down from Scotland, where I supported Celtic. There were two middle-aged men behind me, and one of them got a Rangers scarf out of his pocket and put it on. The other one said, 'You're as safe as houses in there with that on.' It hit me then: 'Is Liverpool a Rangers supporters' club?'

I didn't want it to be a Celtic supporters' club either, though. It was a great relief therefore that, when a chant of 'Rangers' went up from the Kop at half-time, the chant came back just as quickly – 'Celtic'. Ever since then I've kept an ear open for the 'Rangers-Celtic-Rangers-Celtic' chant. I'd say they both seem to have the same level of vocal support, but the chant always seems to start with 'Rangers'. Mind you, it's not a chant you hear very often from the Kop these days.

EILEEN McAULEY
Kopite

Someone pinched my bum once when I was on the Kop. What sort of a sad person does that in any kind of place? It was just ridiculous rather than threatening. It was just silly rather than worrying or irritating. It was a one-off. There is no overriding feeling that the Kop is a heavily macho place, even though it's 98 per cent men.

I was on the Kop for the 5–0 game against Forest. It was 14 April 1988. I'd gone there with a male friend who supports Forest, and at half-time he reached into his bag and got out a tartan flask, full of oxtail soup! On the Kop! I was mortified. I wanted the ground to swallow me up. They play awful records at half-time. They're usually pop by a woman, and there is a rocky edge to them. Either that, or Simple Minds and U2. They must think that the Kop is full of people who are into Adult-Orientated Rock. I wonder if they think about what they are playing.

There is nothing the Kop likes more than to put pressure on the referee. That is why Liverpool get such bad decisions, because the refs don't want to look like wimps. Refs are hard, out to prove that they are not on Liverpool's side. It's really great to be on the Kop for a big match, standing by people who have a common purpose, and when there is a goal it's a brilliant feeling, being with so many happy people bunched up together. That's a lot of the pleasure in being on the Kop: it's not having a better view of the game, it's being there.

LOUISE TOVEY
Kopite

The first time I went on the Kop was the night Liverpool were presented with the 1988 championship trophy. I went with my husband, and the atmosphere was excellent – it couldn't be matched. Any time I've been on the Kop I've had to be right at the front with all the children, or in the part above the Kop stairway, because I'm only short. I have to get there very early. I'd be there so many hours before the kick-off I couldn't go to the toilet or anything. Then I'd get pushed into the wall or barrier at the front. It was uncomfortable, but you didn't mind because you were screaming and celebrating a goal. You almost prayed it would happen more often!

YVONNE McLEOD
Kopite

I don't really know why I started to support Liverpool. I suppose it was when I was watching Bristol Rovers. It was fashionable to watch another team at the time – this was about 1975 – so I'd go to watch Liverpool. I was on the Bristol Rovers supporters' committee, and I had to give that up because I was always away at Liverpool.

I met my husband in Liverpool; he also travelled on his own at the time. It somehow built up from that. I would go to Liverpool matches and meet other supporters from Bristol who were now living in Liverpool, who'd let me stay at their place overnight. I didn't mind travelling up by myself, but I didn't want to go to the match by myself.

I had a season ticket for the Kop in the 1970s. I quite liked it because, at that time, if someone had offered me a stand ticket I would have turned it down. The atmosphere was great, but I do think I missed a lot of the goals. But it was worth it. I particularly remember a Birmingham home game when we were 0–2 down, pulled a goal back just before half-time, and ended up winning 4–3. There was no crude behaviour when I stood on the Kop, I loved it there.

I go to nearly all the matches, home and away. It depends on the ticket situation for a lot of away games, though. I reckon I must spend well over £1000 a season watching Liverpool. A routine for a home match is: get up at six, go and catch a bus at seven which takes me to our picking-up point in Bristol. It's a café, and we all have our breakfast there before leaving Bristol at half-eight. At about eleven, we stop for a break at Roundhill. We usually arrive in Liverpool at about midday and come straight to the supporters' club. We leave right after the game and get back to Bristol about nine in the evening. The worst times for travelling are bank holidays and Sundays; the roads are always mobbed.

GEOFFREY BANFIELD
Kopite

I spend about £450 a season going to the home games at Anfield. It's like a drug. My wife is quite happy about it, but I think she's a bit surprised to see that I'm still so involved. I recently retired, so she looks on it as though I've still got the young spirit in me. Following Liverpool keeps me young. My wife also sees that it gets me out of the house on Saturdays.

On a Saturday, I get up at seven and catch a local bus into Newport. At eight, the Gwent Liverpool supporters' club coach arrives from Caerphilly and picks us up. We stop off at a transport café about ten for breakfast. At half-ten, we set off again, and get to Liverpool about midday. We set off right after the game and get back to Newport about nine at night.

After a game like the FA Cup semi-final replay at Villa Park last season, you'll end up picking up people wandering around the coach park looking for a lift home. The worst times are going to home midweek matches in the winter, when there is fog and the danger that the windows might freeze up or that we break down in the middle of nowhere.

JEFF SCOTT
Kopite

I started the Bristol branch of the Liverpool supporters' club in the 1980s. I'd always gone on the Kop before I joined the army and then the merchant navy. In 1983, I'd left the navy and started going to games even though I was a scouser in exile in Bristol. I borrowed £300 off my in-laws because I didn't have any money. I got in touch with all the people in Bristol who I knew were Liverpool fans. We only had about nineteen people for the first coach, and two of them we'd accidentally picked up as they were waiting for another coach!

I then advertised in the *Bristol Evening Post* asking for supporters to contact me. I've had to make one price for home and away games, so we lose money on away matches. But we make money on the big matches, Man. United and Everton, as more people want to go. We charge the same money as when we started, and it's the same for home and away games, which is £7. We pick up from Bristol, Gloucester and Cheltenham, but a lot of the supporters have to make their way to Bristol first, from places like Bournemouth, Exeter and Plymouth – which is a two-and-a-half-hour drive.

HARRY LEATHER
Kopite

I have a routine, the same every match. I always park in the same place, a piece of waste land opposite some flats, off Walton Lane. There's usually a couple of lads there, as there are just about everywhere near Anfield. 'Mind yer car, mister?', they ask as you park. Woe betide you if you say no. I've come back after the game and seen many a car near me with smashed windows. But so far I've been lucky. I always give them a couple of bob. Usually I say, 'Yeah, will you be around when I get back. I'll see you right then.' I rolled up one game, and this lad – always there, he is – looks at me and says, 'You're not still coming 'ere, are yer?' Another week they'd somehow opened the gates of the local school and were waving all the cars in and parking them in the playground and charging a few bob. Typical Liverpool, but very enterprising.

Anyhow, I park the car and then stroll up Anfield Road and cut up the jigger [alley] that takes me towards the Kop. I always wear the same clothes. Well, almost the same. I have a blue donkey jacket that I wear in summer, and then in winter I put on a large blue coat over it. I also have a tartan scarf. I started wearing that when Liverpool had all those Scottish players – Dalglish, Hansen, Nicol, Gillespie and so on. I've tried wearing a Liverpool scarf, but it never brought much luck so I discarded it. I also have a flat hat in my pocket. Now that goes on if Liverpool aren't playing too well, maybe if they're a goal down.

I always go in through the same gate, have done for years, though I think this might be about to change. There was a huge queue there the other week, and as I was a bit late I opted for another turnstile that had no queue, and Liverpool went and won 4–1. Prior to that they had been rubbish. So I go through the turnstile and then I always buy a programme. There's a ritual to this as well. It doesn't matter who I buy it off, but the thing is that I have to read it before the game. The more I read it, the better the result will be. When I don't get the chance to read it, we invariably lose. Sometimes I can have a good read at half-time, and that helps. But if it's left unopened or, worse still, if all the programmes have been sold, I just know that Liverpool will lose. And, of course, I always stand in the same spot, to the left of the goal, three-quarters of the way up the Kop.

I sometimes have this other ritual as well a couple of days before the match. I'll be walking up the road, and if

I spot a nice little stone on the pavement I run towards it. I'll be saying to myself, 'Molby to Hansen . . . to Rush . . .' And then I kick the stone and, if it shoots between two targets I've noted on the pavement, I shout, 'It's there! Ian Rush, for Liverpool.' Not out loud, of course. That means Liverpool will score, probably Rush. If the stone goes way off target then it bodes ill, but I can always spot another stone somewhere and have another go.

I suppose all these silly rituals come from a time when I wasn't living in Liverpool. I only came back home for Christmas, Easter and the odd weekend, and every time I went to Anfield they either won or drew. I think I went something like ten years without ever seeing them lose at Anfield. Although things haven't been so good lately, there was a time when they rarely lost at home. I sometimes wonder if other people have these rituals, or am I the only barmy one?

LENNIE WOODS
Kopite

It was my dad who took me first. I was about 10 years old then – it was, I think, 1954–55, the season Liverpool had just gone down into the second division. This is the place for me, I thought, and I've been going ever since. I started going in the Boys' Pen until I was about 13 then I went on the Kop and I've been going there ever since, thirty-three years on the Kop. They seem to have flown by. I've stood in the same spot as well, thirty-three years behind the goal, just in line with the crossbar and a bit to the right.

Everything changed with Shankly. He was a Messiah. He had this wonderful rapport with the people. He could convince them of anything. Do you remember when Liverpool got beat 1–5 by Ajax in the European Cup in December 1966? Well, Shankly convinced us all that we were going to score five goals against them. No problem, he reckoned, it was only the fog that helped them score five. Normally, you would have expected Anfield to be empty for the return game, but instead Shankly convinces us all that we're going to win, and 55,000 turn up.

I also remember in 1973 when Liverpool had just won the league title. Shankly came down the Kop end as the team was celebrating, and someone threw a scarf from the Kop and it landed on the pitch close to Shankly's feet. A policeman came over and kicked it away. Shankly was furious. 'This scarf is someone's life,' he told the policeman. He then picked it up, brushed it clean and put it around his neck. That was the sort of person he was, he had that effect on a crowd.

On an average Saturday for a home game, I leave the house at about 12:30 p.m. and go to The Albert pub, next door to the Kop. I meet my mates in there and we have a few pints. Then, at about 2:50 p.m., we make our way to the Kop. After the match, we all meet up again in The Albert to have a natter about the game. We might just have a few drinks before going home or, if Liverpool have done really well, we might stay until closing time. It depends on how we feel. We've been doing that for years. How does the wife feel about it? No, she doesn't mind. She likes football, but she doesn't go to the games. But she'll watch it on the telly.

We used to compose a lot of songs in The Albert. I've heard there are other pubs in Liverpool where groups of supporters get together and write songs. We'd write our songs, then we'd learn them, and we'd start them off on the Kop. After we'd done it a few times, everyone else would have picked the words up, and you've soon got thousands singing the song. We also used to compose songs when we went to away games, especially when we went to Newcastle. We used to come home on a train which we called the '6:5 Special'. We wrote the Rome song on that. Other songs were written in the pub, usually after the game when we'd had a few pints rather than before.

I go to most games; in fact I think I've only missed two games in the past ten seasons – that's home and away, of course. I've also seen most of the European games, going back to the first or second season. Yes, it's cost a few bob over the years. But it's worth it, it's a kind of hobby, like.

JOHNNY KENNEDY
Radio City DJ

There are pubs in Liverpool where songs were worked out. It happened at The Cannon, but it wasn't the main one. I know for a fact that things have been worked out at The Albert, and there may be others I don't know about. What we did in The Cannon – this was before the European Cup final in Paris in 1981 actually – we wrote a song there and rehearsed it. It was a great song which a lot of Liverpool fans learned that year. It was called 'Scouser in Gay Paree'. It was to the tune of 'How would you Like to be Down by the Seine with Me'. We sang it all the way down on the boat; everyone on the boat was singing it. It was an easy song to learn. All the pubs around the ground were singing it. We wrote it in The Cannon, and they still sing it even now.

SCOUSER IN GAY PAREE
(Sung to the tune of 'How would you Like to
 be Down by the Seine with Me')

*How would you like to be
A scouser in Gay Paree,
Walking along on the banks of the Seine,
Winning the European Cup once again.
We'll go up the Eiffel Tower,
And stay there for half an hour,
Cos we won't be late when we celebrate,
Scousers in Gay Paree.*

*We'll visit the Folies Bergère,
They like to see scousers there.
The women are lovely with skin like a peach,
But no one can move it like Kenny Dalglish.*

ANDREW THOMAS
Kopite

It was a record by the Routers called 'Let's Go' that began it all. It came out in 1962 and had a rhythmical handclap in it. The Kop took it up and adapted it, and it became the 'St John Chant'. There had been singing before, but never any chanting and clapping. This was the first time anything like it had been heard. It didn't take long for other fans to take up the same chant and adapt it to their favourites. But it all began with that record.

STAN KELLY
Writer

The first simple but effective chant that caught the head-lines was 'Ee-aye-addio', borrowed from a well-known Liverpool skipping song, 'The farmer's in his den'. Rather like the blues (if the Kop will pardon the expression) in the southern United States, this was a straightforward framework on which the crowd could improvise at will, only four to six syllables being needed to complete the stanza, e.g. 'Sir Roger Hunt', or 'We've won the Cup', or 'Ron likes his beer', following Yeats's appearance in an advertisement.

Many theories have been advanced to explain how 20,000 or so people can simultaneously think of a joke and set it to song. Some claimed Sir Malcolm Sargent was 'in dere somewhere' conducting; if so, when did he hold rehearsals? From time to time there are individual claimants to the title 'King of the Kop' but, characteristically, the Kop has always shunned the cult of the individual. Unlike Stoke City's 'Zigger-Zagger', Anfield's choir works more from a gestalt culture, unified by a fierce devotion to good football (from either side) and a highly-developed love of wise-cracks, puns and Malapudlianisms.

As well as the long tradition of Merseyside comedians, from Billy Matchett via Tommy Handley, Ted Ray, along to Ken Dodd and Jimmy Tarbuck (it was Ted Ray who said 'You have to be a comic to survive in Liverpool'), other patterns can be seen in the Kop tapestry. The post-war folk-song revival in Britain was nowhere more lively than on Merseyside with its natural treasury of shanties, fo'c'sle songs, music-hall ditties and, of course, a direct pipeline to the Irish tradition. While the Beatles, Cilla Black, The Scaffold and Frankie Vaughan were each in their own way putting Liverpool on the international pop scene, folk artists such as the Spinners, Jackie and Bridie, Glyn Hughes and Tony Murphy, poets such as Adrian Henri and Roger McGough, were all spreading the traditional scouse idiom.

The Kop choir borrowed freely from these sources and, in turn, helped spread the gospel that Liverpool was the source of a new articulate culture. The cynic who defined the Liverpool sound as that of a dart piercing the back of a goalkeeper's neck has clearly never been to Anfield, where all visiting goalkeepers (Gordon Banks in particular) receive a sporting welcome from the Kop. Happily, this tradition, like many of the Kop's songs, seems to be spreading to other clubs. 'Da song's Kopyrighted', complained one fan to his mate at an away game. 'Ah, just wave yer scarf an' mime', consoled his friend.

The 'standard' numbers performed by the Kop reveal the wide range of source material. 'We'll fight and no surrender' is based on the Ulster song 'Derry's Walls'. 'Show them the way to go home' is music-hall; 'God save our team' is an inspiration from a royal Wembley; 'We all live in a red and white Kop' is Lennon and McCartney, while 'Mighty Emlyn' is Bob Dylan. 'We're the best-behaved supporters in the land' is originally from the Bronx; 'Tommy Lawrence' is chanted either to 'Trumpet Voluntary' or 'Alouette'; 'Alun Evans' often gets the Hare Krishna treatment, complete with quarter-tones. 'Michael row the boat ashore' is used to send Emlyn Hughes to Mexico or the referee to Vietnam. And, of course, the unforgettable sound of the Kop, the anthem, 'You'll never walk alone', is Rodgers and Hammerstein.

You will often get a chorus of 'Auld lang syne' near the end of a match, but the words are 'sit down, you bums' and are directed at any Kemlyn-Roaders who might fancy slipping away early.

I have often discussed the Kop with Bill Shankly, the players and officials. They are unanimous in affirming the inspiration they all derive from this unique gathering. 'It's more than fanaticism,' says Shankly, who, for once, is stumped for a phrase to describe the Kop's devotion.

The Kop, like the team, raise their performance for the big occasion. At Wembley in 1965, they joined forces with their oft-neglected colleagues from the Anfield Road End and the Paddock and not only swamped the Leeds vocalists but the massed military bands, too. For Inter Milan, down 1–3 at Anfield, they devised the marvellous 'Oh Inter, one, two, three/Go back to Italy', improvised on 'Santa Lucia'.

In a lighter mood, they turned out to pay tribute to a special hero, Gerry Byrne, in his benefit match. Despite sleet and rain there were 41,000, and the Kop enjoyed a night of nostalgia relieved by these bursts of wit. 'Gordon, come and join us,' they yelled at Banks. 'We're scoring goals again', they chanted when the score reached 8–8. Kenneth Wolstenholme was greeted with 'I-T-V, I-T-V', Kenny Lynch with 'Eusebio, Eusebio', and the sight of Bill Shankly in playing kit brought on 'Shankly, Shankly, Mexico'.

No LP, no television camera, no writer, can do the Kop full justice. They will always be there, full of expectation, advice, encouragement, with a thunderous 'No surrender' to inject new life into tired limbs.

'Walk on, walk on, with hope in your hearts,

'And you'll never walk alone,

'You'll never walk alone.'

THE BOYS IN RED
(Sung to the tune of 'Derry's Walls')

We'll fight and no surrender,
We'll fight for the boys in red;
We'll fight the fight for Liverpool,
The team that Shankly bred.

We'll fight for Alun Evans,
We'll fight for Ian St John,
We'll fight the fight for Liverpool
The pride of division one,
Two, three, four,
Listen to the Kopites roar,
LIV-ER-POOL.

GERRY MARSDEN
Gerry and the Pacemakers

The Kop is my biggest choir. They are tremendous, every one of them. It's part of the city of Liverpool. Even now, when the Kop begins to sing 'You'll Never Walk Alone', it sends goose pimples through my body. To stand there and hear them singing your song – or, at least, the song that you helped make famous – is a tremendous feeling. It's very nice.

The record came out in October 1963 and went straight to No. 1 in the charts. Six weeks later, the Kop began to sing it and they've been singing it ever since. I don't know why they started, it just happened, and it very quickly became their anthem. Of course, it is a really appropriate song, because it's about someone having to carry on when life is difficult. But I don't suppose you would ever have guessed that this song would become an anthem for football fans throughout the world. Wherever football is played, they seem to sing 'You'll Never Walk Alone'. I was watching the Italian football on TV just the other day, and there they were, the crowd in Milan, all singing 'You'll Never Walk Alone' in broken English. It was an astonishing feeling. And that goes on in Germany, France and Spain as well as Italy.

The most emotional singing of it came at the Liverpool/Everton Cup final, just after Hillsborough. I was asked to lead off the singing of the song at Wembley as a tribute to those who had died. It was amazing, all those people in Wembley standing up singing 'You'll Never Walk Alone'. You usually get just one set of supporters singing the song, but there we were with both Everton and Liverpool supporters singing, all 80,000 of them. Everyone was in tears, but it was wonderful, just wonderful.

I often wonder who it was who first started singing it on the Kop. There must have been one individual who said one day, 'Hey, let's sing this song,' or maybe they just joined in when it was played on the tannoy. And who had the idea of raising their scarves above their heads and swaying gently with the music? Well, if there was one person, I'd love to shake his hand. I don't suppose that those who first started singing it ever imagined that, thirty years later, football crowds throughout the world would be singing it. Amazing, and so nice.

STEVE SHAKESHAFT
Photographer, Liverpool Daily Post and Echo

I've always been fascinated by how the songs originate. I remember once Tommy Smith came out wearing a pair of silver boots. It was the first time he had worn them, and I think up to that point nobody had ever seen a pair of silver boots. Anyrate, the chant from the Kop was instant: 'Where did you get them boots, where did you get them boots, where did you get them boots?' It was so wickedly funny and so instant. I don't know how it was that so many people were singing it so quickly. He must have got a bit of a ribbing from his team-mates as well, because it was also the last time he ever wore them.

PHIL ASPINALL
Kopite

We used to make the songs up in a pub. In our case it was always The Albert, next door to the Kop. But there are a number of pubs dotted around Liverpool where the same kind of thing goes on. If the songs were long, we'd have to organise it. We'd usually do that before the game, while we're having a few drinks. If the words were easy and the tune was catchy, you might be able to start it that afternoon. Sometimes it would take a few games before it really got going. They're easy songs in the main, and people soon catch on once they've got the tune. On the Kop it would snowball, and everyone would be singing it in three or four minutes.

The best song that I ever wrote was 'Liver Birds'. I'd come home from the pub one night, and the late-night movie was on. It was *The Green Berets*, that John Wayne film. Well, the music was really stirring, and I thought that'd make a great song. So while I'm watching the movie I'm thinking about this, and I started working something out. All week I was trying things out. Anyhow, I went down to the pub before the next game and I'd written it all out, so I let them all have a few drinks and then I told them about it. So they made me sing it. Then somebody started knocking on the bottles, and before long everyone was joining in. We tried it out that afternoon, and it soon became a Kop favourite. That was in the mid-'80s. A few years later Craig Johnston recorded the song, but it was a big flop. I think he lost about £32,000 on it. The problem was that he had some country-and-western singer record it. I could have told him that wouldn't work.

I've been drinking in The Albert since the 1960s. We go there before the game and afterwards as well. We'll be singing most of the night – you know, old Beatles and Elvis numbers – until we get thrown out. We've composed a lot of songs going to away games as well. We used to go to Newcastle on the train, and it was really slow because the line was not electrified. So we'd take crates and crates of beer with us. This was just before Rome, and we wrote a few songs for that. One of them was called 'Roma', which was sung to the tune of 'Arrivederci Roma'. That caught on really well, and everyone was singing it in Rome. It's a great feeling to hear one of your songs being sung by thousands of people on the Kop.

ROMA
(Sung to the tune of 'Arrivederci Roma')

We're on our way to Roma,
On the 25th of May,
All the Kopites will be singing,
Vatican bells they will be ringing,
Liverpool FC will be swinging,
When we win the European Cup.

We'll be drinking all their vino,
On the 23rd, 24th, 25th, 26th of May,
And all the Kopites will be singing,
Vatican bells they will be ringing,
Liverpool FC will be swinging,
When we win the European Cup.

DEREK HODGSON
Writer

Until ten minutes before kick-off, the Kop practises its raucous jeering, shrill whistling and well-drilled chants and shouts. The hard, grey clouds come slanted over the massive roof, as though whipped on by the clamour below. The big Mersey cops prowl on the front, disdain-fully stepping over toilet rolls, outwardly oblivious to the repeated advice to see a taxidermist. Pop music, blasted through giant amplifiers, is mostly ignored unless the Kop's Lennon can hastily improvise a new verse to a current hit. Then comes the moment . . .

Gerry and the Pacemakers, as though singing through a Birkenhead fog, croon as lachrymose a ballad as even Rodgers and Hammerstein could contrive, and the Kop, almost with the surge of a congregation rising to the hymn, join reverently in the chorus. They even adopt the Pacemakers' 'Walk on, walk oo-n, with hope in your heart' in this most bizarre of anthems, for what Bill Shankly has described as the world's only professional supporters.

But, of course, the Kop is one of football's phenomena. It would be a man of thin blood who failed to be stirred by their magnificent array of emotion, expressed in wit and song, in abuse and sometimes obscenity, throughout the ninety minutes of a football match.

Not long ago Arsenal came to Anfield and won, only a few days after Liverpool had lost a Fairs Cup place. The last, heroic charges were being made on a huge, yellow-shirted Arsenal defence, but almost everyone had accepted that no equaliser would be forthcoming. Silently, sorrowfully, small groups of ticket-holders began slipping away from their seats, down the gangways into an icy, starlit evening.

The Kop had suffered silently for a long time. Suddenly, they turned on the deserters with zealous fury; play was almost stopped as this mighty chant, accompanied by 20,000 arms, waving down, rang out: 'Sit down, you bums, sit down.'

PETER MOLONEY
Writer

ODE ON THE KOP

'Go home you bums' swells up the mighty
    roar,
The Reds it cheers, the enemy it daunts,
They go to pieces when they hear the taunts,

Ten thousand take it up, and maybe more,
With songs like this their team just has to
    score.

A new song rises, warm and comforting,
'You'll never walk alone', the Kopites sing.
The anthem then, until the throat is sore.
In three-four time they start to rave and
    swear,
Then 'easy, easy', husky voices bark.
They sway in time and wave scarves in the
    air.
Then sing a Christmas hymn as it grows
    dark.
No other ground has songsters to compare –
Except for Goodison across the Park!

JEFF ANDERSON
Kopite

I remember the day Bill Shankly went on the Kop. I was standing in the Paddock that day, when suddenly every-body starts pointing. There was a mêlée on the Kop. Everyone up there had turned around and was facing in the direction of the Boys' Pen, which was up in the top right corner as you look at the Kop. It was astonishing to see everyone on the Kop looking in that direction, and you could hear the hubbub from them. We wondered what was going on, and then within seconds the word came down from the Kop. Bill Shankly was among them. It was a powerful and moving moment. It was like God among his people.

BILL SHANKLY
Liverpool manager, 1959–74

The encouragement the supporters of Liverpool Football Club have given their team has been incredible. When there is a corner-kick at the Kop end of the ground, they frighten the ball! Occasionally, I would have a walk round the ground before a match, and I went to the Kop one day before it had filled up. A little chap there said, 'Stand here, Bill, you'll get a good view of the game from here!' I couldn't take him up on that offer because I had to look after the team.

I have watched a match from the Kop since I retired as team manager, and that was just the start of going to see supporters in all parts of the ground. I didn't go to the Kop for bravado or anything like that. I went as a mark of respect for people who have been good to me. They used to chant my name as much as they chanted the names of the players, which was unusual. I am a working man and I went among my own kind. Liverpool played Coventry that day, and a crescendo greeted the Liverpool team just as I went into the ground. It wasn't a continuous din. But when we scored our goal the noise was deafening.

LIVER BIRDS
(Sung to the tune of 'The Green Berets')

Now this song's about a football team,
The greatest team you've ever seen,
A team that plays total football,
Won the league, Europe and all.

(*Chorus*)

The Liver Bird upon my chest
We are men of Kenny's best,
A team that plays the Liverpool way,
And wins the league and the Cup in May.

With Kenny Dalglish on the ball,
He's the greatest of them all,
There's Ian Rush, four goals or two,
Left Evertonians feeling blue.

(*Chorus*)

Now if you go down Goodison way

Hard luck stories you hear every day,
There's not a trophy to be seen,
Because Liverpool have swept them clean.

(*Chorus*)

On the glorious twelfth of May,
Walking back up Wembley Way,
We're full of laughs, joy and glee,
It's Everton one and Liverpool three.

(*Chorus*)

AND IT'S LIV-ER-POOL
(Sung to the tune of 'The Wild Rover')

And it's LIV-ER-POOL,
LIV-ER-POOL FC.
They're by far the greatest team
The world has ever seen.

Three

BEFORE THE SEATS

We All Live in a Red and White Kop

BOB PAISLEY
Liverpool manager, 1974–83;
Liverpool player, 1939–54

Shankly and the Kop were made for each other. I knew the Kop crowd from my playing days, and I knew what sort of player and a man they appreciated. The more I saw of the Boss, the more I realised that he and the Kop would soon be married to each other.

BILL SHANKLY
Liverpool manager, 1959–74

It is difficult for me to talk about the Kop without sounding biased, because I am their greatest fan. But then I think there's a soft spot for these people in the heart of anyone who knows anything at all about football. The Kop are unique. They are fair, humorous, well-behaved and very well-educated on the game. They love to see good football being played and, if a team comes to Anfield and uses any foul methods, the Kop will be on them like a shot. But if a team comes and plays well, they will be applauded almost as if they were the home team.

It is said in football that the Kop is worth a goal start to Liverpool, and it may well be true because they do help to raise a player's game. But the other side nearly always play above themselves when they come to Anfield, such is the respect they have for the Kop.

New players at Liverpool usually feel more than a little nervous when they play in front of the Kop for the first time, but they have nothing to fear. For the Kop are warm and they greet new players as though they have been in the team for years. This warmth and behaviour has earned the Kop the title of the best supporters in the land and, believe me, they deserve it.

Forget the Beatles and all the rest. This is the real Liverpool Sound. It's real singing, and it's what the Kop is all about.

MARK LAWRENSON
Liverpool player, 1981–88

When the Kop was full and in good voice, there is no doubt that it was worth a goal start. But, more than that, it's what they did to the opposition. They could destroy teams. When you're out there playing you don't realise it, but when you talk to visiting players after the game you begin to realise just how daunting they had found the experience, especially goalkeepers. I know they used to come down the Kop end and get a good round of applause, but after that the Kop would crucify them for the next ninety minutes.

There were occasions when you were down the Kop end defending and the ball would go out, and there would be silence. Then you'd hear a wise-crack from the Kop. They'd come out with something, and it would crease you up. I remember Johnny Wark playing for Ipswich – this was some time before he joined us – he got hit in the groin by the ball and, as he was lying on the ground, the Kop started singing, 'Are you watching, Mrs Wark?' We were all in stitches at that one.

Before my day, when the Kop could hold 25,000, it must have been daunting. There is no other terrace in British football that can compare with the Kop. The nearest is the Stretford End at Manchester United, but they never had the humour. The one thing that always amazes me is that, when you talk to Liverpool supporters all over the country, the one thing that they want to do is to come to Anfield and stand on the Kop. It has such an aura.

The other thing is that we were never abused by the Kop. I remember playing there one Boxing Day early in my career. We were playing Manchester City in the 1981–82 season, and we got beat and slumped to thirteenth in the table. Any other club in the country, and we would have been crucified by them. But not the Kop. They cheered just the same. A couple of months later we won the league title. Had they moaned at us that Boxing Day, we might well have lost confidence and gone on to lose more games. But because they stuck with us, we were able to shake off our bad patch. We actually clinched the title against Tottenham at Anfield in that same 1981–82 season. We went a goal down to a fierce Glenn Hoddle shot. Then I equalised in front of the Kop, and from that moment on the Kop was trying to suck the ball into the back of the net.

WE'RE GONNA WIN THE LEAGUE (1)

We're gonna win the league,
We're gonna win the league,
And now you'd better believe us,
And now you'd better believe us,
And now you'd better believe us,
We're gonna win the league.

ALAN KENNEDY
Liverpool player, 1978–85

I used to think that all the people on the Kop should wear crash helmets when I was playing. I had a tendency to kick high balls into the Kop. I used to put my head down and run and then, from about thirty-five yards out, have a shot at goal. Invariably, the ball would go sailing into the Kop and everyone would have to duck. The lads on the Kop used to have a real go at me about that. But we had a laugh. I felt I was one of them.

When I first came to Anfield in 1978 I looked up at the Kop and I thought, blimey, some grounds don't even hold that many people. It was such a massive embankment. It was a formidable sight, especially when it was full with 25,000 people. The Kop nicknamed me 'Barney', after Barney Rubble in *The Flintstones*. I suppose it was because of the way I ran, head down, not really looking. Every time you pull on a red shirt you get such a lift, and then you go out there and there's twenty-odd thousand of them cheering you and chanting your name. During my years at Liverpool we weren't beaten too many times at Anfield. The Kop could make you feel ten feet tall. They especially used to appreciate it when one of us defenders – Alan Hansen, Phil Neal or myself – made a run upfield and had a crack at goal. Even if we missed, they would applaud us all the way back. They appreciated us having a try. And that was always encouraging.

I remember one particular game against Manchester City, when someone threw a bottle on the pitch and it hit Joe Corrigan, the City goalkeeper, on the back. This was down the Kop end. The Kop was outraged at this behaviour, and they actually pinpointed the guy who threw it and turned him in to the police. They didn't want their reputation tarnished. I remember the FA took a lenient view because of that. In derby games as well you'd see red and blue scarves on the Kop, often people in the same family, out enjoying themselves. There was rivalry but no bitterness, and never any trouble. People would be there week after week, standing in exactly the same spot. You got to recognise them. I have to say, though, that I have never stood on the Kop. I wish I had. I'd really love to stand there cos, as I say, I feel that I'm one of them. I always regret never having done it.

EMLYN HUGHES
Liverpool player, 1967–79

Teams were physically frightened of the Kop. They would be terrified. No visiting team ever came out of the tunnel and ran towards the Kop; they always went in the opposite direction, down the Anfield Road End. There was this aura about the Kop. They were the people, they were the fans, they were the heart and soul of Liverpool Football Club, and you didn't mess with them. If a team came to Anfield and escaped with a 0–2 defeat they thought they had done well, they were that terrified.

The Kop is an institution. People travel thousands of miles to go on the Kop. They come from abroad, from everywhere, just to stand there and be one of that great crowd. It's strange, because when you see the Kop, as we did most days, with nobody on it, it doesn't look much. It's a bit of a dump. But put 25,000 people on it, and it's a different proposition. It comes alive.

I was lucky to have been playing when the Kop was at its best, with those huge crowds and those magnificent nights in Europe. It gave us a great lift. During the game you're not really aware of the chants, but you are aware of the noise, the rumble. You didn't hear any single voice, but then the Kop always spoke as one voice.

Before the game you're in the dressing-room, and then you come out and you suddenly become aware of the Kop. But within minutes the game has kicked off, and you're concentrating on the match. Then, when the final whistle goes, you're off the pitch pretty quickly. So I was never really as aware as people imagine. I used to hear the Kop sing my name. They adopted this song from that Manfred Mann hit during the 1960s. 'Come on without, come on within,' they used to sing. 'You've not seen nothing like the Mighty Emlyn.' They were great.

STEVE SHAKESHAFT
Photographer, Liverpool Daily Post and Echo

There used to be this old lady who stood in the Kop week after week. She was down behind the goal. And you'd see and hear her there at every match. She'd be yelling, shouting and screaming, and usually at the goalkeepers. She wore an old plastic headscarf and dark glasses and was always swearing. Her language was a disgrace. It was funny really, because outside the Kop she was probably a quite respectable woman – someone's granny, no doubt – but there in the Kop she just let rip and became a different person. She used to have these ongoing conversations with Ray Clemence as well, week after week. But she really hated the opposition goalkeepers and gave them a hell of a time. I've seen young goalkeepers come down the Kop end literally shaking.

RAY CLEMENCE
Liverpool goalkeeper, 1967–81

Goalkeepers have always held a special affection in the hearts of Kopites. I'm told that, going back to the turn of the century, they would applaud 'keepers at Anfield, and over the years they've had some of the best ever here – Elisha Scott, Sam Hardy, Ted Doig. It's a wonderful feeling when you come out at Anfield and you run towards the Kop end. The noise, and all that applause for you. And the Kop is always so generous. When visiting goalkeepers come down for the second half they always get a great reception from the Kop. It can turn average goalkeepers into giants, and that can make life difficult for Liverpool. Visiting 'keepers nearly always play their best games at Anfield, simply because it's a big stage and the Kop responds so positively towards them. It was interesting how that kind of a reception for goalkeepers caught on at other grounds.

I always had a great relationship with the Kop. They appreciated what I was doing, especially in the earlier days when I was still a novice. We all make mistakes, but the Kop was always forgiving and understanding. There would be the same characters standing behind me week after week. I got to know lots of them. They'd try to talk to me, shouting advice, being witty and that, though often you couldn't make it out in the din that was going on, and you were trying to concentrate on the game. But occasionally something funny would come across. Even when I left Liverpool for Tottenham I still got a great reception from the Kop. They don't forget.

IAN ST JOHN
Liverpool player, 1961–71

The one thing I always remember about the Kop was that I had to run up and down it. On wet days, when we didn't go out to Melwood for any training, Reuben Bennett, our trainer, used to take us on to the Kop and make us run up and down it countless times. I don't know how many steps there are, but I do know that they have been covered many times in my sweat.

In my days, the Kop was very inspirational. We were always aware of the heaving mass of people. The gates would be shut at 1 p.m., and they'd be there all afternoon, swaying one way and then the other. Those early days in the second division were memorable. We had some great games then. It was the start of a surge. We led the second division from start to finish, and I particularly remember a crucial game in 1962 against Southampton at Anfield. I had been sent off in a previous match and I was suspended, so I didn't play. But I was watching. The crowd were fantastic. At the end of the game we came back to the dressing-room, and Shanks made us go back out on to the pitch. We all ran around the pitch and then went up the Kop end. I had a nice white mac on, and it got splattered in mud.

We had a great rapport going with the Kop. There were lots of new lads in the side – myself, Ron Yeats, Gerry

Byrne, Gordon Milne. The Kop really took to them. We were running up good scores as well. We needed them to lift us, and they needed us. It was a relationship. But it's not the same any more. They're not humorous, just vulgar these days, screaming at referees. When we got past the half-way line, the roar used to go up. Not any more. It's not as inspirational, it's nothing like as witty. The crowds used to roar. I'll tell you what I think the problem is. I think they've got complacent. Too many good times. They're not hungry any more like they were in the early 1960s. They'd been starved of success for so many years then. Now they win a trophy every season and they automatically expect success.

DAVID FAIRCLOUGH
Liverpool player, 1974–82

People often ask me how aware you are of the Kop as a player. Well, the answer is that you are not always *so* aware as you might imagine. You are very aware when you first come out, and there's the usual two-minute spell when each of the players gets his name chanted. You especially listen out for your own name. It gives you a bit of a kick. And if you've been playing particularly well, then it's often chanted a bit louder.

There are, of course, some who are more popular than others. For me, I was always very aware of the Kop because I was often on the bench. The Kop always played a big part in wanting me on. Things might not be going too well and they'd start chanting my name, or they'd see me coming out of the dug-out and starting to warm up, and a great cheer would go out. They let it be known that they wanted me on. That gave me an enormous boost, just knowing that they want you on the pitch playing. Sometimes the manager, sitting there in the dug-out hearing the call for me, would respond. It was so important to me, it gave me confidence. Maybe that's why I did so well coming on as a substitute.

But once you're on the pitch and playing you don't look up at the Kop much. It's so daunting. You just keep your head down and get on with it. It's only at times that you look up. It can be very frightening. You're not always aware either of the songs because you are concentrating so much, but you are always aware of the buzz, the continuous buzz.

I was born near the ground, and it was inevitable that I soon found my way into Anfield. My first experience was in the Boys' Pen up in the corner of the Kop. This was in the 1960s. I used to join in all the chants, and eveyone in the Boys' Pen always got so excited.

When I think of the Kop and its singing, I always think of that era, the St John clap and the 'Sir Roger Hunt' chant. Then, towards the end of the game, they used to open all the gates. So we would sneak out of the Boys' Pen, round the back and in through the gates of the Kop. And there we would be, on the Kop itself. What a sight. It made us feel like grown men. It was daunting and so dangerous, though nothing ever happened. We always stuck to the sides or the top. We never dared venture into the middle. It was just fantastic to see it all.

CRAIG JOHNSTON
Liverpool player, 1981–88

Old-timers will tell you that singing was first heard on the Anfield terraces way back in 1906, as Liverpool strolled to their second first-division title. Over the years chanting and singing, especially that emanating from the Kop, has become an Anfield art-form. It's spontaneous, humorous and invariably passionate. At times, especially during a poignant moment in a critical game, it can be mesmerising.

The Kop in its glory is an awesome thing, rising and roaring like a volcano, obliterating rival supporters and teams alike. I've seen visiting sides, especially those from the Continent, immobilised by the sheer power and passion of the Kop's support for the home side. Just when you need them most they begin again, right on cue: 'Liv-er-pool, Liv-er-pool . . .' Then comes the anthem of a young scouse soldier dying on the battlefield, softly at first, 'Let me tell you a story of a poor boy who was sent far away from his home . . .', then growing stronger as the rest of the Kop catches on, 'To fight for his King and his country and also the old folks back home . . .' The hairs on the nape of the neck begin to stand on end. 'As he lay on the battlefield dying/ With the blood rushing out of his head/ As he lay on the battlefield dying/ These were the last words he said.' And then everybody joins in. 'Oh, I am a Liverpudlian and I come from the Spion Kop/ I love to sing/ I love to shout/ I get thrown out quite a lot/ We support a team that's dressed in red/ And it's a team that you all know/ It's a team that we call LIVERPOOL/ And to glory we will go . . .' As the sound drops away, the first phrase of the Rodgers and Hammerstein song that will forever be identified with LFC wells forth: 'Walk on, walk on . . .', and instantly 30,000 throats are singing with an intensity that defies description. Uplifted by that tide of passion, Liverpool are unstoppable.

The Kop's faith knows no limit. The Kop is every bit as much a part of the glory of LFC as any of the great players or managers. With the Kop behind us, we had at least a goal start every time.

SCOUSER TOMMY

(The first three stanzas are sung to the tune
of 'The Red River Valley', the last two to
the tune of 'The Sash')

Can I tell you a story of a poor boy,
Who was sent far away from his home,
To fight for his King and his country,
And also the old folks back home.

Now they put him in a Highland division,

Sent him off to a far foreign land,
Where the flies flew around in their
thousands,
There was nothing to see but the sand.
Now the battle it started next morning,
Under the Libyan sun;
I remember the poor scouser Tommy
Who was shot by an old Nazi gun.

As he lay on the battlefield dying, dying,
dying,
With the blood gushing out of his head,
As he lay on the battlefield dying, dying,
dying,
These were the last words he said:

Oh, I am a Liverpudlian
And I come from the Spion Kop
I love to sing,
I love to shout,
I get thrown out quite a lot.
We support the team that's dressed in red,
And it's a team that you all know.
It's a team that we call LIVERPOOL
And to glory we will go . . .

We've won the league,
We've won the cup,
And we've been to Europe too,
And we played the Toffees for a laugh,
And we left them feeling blue, 5–0

KEVIN KEEGAN
Liverpool player, 1971–77

I am not easily overawed. It explains how I was able to take in my stride the fact that I had just left Scunthorpe in the fourth division and was about to make my debut at Liverpool in the first division on the first day of a new season. The reception was something special. The Liverpool players ran to the centre of the field and waved, in turn, to all parts of the stadium. This was traditional before the first game of a season and at the end of the final match, but I did not really feel part of it. I was still very much a stranger.

After waving to the other parts of the ground, the players turned and faced the famous Kop. The ovation was deafening, the red and white scarves and flags appearing to have a life of their own. The whole scene got through to me. I had never experienced anything like it, but I refused to be overawed. I was looking forward to the game and felt I was going to score. The fans on the Kop chanted my name: 'Ke-vin Kee-gan . . . Ke-vin Kee-gan.' It sounded as strange as it had looked on the Liverpool team sheet. No one had chanted my name before. They had just called me names!

The self-appointed representative of the Kop came on the field to greet me. He gave me a kiss, and the smell of booze on his breath almost knocked me off my feet. He needed a shave as well, for his beard was rough. The police accept this ritual whenever there is a new player. This Kopite is a nice old fellow with no harm in him. He kissed me, then kissed the grass in front of the Kop and went back to join his mates in the crowd.

BRIAN BIRD
Former constable, Merseyside Police

I served getting on for twenty-eight years on the Kop. I began in 1964. I was a police constable, and I was there for virtually every game during those years, policing the Kop. Sometimes I was in front of the Kop patrolling – you know, just walking up and down on the pitch behind the goal-line – and then other times I was actually in the Kop itself. It was wonderful for me, because I was such a Liverpool fan. I was being paid for enjoying myself.

There were never any problems in the old days either. It was like a giant family, everybody seemed to know each other. I used always to remember this police sergeant. The Kop knew him as 'The Walrus'. He had a grey beard and a wonderful curly grey moustache. He served for years on the Kop and got the BEM for it. You got the occasional abuse. You'd get called names, but usually only because you were in the way, and they'd yell at you to get out of the effing road. There was also a character used to run on the pitch every week. He'd run up to the players, give them a kiss or whatever, and I'd have to chase him off the pitch. Many was the time I'd be running across the pitch after him. I'd grab him and then finally throw him back into the Kop. Well, what else could you do? You don't book someone like that.

But it all changed in the early 1980s. It stopped being as humorous. Suddenly, the fans decided they didn't like the police. There still wasn't any real trouble on the Kop, it was just that they were not at all friendly towards us. I think the riots of 1981 had a lot to do with it. The youngsters today don't like the police at all.

JIM HESKETH
Former sergeant, Merseyside Police

I was known by everyone on the Kop as 'The Walrus'. That's because I used to have a huge white moustache. It's a bit shorter these days. They all used to call me 'The Walrus', and some of the younger ones even called me 'Mr Walrus'. The Kop just gave me that name. They chanted it on more than a couple of occasions as well. I was the sergeant in charge of the pitch at one time, and I would be marching up and down and the Kop would be chanting, 'Walrus, Walrus' ! Then there was another time, I remember. I was parading along the bottom of the Kop when they all starting singing, Ee-aye-addio, the Walrus is a queer'! It was all good sport, and I took no offence because I know they meant no offence. I loved the Kopites. I got on very well with them and always found them most helpful.

I started policing at Anfield in 1947, both inside and outside the ground. I became a sergeant in 1953 and then, in 1956, I became the sergeant in charge of the pitch. I had an awful lot of friends there. I would see the same people in the same spot week after week, and they would always say hello and be as helpful as they could. We rarely had any fights, and if we did we nipped them in the bud quickly. I remember the lad from Barker and Dobson who used to go around with his sweets tray coming over to me one week. He'd had a box of chewing gum pinched up by the Boys' Pen. So we went over there, and I said to the lads there, 'Look, this man seems to have lost a box of chewing gum. I think it must have fallen on the floor. Could you please have a look and see if you can find it?' I turned away for a second and, of course, they suddenly produced the chewing gum. You have to apply a bit of psychology. So everyone was happy.

We used to have the occasional person run on the pitch, but it was always done in good spirit and with the best of intentions. There was one guy who would always come on to welcome new players to the club when they were making their debut. I would just let him do his business, and then I would escort him off the pitch and back into the Kop. I always used to wonder as well how the singing on the Kop was organised; then one day I spotted a lad giving out song sheets. They must have made the words up beforehand, and they were handing them out to a group in the middle of the Kop behind the goal. They were wonderful times and wonderful people.

INSPECTOR BERNARD SWIFT
Football liaison officer, Merseyside Police

It's very pleasant being the football liaison officer for the police, as I've been a Liverpool fan all my life. I first started coming here when I was 13. I think the first match I ever saw was Liverpool against Honved, back in the mid-1960s. I also remember coming to see that famous

Everton/Liverpool Cup-tie, the one that had television screens here at Anfield.

I joined the police force in 1972, and I had ten years policing football matches. Part of that was with the mounted force. Anyhow, for the past two years I've been in charge of all the policing, not just for Liverpool but for Everton as well. Everybody thinks our day starts at about 2 p.m., but it doesn't, it begins at 10 o'clock in the morning. We have 200 police on duty each Saturday that there's a game. Most of them are employed outside of the ground itself. We have to be down at Lime Street Station or Edge Hill awaiting the arrival of the away fans, then we have to escort them to the ground. We also have to have police on traffic duty, especially after the game, so that we can clear the roads as quickly as possible. Then, of course, we have policemen outside the ground at the turnstiles, some mounted, and there will be others in reserve. It's a big operation, but I'm glad to say we don't have much trouble here.

On the Kop itself we have one sergeant and eight constables. They're usually at the turnstiles, making sure nobody is bringing in drink or offensive weapons. It's not a lot of policemen, considering you get 16,000 on the Kop. It's an offence to bring drink into the ground, but then the club itself serves drink, so it's a bit of a dilemma for us. We obviously don't arrest anyone for bringing drink on to the Kop, but we would confiscate it. Some people genuinely don't know that they are not supposed to bring drink in. In the 1960s, it was traditional to have a pint in the ground, but you can't buy drink on the Kop now, only in the executive places. Most people who come on the Kop have a drink in the pub beforehand anyhow, but if they're drunk then we would not let them into the ground.

The other week we arrested someone who was drunk in charge of a six-month-old child on the Kop. Can you imagine? Any can is what we call a controlled container; that means it is potentially a dangerous weapon and could be thrown at people. So again we have the right to confiscate, but sometimes you turn a blind eye. You have to make a judgement.

At the moment, we are looking to decrease the number of police officers inside the ground and increase the number of stewards. Of course, all the stewards will have to be trained up, but we think this is the direction to go in. This all came out of the Taylor Report. It will also be cheaper for the club, who have to pay for all the policemen inside the ground, and because football is played on a Saturday or in an evening it means that the police are on overtime. We have about eighty police inside the ground altogether, so it costs the club between £10,000 to £13,000 a match for policing. It's a lot of police we are using, and it means that other areas of the city are not policed. Naturally, some of the public don't like that, especially as the police are drawn from all over Merseyside. Someone on the Wirral, for instance, might well complain about their police being used to control a football match in Liverpool.

Since Hillsborough, most of our efforts are focused on increasing safety. It means that we now have more policemen than ever at the ground. I'm always on the look-out for potentially hazardous incidents, such as places where you might get a build-up of people in a confined or restricted area. If we think it is potentially dangerous then we will talk to the club about improving the situation.

The hooliganism element seems to be on the decline. I can recall in the mid-1970s when it was at its peak. I was on the horses then and escorted fans to the stations. We had running battles. It was still going on up to about 1986. There's still a bad element, but I think we have it under control. We get very few incidents on the Kop, maybe the occasional coin-throwing, but not much else. The Kopites don't always like us, but there has been a change in attitude since Hillsborough.

We had a fellow collapsed with a heart attack on the Kop last season, and the paramedics needed to get to him with their equipment which, as you can imagine, is pretty difficult when this bloke is right in the middle of the Kop. So I went on the tannoy. Now I'm very reluctant to go on the tannoy and make an announcement, because it's usually greeted with derision and you get a bad response, but on this occasion I decided to. I explained the situation and I asked the Kop to make way for the paramedics and their equipment. And you should have seen the Kop. It was like the Red Sea parting. In an instant, a huge corridor had been made for the medics. And the corridor stayed there for ages until they had finished and got the bloke off the Kop. I was so impressed I went back on the tannoy and thanked them all for their help. And you know what? They applauded.

INSPECTOR JOHN JEFFREY
Football liaison officer, Merseyside Police

We have some very sophisticated technology these days to help us. For instance, all our turnstiles are computerised so that, at any given moment, we can tell how many people are in the ground and how much room is left. The computer also breaks it down to numbers on the Kop, in the Paddock, the Main Stand, the Centenary Stand – both upper and lower tiers – the Anfield Road End and the visitors' section. With the Kop, we can also tell you how many paying customers we've let in and how many season-ticket holders.

There are 16,480 people allowed on the Kop these days, and only 7,320 are paying customers. The rest are season ticket-holders. We have to know the number of paying customers because we cannot allow more than the 7,320 in. It may be one minute to three with only 1,000 season ticket-holders inside, but we still can't let more than the prescribed number of paying customers in. Who knows, the other 9,000 season ticket-holders might turn up at one minute past three. It also helps us know when to warn the fans in the queues that they are not going to get in.

I'll give you the other breakdowns if you like. The capacity of the Main Stand is 8,771, the Paddock takes 2,578, the Anfield Road End 2,392, the visitors' section 3,120, the Lower Centenary 6,809 and the Upper Centenary 4,595. That gives a total ground capacity of 44,245.

So, as the ground is filling up, I can give you a reading of the numbers anywhere inside at any second. I can also get a hard copy printed off the computer. Now the other thing that our computer does is to show you the flow per minute, i.e., how many people are going through the turnstiles. Now here, for the game against Middlesbrough, we can see that the maximum flow through the turnstiles was between seven minutes to three and just after, when 300 people per minute were entering.

We can also look back and see how the Kop filled up for that game. The gates opened at 1:02, and at 2:10 there was a total of 3,041 people on the Kop, of whom 2,061 were paying customers. You'd expect that. The paying customers always come early to make sure they are going to get in. At 2:35 p.m., there were 6,038 on the Kop, with 3,335 of them paying. At 2:45 p.m., the number had risen to 8,031, with 3,853 paying. At 2:53, the total was 9,800, with 4,162 paying. Then, with five minutes to go, the number had shot up to 10,520, and of those 4,298 had paid. As the game kicked off, the figure was 11,796, with 4,463 paying. The final official figures showed 13,332 on the Kop, with 4,627 paying.

So what can we say about these statistics? First, that the Kop was not full. Nearly all the season ticket-holders came that day, but there was still room for another 3,000 paying customers. The other thing that is interesting is that we can trace how quickly the Kop fills. Compared to other parts of the ground, it begins to fill up earlier. This is simply because of the paying customers and people wanting to get a good spec. Between 2:35 and kick-off, only 5,000 went on to the Kop. But if you look at the ground as a whole: at 2:35 p.m., there were 14,386 people inside, whereas at kick-off there was 31,916. The other thing is that 3,000 people arrived after the game had kicked off.

Anfield can be filled very quickly and, of course, it can be emptied even quicker. That day it took precisely seven and a half minutes to get all 34,570 people out of the ground. That's from the final whistle to when it is completely empty. If you look at these photographs as well, which were taken at ten- or five-minute intervals from 1:00 p.m. onwards, you can see the way the Kop fills. Everybody makes for the centre behind the goal. It starts filling up there straightaway. By 2 p.m., the middle of the Kop is densely packed. After that, people start going to the sides.

All the exit gates are also computerised, so that we immediately know up here in our control room if there is a problem with one of the gates, if it is insecure or anything like that. It would immediately show up on this plan, where all the exits are marked. And we can also open any gate or all the gates by simply pressing a button here. Press that, and every exit gate in the ground will automatically open. So if there was a major problem, we could get people out quickly and wouldn't have to go looking for a key or a steward or anything like that.

We also have thirteen video cameras inside and outside the ground. Four of them are outside, four inside, three are underneath the Anfield Road visitors' section, and then one is a hand-held camera on the gantry of the Centenary Stand. All the cameras outside and inside, except for those under the visitors' section, can be moved through 180 degrees or more and tilted up and down. They can also zoom in on anything.

A policeman sits here in the police control room during the game and watches all these thirteen monitors. If he sees anything suspicious or is asked by another police officer to look at something in particular, he can move a camera and home in on any individual anywhere in the ground. Everything is recorded in case we need to look at it again. We can also take a photograph which is instantly available of anything on the monitor.

We can even home in on individuals in most places outside the ground. For instance, what is that man doing there outside the Anfield Road turnstiles? There is a crowd around him. Is he selling tickets, or are people signing a petition? It looks to be worth investigating, so I shall give a call to an officer nearby to walk up and investigate. And all the time everything is being recorded.

It's also useful for when the team coaches arrive. We always know precisely where the coaches are. When they leave their hotel for the ground they inform us. The away coach will have a motor cycle escort and as it nears the ground will also have a mounted police escort. The coach always comes in the same direction, and we can film it as it approaches and turns through the Shankly Gates to the players' entrance. So if anything was to happen, we would spot it straightaway, be able to get reinforcements there, know our culprits and have it all recorded.

Let me give you another example. There was an incident the other week when, during the early kick-about, the ball shot into the Kop and a young lad decided he'd like to keep the ball. Well, of course, he shouldn't. So we zoomed in on him and he clearly was not going to release the ball. He stuffed it under his pullover and had a good giggle with his pals. We could see all this, and it was being recorded. He then decided to move away, but our cameras followed him. Then he decided to take his hat off so that he wouldn't be recognised, but we still knew him. We were, of course, recording all the time, and we also took a photograph of him where we could quite clearly see the ball hidden under his jumper. But he clearly had no idea that we were watching his every movement.

Our man on the monitor was able to give his description to a police officer on the Kop, as well as to the officer on the gantry with the hand-held camera. Then we do what is known as 'the golden shot', where we direct the police officer down the Kop through the crowd and to the individual. It's a process of 'down a bit, now go left, down a bit further, left, and there he is in front of you, the boy with red hair'. And that's it. The lad is arrested.

It's strange because people just don't realise that if they get up to mischief, we could be watching them all the time. In this case, it was taking a hammer to crack a nut, but in another instance it would be of extreme value.

I joined the police force in 1967, and I'll never forget the first game I was asked to police. I thought it was going to be great. I was a Liverpool fan, always have been, and been on the Kop plenty of times. So I thought I was going to be in there, seeing the game free, walking up and down in front of the Kop. It was a midweek game, and I went down to the station to get my orders. It was pouring with rain, and they gave me this big white mac, clearly designed for someone about 6ft 6in. I was only 5ft 9in, and they told me to go down Everton Valley and direct the traffic. I was there in this appalling white mac ten sizes too big for me, directing the traffic in the cold and the wet from 6:30 p.m. until 9:30 p.m. Blow this, I thought, next time I won't volunteer, I'll pay and go on the Kop like the rest of the lads.

BOB LYONS
Constable, Merseyside Police

Generally we don't get many problems on the Kop, though we had to go in there when Liverpool played Spartak on 4 November 1992. A couple of flares were set off, and we just don't allow that. We were able to spot the culprits via our video camera and we sent some bobbies in to arrest them. One of them turned out to be a Norwegian as well. The Kop fans are pretty good and a lot more helpful than they used to be. They'll assist us where they can, but we tend not to send anyone into the Kop alone. The main problem is drunkenness, and if we think someone has had one too many he gets ejected.

The other problem is pickpockets, especially in the Kop. Thieving is a big problem in Liverpool. Our lads spot the pickpockets in the queues and just go up to them and let them know that we know. We tend to know most of them, they're not amateurs. They go all over, wherever there is a big crowd: pop concerts, car boot sales, sports events, Marks and Spencers. You get them everywhere. The Kop is ideal for them. Some of them come to watch the game, but most are there to do a bit of business. I spotted one outside Goodison some time ago in the queue, so I just shouted to everybody, 'Be careful, gentlemen, there are known pickpockets about.' We will, of course, search them if we have good reason to believe that they may have stolen goods about them, but often it's a case of simply warning them off and just letting them know that we're watching them. You get them at away games as well, and we help to identify them.

Another thing we don't allow is for anyone to go on the pitch. It's quite difficult to get on the pitch from the Kop, but if they did they would be ejected straightaway. We don't have any transfer policy at all here. People stay where they are, and that's it. If they try to go anywhere else they're out. I have to say that I have never in my years seen any fighting on the Kop.

Another problem we have are the touts. They are not illegal but they are a nuisance. They'll sell Kop tickets or whatever to away supporters, and that causes problems for us. Half a dozen away supporters on the Kop can be a potential problem, and it means we have to sort it out. Usually, it means having to guard them or get them to a place of safety.

Oddly enough, the clubs that cause us the biggest problems are the smaller clubs like Chesterfield and Swansea. They usually arrive with a big crowd. Coming here is a bit special for them, a sort of Cup final, so they make the most of it. They're excited, it's a big occasion, they have a bit too much to drink. Then if their team goes ahead, as Chesterfield did during the 1992–93 season, they get even more excited. And it can all lead to trouble.

We're in regular contact with police forces around the country, and in the week before a game we have meetings with the other relevant police force, and usually we send a couple of our officers on the away trips while a couple of their officers will come here for the home games. When we go away we travel in uniform. We mingle with the Liverpool fans, by the tea bars and that, and then link up with the other force and pass on any intelligence information that we might have gathered. If we spot a lad who has a known record, we just go up to him and say, 'Didn't know you were coming today.' We can even be a bit jokey about it. It's just a way of warning them. We then let the home police force know that such and such a person is here, and we help identify them.

But I have to say that the Liverpool fans are pretty good. We don't have a lot of trouble other than a bit of drunkenness and a bit of thieving, but then you can get that anywhere. There's usually four to seven thousand of them going to an away game, but there's not much thuggery these days. A good indication of the changing attitude is that we have never had any damage whatsoever to the Hillsborough memorial. Years ago someone would have painted on it or thrown eggs at it. But not any more. It's quite common to see the away fans laying flowers.

JAMES CATLING
Cleaner

I've been sweeping and cleaning the Kop for eight years. I quite enjoy it. There's three of us work the Kop. We come in on a Monday morning if there's been a game on a Saturday. We start about 8 a.m. and work through to twelveish. We have these large brooms, and we sweep everything into piles and then put it into black bin-bags. The bags are then put into those bins down at the bottom there, and finally it all gets put in a skip. I suppose we fill about twenty bins after each match. If it's not a full house then it's less.

Two of us do the sweeping, and the other cleans the toilets, the stairs and the cafeteria. It takes us four mornings to get it all cleaned up properly. Yes, there's a lot of rubbish here, mostly tin cans, sweet wrappers, cigarettes, newspapers, the likes of that.

Occasionally, you find something interesting. This morning there's been a couple in. She lost her engagement ring and wedding ring on Saturday, so we're keeping our eye out for it. But we haven't found it so far. We get a lot of requests like that; people come to the club, and we try to help. Sometimes we find things. We always find lots of scarves, hats and gloves, and we take these down to the office, so if anybody loses them they can come and reclaim them. I found a wedding ring last year, and some people came and got it back.

What else have I found? I've found a couple of gold bracelets, that's the kind of thing that always comes off at football matches; watches, that's something else that we regularly find; and credit cards as well. It's probably easier to find things these days, as there's only 16,000 allowed on the Kop now. Back in the old days, when there were 25,000 on here, if you dropped something it was impossible to bend down and pick it up. It was lost forever, or at least until the end of the game, and by then you'd likely be twenty yards from where you dropped it.

JOHN CULL
Chief programme seller

There is a pecking order in selling programmes. When I began in 1951, the place to start was the Boys' Pen. That was up in the corner of the Kop. You started there because there were not so many programmes to sell. You only sold 200 there, and you could get them all sold before kick-off. It gave you an idea of what the job was like and how you coped. I used to get a commission of 1s. 3d per hundred, so on most match-days I would make 2s. 6d.

Once you have proved that you can do the job you go on to the 'spares list', and you get the chance to stand in for someone else if they are not available. Eventually, you begin to move up in the pecking order and get a proper posting. You'd go to do the Paddock or maybe the Kop, and finally you would wind up doing the stands.

I stood down the Kop end of the Paddock for near twenty-five years selling programmes. It works pretty much the same these days, although there is no Boys' Pen. Today you might start at the Anfield Road End, either in the home supporters' section or the away section. Not as many programmes are sold there. We have nicknames for all the selling spots, such as 'Flagpole Corner', 'Underneath the Arches', and so on.

Back in the 1960s, we would sell programmes to one in two spectators, but it's gone down a bit now. It probably averages out at around one in three today. It varies slightly according to the visitors. A club like Wimbledon, for instance, bring in very few visitors. When they played here recently, we only sold fifty-four programmes in their section, but with someone like Manchester United or Tottenham we can probably get rid of 1,500, or maybe even 2,000. So that boosts the sales considerably. The higher cost of programmes nowadays has been the main cause of the drop in sales. This season we charge £1. 10. When I started it was 3d, which is little more than one penny now.

The best visitors for selling programmes to are Manchester United. That's because they not only bring a lot of support but they have a system whereby they have to have so many tokens from their home programmes as well as so many away programmes to make them eligible for Wembley tickets. That's if they ever get to Wembley! So, their supporters are always keen to buy programmes.

Tottenham supporters are big buyers of programmes too. The funniest thing that ever happened to me was one day when a Tottenham supporter came up to me. He said, 'How many programmes have you got there?'

I said: 'Four hundred.'

'Right,' he said, 'I'll have the lot,' and he gave me £400 in cash. I couldn't believe it. I took the money, dashed round to the office, and then got a bit of a telling-off. They were most annoyed that I'd sold all the programmes to one person. Now that they sell programmes in the Development Office, you're supposed to direct people there if they want to buy in bulk. I heard the police later stopped the Tottenham bloke, wanting to know why he had 400 programmes. They must have thought he had stolen them.

It might surprise you, but one of the worst clubs of all for selling programmes to are Everton. Of course, they know all the players and that, so I suppose the programmes aren't much use to them. But the truth is that no true Evertonian would ever want to take a Liverpool programme home with him!

We don't sell programmes on the Kop itself, never have. They're all sold by the turnstiles as you come in. In fact, Liverpool have never even sold programmes outside the ground. We've always sold inside the ground. The favourite selling spot for the Kop is called 'Flagpole Corner'. It's at the *Great Eastern* flagpole which, as you probably know, is down at the back of the Kop. Although we always sell a lot of programmes there, it wasn't always popular with us because, if it was raining, you got soaked. But in the last few years they've started putting up huts for us, mainly as a security precaution. We have four sellers there who usually sell about 2,000, that's out of a total of around 4,000 sold on the Kop. The other sellers on the Kop are at the corners, where three of them get rid of about 1,200. Then there's a guy at what we call the Walton Breck Road, he's just at the bottom of the staircase, and he sells about 600. A third of all our programmes are sold at the Kop. Elsewhere in the ground we sell 1,500 to the Anfield Road visitors, 700 to the home supporters, 700 to the Paddock stands, 2,000 in the Main Stand, and 2,200 in the Centenary Stand.

On match-days I usually arrive at the ground by 12:30 p.m. The sellers drift in over the next half-hour or so, and I dish out the programmes to them. The gates open two hours before kick-off, so I like to have everyone in their spot by 1 p.m. At about 1:30 p.m., I go on a walkabout, visiting all the sellers to make sure everything is all right. By 2 p.m., I'm back in my office in the Centenary Stand, ready for the sellers to return with their money. I take the cash off them, check it, sign the forms, pay them the commission. They get paid £3 per one hundred programmes but they have to pay tax on that, so it really works out at £2.25 per hundred, unless you're a student or are exempted tax. We have a new rule now that nobody gets less than £7.50. That's because sometimes the sales at the visitors' end can be so low you'd only be picking up a few pounds, and it wouldn't be worth it or even fair. Once they've been paid they can go off and watch the game. Most of them go into the Kop. Unfortunately, I still have a few things to do like totting up all the money and taking it to the cash office, so I often don't finish until it's well into the second half.

We don't get much trouble selling programmes. I can't remember anyone being beaten up or anything like that. The funny thing is that, if there is an incident, it's people stealing programmes. They don't seem to be bothered about stealing the money, they just take the programmes. It seems a bit odd, you'd think they'd be more interested in the money. Of course, there was a time when we just put the bundles down, and people picked up the programmes themselves and gave you the appropriate money. But not any more. The police have made the club give us security huts.

HUGH O'NEILL
St John Ambulance

I first went to Anfield as a representative of the St John Ambulance when I was a 15-year-old cadet. That was in 1968. In those days you certainly needed us, and we were kept pretty busy but these days, with the lower capacity, particularly on the Kop, we are not brought into action as much. I am now the longest serving St John Ambulance man at Anfield.

On an average Saturday, there will be as many as twenty-four of us attending to the Kop, with another sixteen or so around other parts of the ground. I usually arrive about noon, get the keys and open up the first-aid rooms. Most of our people arrive about oneish. I then allocate people to their various posts, and we put the stretchers out – a wheel stretcher and a canvas stretcher to each corner of the pitch, and also a canvas stretcher behind the Kop goal.

Everyone has to be standing in their posts half an hour before kick-off. I'm usually in the Kop, close to the first-aid room, and I've been there around twenty-five years or more. We get our calls from either the police, the fans or the stewards. Once we have our injured person they are taken to the first-aid room, where we diagnose them. The first-aid room is manned by women, and there is a doctor in attendance at the ground. Once we have diagnosed them we can give them the appropriate treatment. In some cases they will then have to go to hospital, in other cases they may just go home, or if they are fully recovered they can go back and watch the match.

I suppose we treat about twenty-four or so on the Kop each match. The most usual complaint is fainting. People come to the ground in winter with a lot of clothes on, and then they get in the Kop where they're huddled up together and they soon get too hot. We've never had any problems from people on the Kop. I think they all respect us, especially after Hillsborough. These days, if we have to go on the Kop with a stretcher, everyone makes way and, when we're coming back with an injured person on a stretcher, the crowd parts like Moses and the Red Sea.

It's so much better now than it used to be. We've been very lucky not to have had a serious tragedy here. And those steps that used to be at the back of the Kop . . . How we never had an accident similar to Ibrox I'll never know.

The worst time on the Kop? Well, you'll be surprised. The worst time we ever had was when Billy Graham came. It was the busiest we have ever known from our point of view. We had seven ambulances on duty each night, and all of them were used every night. The trouble was that most of the people who came had never been to a football ground. They were unfamiliar with the steps and so on. There were also a lot of old people on the Kop. And because there was not a big crowd, it was easier to slip. When you are all crushed up together, it's almost impossible to slip and fall to the ground. But people were tumbling all over the place at the Billy Graham meetings. They just were not used to the steps. We had fractured ankles, legs and wrists galore.

In all the years I have been in attendance on the Kop, only one person has died, and that was on 10 March 1992 at the West Ham United game. It was someone who had a massive heart attack. There was nothing we could do about it. We get quite a few people who have heart attacks. I think we had about three or four last season, but the season before that there were about seven. It's men usually in their 50s. It's the crush, the excitement, the tension. People really should not go in the Kop when they get to that age. Most people of that age go in the stands, though they still have heart attacks even there. If we get called to someone in the stands, the chances are that it will be a heart attack.

Back in the 1960s and 1970s, the Kop was packed. It was really dangerous, and it was a miracle that there was never a major disaster. It was impossible for us to get on to the Kop when someone was hurt or had fainted, it was so packed. So they just used to pass the bodies over everybody's head, all the way down the Kop. These days, with the lower capacity of the Kop, we are able to go in and deal with the problem, but it wasn't always like that. When there were fences at the bottom of the Kop, they used to cause real problems for us. Someone once got an arm impaled on the spikes. But the biggest problem of all was that, as the bodies were being passed overhead, we had to direct them towards the openings in the fences in order to get them out. You can imagine how difficult it was trying to direct people to pass the bodies in another direction. Most of the casualties had fainted, some had broken ankles or crush injuries. We rarely had injuries such as knifings.

There was the occasional skirmish when punches were thrown, and these were generally between Liverpool supporters, but it never resulted in too serious an injury. I always remember a couple of lads being pulled off the Kop. One of them had a badly bleeding nose, and the other was apologising all the time. Apparently they were mates and, when St John scored, the one who ended up with the bleeding nose turned round and said it was a bit of a flukey goal. So his mate immediately punched him in the face. It was just a natural reaction, and he was terribly upset at what he had done.

I sometimes have to deal with the players. I well remember Stevie Heighway got a bad cut on the eye in a game against Ipswich, and we had to take him to the first-aid room and give him an injection above the eye so that stitches could be put in. He was screaming with pain as we put the injection in. It was half-time, and Kevin Keegan popped his head round the door to see how he was. 'Don't worry, Steve,' he said, 'we'll do them for you.'

The funniest was an incident with Neville Southall, the Everton goalkeeper, in a derby game. He had collided with the goalpost down at the Kop end and was laid out flat with concussion. He was in a bit of a bad way, and the Everton physio called for the stretcher. So we ran on to the pitch and started to put him on the stretcher. Then Howard Kendall comes running on, wanting to know what we were doing. He was furious. He didn't want Southall off at all and overruled his physio. At this point, Graeme Souness, then a player with Liverpool, wanders over and has a look. 'No way,' he says, 'you've got to get him off, he's out of it, Howard.' It was obvious what Souness was playing at. I had to laugh to myself. But Kendall had his way. Southall stayed on. He played a blinder the rest of the game, but he didn't know where he was.

I once broke my own foot on the Kop. It was a game against Leicester at the end of the 1972–73 season. Liverpool needed a draw to win the league title. Anyhow, a young kid had fallen off a wall, and I had to climb over this wall on the Kop to get to him. Someone kindly lent me a small ladder. As I was coming back up the ladder, it slipped and came down on my foot, breaking it. I was in agony but I refused to leave my post and go to hospital. It wasn't dedication to the job, mind you, it was just that I wanted to see Liverpool win the title. No way was I leaving Anfield before the final whistle.

WE'RE GONNA WIN THE LEAGUE (2)
We're gonna win the league,
We're gonna win the league,
We're gonna win, win, win, win,
Win the league.

SYDNEY MOSS
Former Vice-Chairman, Liverpool Football Club

As a club, not only have we always carried out the instructions of the City Surveyor who grants our safety certificate, but we usually go much further. Well, one year we had checks done on the crush barriers. One of them was taken out for inspection, and it was discovered that it had badly deteriorated. We then had a stress machine check the barriers, and it was clear that this one had rotted. The City Surveyor said, quite rightly, that they would all have to be replaced, but he said that we could do it over a period of five years. Well, we said, 'No, let's do it all at once. We're not going to take any risks.' So, in the summer of 1988, the contractors moved in to replace all the barriers. Well, it was a good job that they did, because we discovered this huge hole under the Kop.

When they built the Kop back in 1906 they had thrown all the rubbish they could find on to the mound to make it bigger. Apparently, the surveyor had then come along and had said, 'You can't do that, because there is a sewer running beneath it, and it has to be checked regularly.' He told them they would have to knock it all down. Well, at the time the club didn't want to do that, so they agreed to build a manhole from the top of the Kop down to the sewer. Anyrate, it was the brickwork on this manhole leading down to the sewer that went. The bricks started to come out and the manhole collapsed, causing a big hole. The whole Kop could have collapsed. It was very dangerous.

We were already behind schedule when that was discovered, so it caused a major problem as the new season was fast approaching. Specialist contractors were brought in, and work was carried out around the clock, a full twenty-four hours. It was the only way we could meet the deadline. It involved a lot of heavy machinery, and it was very noisy. Before long, the neighbours started complaining, and the police informed us that one old lady was going to take out an injunction to stop the work. She said that she could not sleep. Well, that was a potentially serious problem.

We owned her house so we sent Jack Cross, one of our directors who is chairman of our Grounds Committee, to see her. Well, he knocked on the door, and she answered. 'Who are you?' she asked rather gruffly.

'I'm Mr Cross,' he said, 'and I've come to see you about the injunction.'

She wasn't at all friendly. 'You'd better stay there,' she told him. 'There's a rottweiler here and he'll have your hand off. You can't speak to my husband either, because he's gone away. He can't stand the noise, and I'm going to see him tomorrow for a week.'

Well, that gave Jack an idea. And he asked her if there were any jobs needed doing on the house. She told him we had a week. So we took advantage of her absence, carried out a few repairs on the house for her, and got the contractors on the Kop to hurry up with the job before they returned. Well, when they returned, Mr Cross went round to see them, and she greeted him very differently.

'Oh, thank you very much,' she said, 'do come in.' The rottweiler was still there chained to the banister, so Jack edged his way carefully past it, when suddenly the dog broke away from its chains and came charging towards him. It pounced right up at him and placed its paws on his shoulders and then just licked his face. Even the dog had been won over.

STEVE SHAKESHAFT
Photographer, Liverpool Daily Post and Echo

I've been lying on my stomach in front of the Kop for twenty-five years as a photographer for the *Liverpool Daily Post and Echo*. It might sound wonderful, but I can assure you that it is not always so. For a start, it's frightening. There is this great wall of heat behind you. You notice it particularly on cold or wet days when you walk towards it. Steam is rising from all the bodies and hanging just below the roof of the Kop itself.

I can still remember the first day I went there as a nervous 19-year-old. Up until a few years ago, the crowd came right down to pitch level. But there's a moat there now, and it's not quite the same. But before that all the kids were at pitch level, heads and faces peering at you over the edge, and only a foot or so away. All the time you're concentrating on getting a photograph, but you are always aware of this huge wall hanging over your shoulder. And if you turned around and looked up, it was terrifying. It seemed to go on forever. And when the crowd swayed and started cascading downwards, you thought they were all going to land on top of you. All the time you were looking through your lens you could hear this noise vibrating through you.

The other problem was that, as a photographer, you'd be lying at the side of the goal and, inevitably, you would be blocking the view of someone behind you. I could sympathise with them, but there was little I could do about it. In fact, the Kop at that time was one of the only grounds in the country where you had to lie on your stomach. I suppose we could have sat, but that would have made it a lot worse for those behind. As it was, we were doing them a big favour by lying down. But still we got it in the neck. You can imagine their reaction. 'Ay, mister, gerrout of the effing way,' was about the politest request. I used to think, 'I bet you wouldn't like to have to lie here.'

And when it was raining it was even worse. The wet would seep through, you'd be cold, and there was no cup of tea at half-time. It wasn't much fun. And then when they'd shouted to you to move and you hadn't, they would start spitting. That was the worst and, if it didn't work, they would start throwing things at you. The favourite used to be the half-crown piece. It was heavy. They weren't always throwing things at us, sometimes it would be at a particular defender as he came close to the goal-line. The half-crowns would come hurtling down. Inevitably, one or two would hit us. One Saturday I saw someone with a half-crown embedded in his face. The one good thing was that some of the coins would land in front of me. Many was the Saturday when I collected enough half-crowns to buy myself a few rounds that night.

But it wasn't just half-crowns that I've seen thrown. Once I saw someone pulled out of the Kop with a dart in his head. But, most frightening of all, somebody once had a gun, an air rifle or something, because the pellets came whistling past me and one of them actually hit me. The other thing that used to get thrown were cigarettes. It's quite difficult when you're standing in the Kop to get rid of a cigarette. You're so huddled together you can't drop it on the floor and stamp on it. It's much easier to throw them. There were plenty of times when I'd come away with holes burnt in my coat. So, as you can imagine, it hasn't always been fun lying in front of the Kop. I used to quite welcome it if Liverpool were kicking towards the Kop in the first half, then you'd get it over and done with quickly and could look forward to the second half up at the Anfield Road End.

Four

THE WIT AND WISDOM OF THE KOP

Careless Hands

ERIC DOIG
Kopite

Everyone remembers the Gary Sprake incident. It was on 9 December 1967. If you were there you would never forget it. It must have been the most embarrassing moment of his life. But it will always be remembered not because Sprake made the most awful error, but because of what happened afterwards. I was in the Kop that day, just behind the goal. Leeds, of course, were a great side in those days.

I can see it now. Sprake has the ball, and all the Leeds players are running back upfield. He holds the ball in his left hand wondering who to throw it to, bounces it, then draws his arm back and goes to hurl it upfield. Unfortunately, the ball flies out of his hand just as he has pulled his arm back. The ball shoots into the goal. It's a goal for Liverpool.

There was total disbelief. Then from somewhere on the Kop comes this almighty chorus: 'Careless Hands,' they all start singing. It was a big hit at the time and, within a second, the entire Kop was singing, 'Careless Hands', even before Sprake had had time to go and pick the ball out of the back of the net. It was that instantaneous.

ROGAN TAYLOR
Kopite and a founder of the Football Supporters'
Association

Tommy Smith's testimonial in 1977 was unique. It was one of the greatest occasions I've ever seen at Anfield. I don't expect it could have been bettered anywhere in the world, and I'll never forget it. It came just two days after Liverpool had won their first European Cup. Liverpool had beaten Borussia on the Wednesday, and then on the Friday evening they lined up at Anfield against a Bobby Charlton XI. Smith was supposed to be retiring and, of course, in his final game in the European Cup final he had headed that glorious goal which put Liverpool on the road to victory.

Anyhow, there was a huge crowd and they were all in celebratory mood. The Kop weren't really interested in the game as a contest and were getting a bit bored, so they decided they were going to entertain us all. First of all, they began singing to the Anfield Road End and instructed everyone down the Annie Road End to sit down. And, to the amazement of everyone, the entire Anfield Road End of the ground sat down. Next in line was the Kemlyn Road Stand: 'Kem-lyn Road, Kem-lyn Road, stand up.' And again, to everyone's astonishment, everyone stood up.

By this time the entire ground was in fits, and the Kop was beginning to get a bit cocky at its superhuman powers. So they turned their attention on the directors' box. Surely they would not respond. But they did. 'Dir-ectors' box, dir-ectors' box, stand up,' they demanded. And, of course, the directors all meekly stood up. But then, best of all, in what proved to be a prophetic instruction, they sang to themselves: 'Kop-end, Kop-end, sit down.' And the entire Kop suddenly sat down, every one of us. I've never seen anything like it. What they were really doing was to tell the club who was in charge. It was really the Kop who ran the club, the Kop who were the heart of Liverpool Football Club. It was a proletarian moment, a moment of universal democracy. It was a little bit of genius.

IAN SERGEANT
Kopite

During the early 1980s, there was a famous case in Liverpool of a certain Jimmy Kelly, who had died while in police custody. There were a lot of accusations that the police had manhandled him, using unnecessary force, and that this had resulted in his death. The case had received a lot of publicity, and there was all sorts of graffiti around Liverpool along the lines of 'Who killed Jimmy Kelly'.

Well, one Saturday on the Kop there was a bit of pushing and shoving somewhere behind the goal, and the police were forced to move in. Suddenly they hauled this body out of the Kop, and about six coppers tried to drag this guy on to the running track and take him out of the ground. But he was struggling like mad, and the police were having a terrible time trying to control him, so a couple more dived in. There were at least two of them to each arm and leg, and this poor bloke was being pulled all over the place. He was putting up a tremendous struggle that had the Kop cheering like mad, but with so many coppers he was never going to win. Then, suddenly, the Kop all started singing: 'One Jim-my Kelly, there's only one Jim-my Kelly, one Jim-my Kelly.' It was so funny. This was then followed by, 'You're gonna get what Jimmy Kelly got, you're gonna get your f***ing 'ead kicked in!'

It was the Kop voicing their natural distaste for the police, as well as showing that they had a few political opinions of their own. Here was a political awareness that you would not find anywhere else in football.

TED ROBBINS
Comedian

I first went on the Kop with my Uncle Bert when I was about ten years old. Now the thing about my Uncle Bert is that he's 6ft 3in tall. Anyhow, we're standing there and some scouse wit behind us says, 'Hey, youse. Are you standin' on a horse, or am I standin' in a hole?' I also remember this bloke who used to go around selling Wrigley's chewing gum. He had a really sophisticated sales patter: 'Ere are, lads, chewy,' he used to shout.

The other thing, of course, was the problem of having to wee after you've drunk five pints of Higson's before the game. The fellas used to take the *Echo* with them, and I have actually seen that. I used to go with my mate, and I said to him at half-time, 'I'm dying for a pee.'

'There y'are,' he says, 'why don't you do it in dat fella's pocket?'

'I couldn't do dat,' I says.

'Why not,' he says, 'I've just done it in your pocket, and you didn't notice.'

They were great times. I started going in the Boys' Pen and then I went on the Kop. I went in the stands once but I didn't like it, it wasn't the same. I think every bloke in the city of Liverpool must have been on the Kop at some point in their lives. It's really hard to find anyone who has never set foot on the Kop. That's a lot of people.

PHIL ASPINALL
Kopite

It was one of the funniest things I ever heard. It was actually at Old Trafford. They'd kept us in the ground until after the match, and then they let all us Liverpool fans out. There must have been about three or four thousand of us. Anyhow, as you know, you can walk all the way around the perimeter of United's ground. So we've come out and we're starting to walk around the

The Kop after the introduction of a roof in 1928 (© Steve Hale)

You always had to get there early. The Kop filling up in the 1992–3 season (© Steve Hale)

The Kop as it is now
(© *Liverpool Daily Post and Echo*)

△Even though there are seats, the rendition of 'You'll Never Walk Alone' is still rousing
(© Steve Hale)

◁The stampede to
get through the
turnstiles and onto
the Kop...
(© Steve Hale)

▽...and the crush
once on it
(© *Liverpool Daily
Post and Echo*)

▽Celebrating the
1974 FA Cup
victory with a
drive past the Kop
and the Albert
(© Steve Hale)

◁Bill Shankly, the very embodiment of the Kop, salutes the fans...
(© Steve Hale)

▽...and the fans remember Shankly – early 1980s
(© Steve Hale)

△The Kop from the pitch... (© Steve Hale)
　　　　...and the pitch from the Kop (© Steve Hale)▽

In the aftermath of Hillsborough, the Kop became a shrine △ (© *Liverpool Daily Post and Echo*) (© Steve Hale)▽

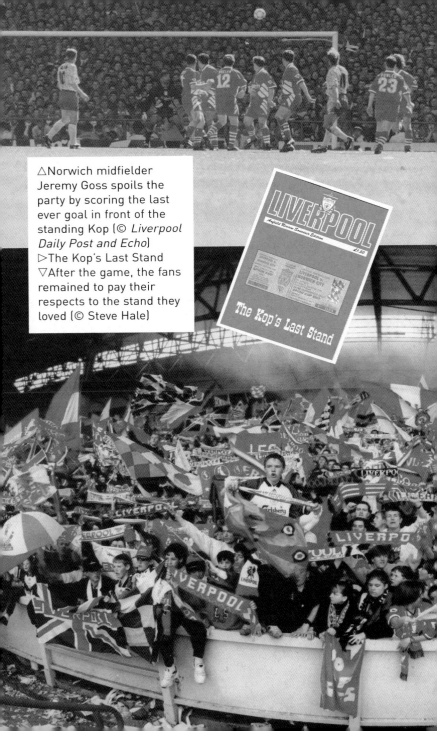

△Norwich midfielder Jeremy Goss spoils the party by scoring the last ever goal in front of the standing Kop (© *Liverpool Daily Post and Echo*)
▷The Kop's Last Stand
▽After the game, the fans remained to pay their respects to the stand they loved (© Steve Hale)

LIVERPOOL

Anfield Review Souvenir Edition

£1.50

The Kop's Last Stand

LIVERPOOL
CLUBCALL
0898 121 184

savers BIG

△The tea bar on the Kop awaiting the pre-game rush (© Steve Hale)

▽The end of the standing era. Workmen look on as the Kop is pulled down (© *Liverpool Daily Post and Echo*)

DANGER DEMOLITION

The Kop's 12,000 seated supporters – still Liverpool's twelfth man (© Steve Hale) ground, when this guy with a noisy old tin tray starts banging it and singing the HP baked beans song. And suddenly, within a matter of seconds, this huge crowd, about 4000, are all marching around Old Trafford singing, 'HP baked beans, they're the beans for me'. It was bizarre.

JOHNNY KENNEDY
Radio City DJ

Of course, the humour was always an important element of enjoying yourself while you were there. There was always a great humour in the Kop, the repartee from the fans, some great one-liners which emanated from the Kop. A player who hadn't been playing well and is lying on the ground, and the St John Ambulance come on with a blanket, and someone shouts, 'Gor blimey, don't put a blanket over him, he'll go to sleep altogether.' You know, lovely humour like that. 'Seen more life in our kid, and he's on an urgent note.' Stuff like that.

The chants I particularly remember were against Inter Milan. 'Ee-aye-addio, Mussolini's dead,' was the most popular. Then there was, 'Ee-aye-addio, We beat yer in de War'. And then they were singing, 'Go back to Italy', to the tune of 'Santa Lucia'. That was a beauty.

Another funny memory of the Kop. This was a derby match, Liverpool and Everton. Again, it was in the great days of the Kop, in the 1960s, when Evertonians still went on the Kop, which was great, there was no problem at all. This particular day I was with my Uncle John, who's as rabid an Evertonian as I am a Liverpudlian, and we're standing side by side. It's all part of the atmosphere, shouting for your team, arguing and all that. But he got into an argument. One of the Liverpool players fouled one of the Everton players. That never goes down well in a derby match, so my Uncle John, who was a lone voice in this immediate area, is shouting at the Liverpool players for fouling the Everton player.

Anyhow, this fella behind him says, 'Shurrup, mate, you dunno what yer talking about. It was a foul, anyrate.' So they're arguing, aren't they? You get carried away in the heat of the moment. So my Uncle John is continuing this argument, and it's getting quite heated. I just glanced back, and I realised that I knew the guy. So I said to me Uncle John, 'If I was you I'd stop this argument now.' And he says, 'What do you mean, like, shurrup. Don't you start on me.' So I said, 'Er, well, he won the British welterweight title last Saturday, that fella.' It was Johnny Cooke, from Bootle. So he says, 'Sorry, Johnny lad, it probably wasn't a foul after all.'

LIVERPOOL 3 EVERTON 2
(Sung to the tune of 'Who do you Think
   you're Kidding, Mr Hitler')

*Oh, who do you think you're kidding, Harry
   Catterick,*
If you think the Pool's no good.
*There's Steve Heighway, John Toshack and
   Christy Lawler too,*
They scored three goals for Liverpool,
And worked them right up you.
*Oh, who do you think you're kidding, Harry
   Catterick,*
If you think the Pool's no good.

Now the Kop was here, all came to cheer,
A famous victory,
With Alun Evans, Tommy Smith,
And our king, Bill Shankly.
*Oh, who do you think you're kidding, Harry
   Catterick,*
If you think the Pool's no good.

Well, the Everton supporters,
They have had just quite enough,
They'd seen their team two goals in front,
Then Shankly called his bluff. 1-2-3,

*Oh, who do you think you're kidding, Harry
    Catterick,
If you think the Pool's no good.*

JOHN STILE
Kopite

A few seasons ago, when feelings between Liverpool and
Manchester United supporters were at an all-time low, the
two clubs decided to try and improve matters with some
pre-kick-off gestures. First of all, the two teams came out
of the tunnel side by side, which in itself was quite unusual,
but even more unusual was that they then both ran to the
opposite ends they would normally go to. So Liverpool ran
down to the Anfield Road End, while United came up the
Kop end. The intention was to wave to the supporters and
kick a dozen or so balls to the fans for them to keep, before
going down to their normal end. So United came racing
down to the Kop to be greeted by a wall of whistles. They
then proceeded to kick all these balls into the Kop. But
then, in an equally symbolic gesture, the Kop threw the lot
back at them. You had to laugh. It was brilliant.

STEPHEN F. KELLY
Writer

A couple of seasons ago, Liverpool were playing at Stoke
City in the FA Cup. With the capacity of Stoke's ground
restricted to not much more than 30,000, the demand for
tickets was particularly heavy and meant that a great
many Kopites simply had little chance of getting to the
game. This, in turn, meant that the scheming and devious
ways of getting into a football match without a ticket
reached new heights.

Apparently, that night a number of Kopites, said
to be at least four, arrived separately at the main
reception area of Stoke City's ground, all smartly dressed,
and each carrying a small holdall. They each told the

commissionaire on the door that they were the linesman for the game. They gave the correct name and promptly strode nonchalantly down the corridor towards the referee and linesmen's changing-room, past the door, straight through the tunnel, on to the pitch, and walked up towards the end where all the Liverpool supporters were massed and joined them.

This cunning ploy was said to have been successful on four occasions, and it is believed that at least a further four Liverpool supporters tried the same trick, though unsuccessfully. By then, the commissionaire had cottoned on. When the genuine linesman finally arrived, the commissionaire refused to believe who he was and told him in no uncertain terms where to go.

JEFF SCOTT
Kopite

The two chants or songs I remember most from the Kop were both at away matches. There was the famous 5–1 win at Burnley in the fog sometime during the 1960s. At the time, there was a song in the charts by the Searchers called, 'What have they Done with the Rain?' We were standing there at Burnley in the fog and the rain, and that was our song that day.

The other incident was at West Brom in 1965–66, I think. There was no nastiness meant in this incident. There were a lot of West Indians in West Bromwich at the time, and there was a lot of them in their support. When Liverpool scored, the fans spontaneously waved their hands in the air and went, 'Hallelujah!' It was a one-off, and I've never heard it since. I suppose it would be frowned upon today but there was no nastiness meant.

STEVE CAIN
Kopite

One of the best Kop off-the-cuff chants that I ever heard was one time we were playing Everton in the 1970s. The

Everton fans started singing, 'Latchford walks on water, Latchford walks on water', and straightaway the Kop comes back with, 'Latchford is a duck, Latchford is a duck'! It came back so instantly it was like the whole thing had been rehearsed.

In the early 1980s, we were playing Ipswich, and Paul Cooper came running down to take his place in goal and, as usual, he was applauded by the whole Kop. And, in turn, he applauded us back. Then the Kop starts chanting, 'Eric Gates, Eric Gates', as he was running towards us ready for the kick-off. So he starts applauding the Kop as well. Unfortunately, he didn't wait for the Kop to finish, and they continued with, 'You're so f*****g ugly'! He fell for it, and his face was nearly as red as the Liverpool tops.

STEPHEN F. KELLY
Writer

The Kop can be wickedly cruel. Tommy Docherty once felt their barbed sense of humour following a marital misdemeanour. It was after his affair with Mary Brown, the wife of Manchester United's physiotherapist, had been exposed in the newspapers. When Docherty next appeared at Anfield, the Kop was in full voice: 'Who's up Mary Brown, Who's up Mary Brown,' they sang to the tune of 'Knees Up Mother Brown'.

But perhaps the most memorable was the day Peter Shilton came, a great goalkeeper and always one of the Kop's favourites. Only weeks before, Shilton had hit the front pages after he had been caught with a certain lady called Tina. The Kop was ready, and they ribbed him all afternoon. As he came running out towards them, up went the cry, 'Who were you with last night'. A little later it was followed by, 'Don't Cry for me, Tina, Tina'! Poor Shilton, But you had to smile. The Kop could be very moralistic.

BILLY O'DONNELL
Kopite

Me and my mate went on the Kop one day. It was during the 1930s. Liverpool were playing Bolton. My pal, a little bloke he was, was a dead keen fan of Gordon Hodgson. Loved him, he did, couldn't do wrong for him. Anyhow, Hodgson was playing that day with Sam English alongside him at centre-forward. Bolton had this big defender, and English wasn't a particularly big bloke; he was built a bit like Kenny Dalglish. But, you may remember, he was the former Glasgow Rangers centre-forward who had been involved in an horrific accident that led to the death of the legendary Celtic goalkeeper, John Thompson. Racing into the area for a loose ball during a Rangers–Celtic derby game in 1931, English collided heavily with Thompson as the giant goalkeeper dived at his feet for the ball. Thompson suffered a fracture to his skull and was immediately rushed to hospital but died later that evening. Although there is no doubt that English was not to blame he was nevertheless accused by one half of Glasgow and was barracked wherever he played. Eventually he left Rangers and came south to Liverpool in the hope of escaping the barracking. Unfortunately it followed him and he remained just two seasons at Anfield.

Wherever English went after that, the crowd would get on his back. Anyhow, this particular day, the Bolton defender must have said something to English because suddenly there they were, throwing punches at each other. So big Gordon Hodgson jumps in to separate them, and this Bolton defender starts having a go at Hodgson as well and pushing him around.

Well, my mate was furious. 'Hang on,' he says to me, 'I'll be back in a minute.' I thought he was going off to the toilet or something. He said it quite casually. Well, off he goes, straight down the Kop, over the wall, on to the pitch and makes for Hodgson and the Bolton defender. It all happened so quickly. The next thing, my little mate's throwing punches at the big Bolton defender. Then a policeman comes diving on to the field, and my mate turns round and punches the policeman as well.

'Hang on a minute,' he'd said. It was six months before I saw him again. He spent the night in the Bridewell and was in court first thing on the Monday morning. The magistrate gave him six months inside.

PHIL THOMPSON
Liverpool player, 1971–85

Oh yeah, I always remember my first game as captain of Liverpool. I was dead proud. I was a Liverpool lad and here I was, captain of the side. Anyhow, that first game, we were all in the tunnel ready to come out and we got the signal to lead off. So I ran down the tunnel, up the steps and on to the pitch. I made straight for the Kop, pleased as anything. There was a bit of a cheer to begin with, but then everybody started laughing. I couldn't understand it. Why were they laughing at us? Then I turned round and, to my horror, I saw that I was all by myself. The rest of the lads were up at the tunnel, laughing themselves silly. They knew I was all keyed up for it and really looking forward to leading the team out, so they thought they'd let me go by myself. I was so embarrassed.

HUGH O'NEILL
St John Ambulance

Liverpool were playing a match one day, and it was very foggy. Tony Hateley scored down the Anfield Road End, and although the Kop heard this terrific roar they could not see who had scored. So they all started singing, 'Annie Road, Annie Road, who scored the goal?' The reply came back instantly, 'To-ny Hate-ley, To-ny Hate-ley.' And then, funniest of all, the Kop, not to be outdone, replied to the tune of The Scaffold's famous song 'The Aintree Iron': 'Thank you very much for the information, thank you very much, thank you very, very, very much'!

GEORGE EDWARDS
Kopite

It was just after the John Barnes affair, when there had been considerable criticism about racism at Anfield. There had been a couple of games against Everton, when some appalling racist chanting had been aimed at Barnes by the Everton supporters. Anyhow, a few weeks later, Liverpool were at home against some mid-table team, when the referee blew up for yet another foul in favour of Liverpool. The opposition fans squeezed into the Anfield Road End were getting a little tired of this and, when the whistle blew against them yet again, they began to direct their anger at the referee. 'Who's the scouser in the black?' they sang, not, of course, expecting any answer. But they got one. Quick as a flash, the Kop answered them back: 'Johnny Barnes, Johnny Barnes, Johnny Barnes,' they chanted.

RON PAWSEY
Kopite

The Kop loves an oddball. Half-way through some game at Anfield, the opposition – I think it was Derby – decided to bring on a substitute. And out of the dug-out emerged this giant who began to pull off his tracksuit. It was Kevin Francis. He was all of 6ft 7in and towered over everyone, especially the linesman. He looked like he should have been on a basketball court rather than a football pitch. The entire ground was agog. You could hear everybody nudging each other. Then, as he finally took the pitch, the Kop decided to rib him and began to sing: 'One Blackpool Tower, there's only one Blackpool Tower, one Blackpool Tower ...' As if that wasn't enough, they then started singing, 'What's the weather like up there?'

ROGAN TAYLOR
Kopite and a founder of the Football Supporters'
Association

The Kop at its wittiest? It had to be a game against Grimsby Town. It was early January during the 1979–80 season, and it was a League Cup match. Liverpool led 2–0 at half-time and eventually wound up 5–0 winners. As usual, the Kop was getting a bit bored during the second half and decided to provide the in-house entertainment. Suddenly they all began, 'Sing when you're fishing; you only sing when you're fishing; sing when you're fishing . . .' An obvious reference to the fishermen of Grimsby.

The next minute they started to chant the name of every Liverpool player, but attaching to it the name of a fish. First of all, they started with Dalglish: 'Ken-ny Dog-Fish, Ken-ny Dog-Fish,' they chanted. It was absolutely spontaneous. Then they came up with, 'Sting-Ray Kennedy, Sting-Ray Kennedy', followed by, 'There's only one Phil Eel, one Phil Eel'. They went through the entire team. We also had 'Sword-fish Souness, Sword-fish Souness'. Finally, they came up with the best of all and started singing, 'Jim-my Plaice, Jim-my Plaice, Jim-my Plaice.' It was all so witty, so spontaneous, and so clever.

IAN SERGEANT
Kopite

The Kop is full of comedians. I suppose it's just a reflection of the city of Liverpool. The wonderful thing is that you can go on the Kop, and you don't have to go with anyone. Normally you would go to a match with a pal, but on the Kop you have thousands of mates. Everyone talks to each other. You're all squashed together, shoving and pushing, so it's natural that you natter.

I used always to go to this regular spot not far from one of the posts. It used to be less congested, and every week there was this bloke behind me. He was a policeman, but he would never volunteer to do duty at Anfield. He wanted to be there on the Kop with everyone else. He was also something of a comedian and used to tell the most wonderful stories; they were so funny. But the best he ever told was about a wedding. It seemed that the bride's father had been to the police station one Sunday to report that his wallet had been stolen the night before at his daughter's wedding. He didn't know where it had gone, and although they had searched high and low they had not been able to find it. He last remembered that he had put it in his back pocket after buying a round of drinks at the do. He could only suppose that it had been stolen.

Anyhow, a couple of days later, he turned up again at the police station and asked for the search to be called off. They knew where the wallet was. It seemed that, a day or so after the wedding, his brother had shown up at his house with a video of the wedding, and as they watched it they saw to their horror the full saga of the missing wallet. There he was dancing with his wife, when suddenly this hand appears behind him and nicks the wallet out of his back pocket. And who does the hand belong to? None other than the groom. We all fell about laughing.

'And what are the police going to do about it?' we asked. 'Oh, nothing,' he says. 'But the bride's father and brothers have assured us that they will be going to the airport to meet the couple when they return from their honeymoon!' It was a typical Liverpool tale.

WENDY DOIG
Kopite

The fanaticism of Liverpool fans seems to know no bounds. We had a patient came to us one Wednesday evening when I was working for a dentist as a dental practice manager. He had twenty-eight teeth out, yes, twenty-eight. And, would you believe, he went straight from us at the dentist's to Anfield to watch a match. I don't suppose he did much shouting though. Then, one Saturday morning, we had another patient. He came and had a new set of dentures fitted. Anyhow, when I arrived at work on the Monday morning, he was there again, on the doorstep. He'd lost his new teeth at Anfield that same afternoon and hadn't been able to find them anywhere. So we had to give him another set and told him not to wear them when he went to the football in future.

BOB GREAVES
Television presenter

The Kop doesn't just reserve its barbed sense of humour for those it hates. It can be equally sniping about its own kind. I remember early on in the 1992–93 season when Liverpool's new Centenary Stand was opened. The new chairman, David Moores, came on the pitch with the president of UEFA to open the stand. David Moores, as we all know, has rather long hair and used to wear an earring, not quite the traditional image of a Liverpool chairman – something, of course, which the Kop recognised.

Anyhow, there was David Moores waving to the Kop as he wandered across the pitch towards the new stand, when the Kop suddenly begins singing, 'One Fred-die Bos-well, there's only one Fred-die Bos-well'. That was funny enough, but then some punter behind me says in a loud voice: 'I suppose that's because he's got a lot of bread!'

JEFF ANDERSON
Kopite

Towards the end of the 1973–74 season, Liverpool played Manchester City at Anfield. We were through to the Cup final, and I don't think we had much hope of winning the league, so the game was played in a fairly relaxed atmosphere. There were over 50,000 in the ground, and it was something of a celebration. The Kop was barely interested in the football and started entertaining everyone almost from the kick-off. It was a wonderful night as they came up with one song after another. And poor old Manchester City were on the receiving end of most of the humour. Fortunately, they saw the funny side of it and joined in.

At one point Francis Lee, who had been repeatedly mocked for his lack of hair, crashed into the photographers at the side of the Kop goal. The Kop burst out laughing, and Lee responded by grabbing a camera with the most enormous zoom lens off one of the photographers and spraying the Kop with it as if it was a machine gun.

Denis Law was another who was on the receiving end that night. He was getting on a bit then and was in his final season with City, having joined them from United. In fact, it turned out to be almost his last game in football. 'Denis Law, Denis Law, is it true what Shankly says, you're sixty-four,' sang the Kop. Standing on the Kop we could see Law laughing his head off at all this. He loved every minute. It was a memorable night.

Five

MATCHES TO REMEMBER

Ee-Aye-Addio, We've Won the Cup

HARRY WILSON
Kopite

DIVISION ONE, 25 FEBRUARY 1928

Liverpool 3	Everton 3
Hopkin, Bromilow,	
Hodgson	*Dean 3*

Attendance: 56,447.

The best game I ever saw at Anfield was a 3–3 draw with Everton in the late 1920s. Dixie Dean scored all three Everton goals that day. He was magnificent. The crowd called Dean for all kinds, but he kept on scoring the goals. And every time he scored he turned to the Kop and gave a matador-like bow. It really got the Kop going, but they had to admit he was good. It was an outstanding game; in fact, the greatest game of football I have ever seen. There was a big crowd, I remember, and both sides were just wonderful. I've never seen football like it before or since. Oh, the atmosphere on the Kop was electric. I remember Liverpool went into an early lead, but Everton fought back and took a 2–1 lead at half-time. Then, late in the game, Liverpool fought back to get a draw. It was magnificent stuff. Everton went on to win the league title that season, and Dean scored his sixty league goals.

Liverpool: Riley, Lucas, McKinlay, Morrison, Jackson, Bromilow, Edmed, Hodgson, Race, Chambers, Hopkin.

Everton: Hardy, Cresswell, O'Donnell, Kelly, Hart, Virr, Critchley, Forshaw, Dean, Weldon, Troup.

JACK PAYNE
Kopite

DIVISION ONE, 11 FEBRUARY 1933

Liverpool 7   Everton 4
Barton 3, Hanson,
Morrison, Taylor, Roberts   Dean 2, Johnson, Stein
Attendance: 50,000.

Everton in the 1930s had a wonderful team. They were brilliant, with players such as Dixie Dean, Cliff Britton, Ted Sagar and so on. They won the second-division title, the first division and the FA Cup, all in three years. Anyhow, they came to Anfield in February 1933 when they were just about at their best. They'd beaten us 3–1 at Goodison earlier in the season, and we didn't expect to get much out of them at Anfield, especially as we were introducing a few new lads to the side. Well, blow me if Liverpool didn't go and win 7–4. It was probably the greatest derby game ever – it was certainly the highest scoring derby game ever played – although we beat them 6–0 a couple of years later. At half-time, Liverpool were only just ahead, 3–2, but by full-time we had totally overpowered Everton. Dean scored a couple for Everton, and Barton hit a hat-trick for Liverpool. The Evertonians on the Kop that day were sick. They were so down in the mouth. It was one of our greatest games.

Liverpool: Scott, Steel, Jackson, Morrison, McDougall, Taylor, Barton, Roberts, Wright, McPherson, Hanson.
Everton: Sagar, Cook, Cresswell, Britton, White, Thomson, Geldard, Dunn, Dean, Johnson, Stein.

SHEILA SPIERS
National Secretary, Football Supporters' Association

FA CUP, SEMI-FINAL, MAINE ROAD, 25 MARCH 1950

Liverpool 2	Everton 0
Paisley, Liddell	

Attendance: 72,000.

I went to the 1950 FA Cup semi-final at Maine Road with my dad. Liverpool were playing Everton and, of course, everyone wanted to go. I don't think the two teams had ever met at such a stage in the Cup before, and it was billed as the most important derby game in history. I remember it was a bright sunlit day, and the whole of that bank of the Kippax was red and blue. That was at a time when the Kippax didn't have a roof, and as we came to the ground we could see this mass of people standing on it in their colours. I'd never seen so much colour before. People didn't normally wear much in the way of colours except for a rosette, but this day they had scarves on as well. It was a fantastic sight and a marvellous atmosphere. Liverpool led 1–0 at half-time through a Bob Paisley goal. He was deputising that day for the injured Laurie Hughes. And then, midway through the second half, Billy Liddell scored Liverpool's second to give us a trip to Wembley, the first ever in Liverpool's history. I was so excited.

Liverpool: Sidlow, Lambert, Spicer, Taylor, Jones, Paisley, Payne, Baron, Stubbins, Fagan, Liddell.
Everton: Burnett, Moore, Hedley, Grant, Falder, Farrell, Buckle, Wainwright, Catterick, Fielding, Eglington.

BILLY O'DONNELL
Kopite

In 1950, I went to see Liverpool in the semi-final at Maine Road against Everton. There were eight of us went, on the train, four Liverpool supporters and four Evertonians. We all had our scarves and hats on. Well, they couldn't make us out in Manchester. They just didn't understand. We had dinner at Woolworths and then went to a pub I knew near the Mancunian Way, where we had a good singsong. Then we all went to the game together. The woman who ran the pub really liked us and told us to come back after the game.

Well, it was a great match. Liverpool won, thanks to Bob Paisley's goal, and we were in the final, only the second time we had ever reached the Cup final. We went back to the same pub after the match, and the landlady had done this big spread for us, sandwiches, pies, cakes and tea. It was great. We all had another singsong, and a band turned up. But none of the Mancunians could understand why we Liverpool and Everton supporters were mixing and so friendly to each other. It was something they had never experienced in Manchester.

SHEILA SPIERS
National Secretary, Football Supporters' Association

FA CUP FINAL, WEMBLEY, 29 APRIL 1950

Arsenal 2   Liverpool 0
Lewis 2

Attendance: 100,000.

I was in our pub, the Sandon Hotel, one evening and there was a man sitting in the corner. I thought I recognised him, so I said to my dad, 'I think that's Joe Cadden.' He was an American who had signed for Liverpool. So my dad went up to him and asked him, and it turned out he was. He was sitting there with one of the club's mothers. But he was desperately lonely. He didn't seem to have made many friends. Anyhow, after that he soon became a great friend of the family. He would come and play with us, and we all liked him. He used to come to the pub so often that word got back to Anfield, and they told him off about his drinking. In fact, he rarely drank when he came to the pub. He only came for a chat.

Anyhow, Joe managed to get us a couple of tickets for the Cup final. No Liverpool supporters had ever seen

Cup-final tickets. Liverpool hadn't been in a final since 1914, and the clubs were only allocated 15,000 tickets each. So to see a Cup-final ticket was quite rare. I used to chase upstairs and bring my ticket down and show it to people in the pub. We had planned to go down on the train. But it was a bit of a problem, because the pub needed to be opened.

Anyhow, my dad saw this advert for flights to London, so he booked us on a plane and we flew down to London on an old Dakota. We were back home by 8 p.m. that night. But Wembley was terribly disappointing after that semi-final at Maine Road. There was no atmosphere at all. There were only 30,000 fans from the two sides, and it was very quiet. It was weird, really. Liverpool were never in the game. We lost, and I cried all the way home.

Arsenal: Swindin, Scott, Barnes, Forbes, L. Compton, Mercer, Cox, Logie, Goring, Lewis, D. Compton.
Liverpool: Sidlow, Lambert, Spicer, Taylor, Jones, Hughes, Payne, Baron, Stubbins, Fagan, Liddell.

JOHN CULL
Chief programme seller

FA CUP, FOURTH ROUND, 2 FEBRUARY 1952

Liverpool 2   Wolverhampton Wanderers 1
Paisley, Done   *Mullen*
Attendance: 61,905.

I was selling programmes that day, and I still remember it well. It was Anfield's record attendance. The gates were closed by 2 p.m., so all my programmes had gone shortly before that and I was able to watch the whole match from the Kop. The Kop was swaying all over the place, but there were never any accidents. There were at least 25,000 of us on it that day. It was wonderful.

It was the switch that made it so memorable. Poor Billy Wright didn't know what he was doing. He was supposed to be marking Liddell, who was normally out on the wing. But Liddell reverted to centre-forward, even though he wore the No. 11 shirt, and Cyril Done went to outside-left. The Wolves defence was all over the place and couldn't understand what was going on. By the time Wright had sussed it all out, Wolves were two goals down and on their way out of the Cup. Paisley scored the first after a couple of minutes, and then Cyril Done had us two up within ten minutes. Wolves never recovered.

Liverpool: Crossley, Jones, Lambert, Taylor, Heydon, Paisley, Williams, Balmer, Done, Payne, Liddell.

Wolverhampton Wanderers: Parsons, Shorthouse, Gibbons, Wright, Chatham, Baxter, Hancocks, Broadbent, Swinbourne, Pye, Mullen

IAN ST JOHN
Liverpool player, 1961–71

EUROPEAN CUP, FIRST ROUND, FIRST LEG, 25 NOVEMBER 1964

Liverpool 3   Anderlecht 0
St John, Hunt, Yeats
Attendance: 44,516.

Those early European games in the 1960s were memorable. On one particular night against Inter Milan the Kop was inspirational, just as they were in an earlier game against Anderlecht. That was the first really big European night at Anfield. We'd played Reykjavik in the first round, but they were a small unknown club and they didn't really matter. Then we faced the Belgian champions. They had a great team that formed almost the entire Belgian national side. Not long before we played them, Belgium had taken England apart. Shankly was very impressed by them. They were all wonderful players.

That night was the first time Liverpool played in all red. Shanks had decided that we should wear red shorts as well as red jerseys. We tried them on, and we all liked them. Then Ron Yeats and I said, 'Why don't we have red socks as well?' So Shanks says, 'OK, let's see what they look like.' He found a pair of red socks and put them on Ron, and he looked like a giant, very fearsome. So that was it. Shanks said, 'All right, we're in all red from now on.' I think the Kop was a bit shocked when we appeared in this new rig-out. But it seemed to make them roar us on even more. And after that we had to stay in red.

It was also the night Tommy Smith made his European debut. Shanks was a bit worried about playing him, because it was such an important game and he was so young. So he had a word with Ron and me on the quiet. 'Don't worry,' we told him, 'he won't let you down.' Smith was a man when he was eight years old. So Smithy made his debut and he didn't let anyone down either. We won 3-0. I scored the first goal after just nine minutes, much against the run of play. Then, just before half-time, I managed to get the ball off one of their defenders and passed it to Roger Hunt. That was 2-0. Then Ron Yeats headed a third minutes after the interval. Before the game, Shanks had been telling us that Anderlecht were no good and we'd easily beat them, but after the game it was a different story. He was going around telling the press that Anderlecht were one of the finest sides he had ever seen. Anyhow, the Kop loved that night, and it gave them a taste for European football.

Liverpool: Lawrence, Lawler, Byrne, Milne, Yeats, Stevenson, Callaghan, Hunt, St John, Smith, Thompson.
Anderlecht: Trappeniers, Heylens, Cornelis, Hanon, Verbiest, Plaskie, Stockman, Cayulea, Jurion, Van Himst, Puis.

GEOFFREY GREEN
Sportswriter

EUROPEAN CUP, QUARTER FINAL, SECOND LEG, 3 MARCH 1965
Liverpool v Cologne

(The first, away, leg of this European Cup quarter-final had ended in a goalless draw. The Anfield leg had to be postponed shortly before the kick-off because of snow. After the postponed game, the second leg was finally played a fortnight later. This, too, ended 0-0. The replay in Rotterdam was also drawn, and Liverpool eventually went through to the semi-final on the toss of a coin.)

It was the mid-1960s. Liverpool were due to play Cologne on Merseyside in the second leg of a European Cup quarter-final. For hours the city was wrapped in the white arms of a blizzard. The snow lay deep everywhere, but for some unaccountable reason the gates of Anfield were opened some half an hour before the night kick-off to let in a shivering 45,000 crowd.

The Cologne players duly came out stripped for a warm-up before the start, kicking about a white polka-dot ball on a frosty white surface. All you could distinguish of the ball itself were those moving dots, as if it were a dice being rolled on the icing of a Christmas cake. The conditions, of course, were impossible, and the referee called it off before the start, without Liverpool even bothering to take the field.

At some grounds there might well have been trouble, and that Anfield crowd had queued for hours in the snow to get in. Their money had been taken, virtually under false pretences. Yet there is nothing, anywhere, quite to measure up to the Kop at Liverpool. It may contain some villains within a family ranged – some 22,000 strong – behind one goal. But it bursts with original, unpredictable wit and generosity, and when it sings its own adopted battle hymn 'You'll Never Walk Alone', there is about it all the fervour and moving quality of a vast cathedral choir, as it sways and countersways to the music. It sends an endless tingle up the spine.

But in spite of that blank night and the disappointment, there was no explosion. Instead, as the snow still fell in a thick, feathery cloud, there suddenly appeared a dozen or so characters out on the pitch imitating the gyrations of international ice stars one sees on television. And there, too, in the background was one wry wag lampooning the official markings of skating judges, as he held aloft the numbered figure plates usually used to convey the half-time scores at other matches. It was a brilliant piece of inspired mime and, but for that, the night would have long since passed as a frozen waste into the limbo of forgotten things.

To me, that was another small but 'great' moment of football, stemming from unexpected, unexplored depths of the human spirit that makes light of adversity.

JOHN CULL
Chief programme seller

Liverpool v Cologne

I was selling programmes the night of the Cologne game. The gates opened at 5:30 p.m., and it started snowing at just about the same time. There had been a light covering of snow very early that morning, but it had all but disappeared by the afternoon. But it was bitterly cold. Then the snow started coming down heavier. At 6:30 p.m., the ground staff came out and started painting the lines on the pitch blue. But, by 7:30 p.m., even the blue lines had all but disappeared. There was a full house inside Anfield, and a lot of Cologne supporters had come over as well. Then the referee came out. The snow was coming down even more, and he finally decided to call the match off.

Nobody knew quite what to do. There was an announcement over the tannoy that if you kept your ticket stub you could get into the replay, whenever it was played, for just 10d. Now what usually happens at Anfield is that, half-way through the second half, they open the big gates. But for some reason they were not opened that night. The whole system had been thrown into chaos. So the Kop gates were closed. They did not have reversible turnstiles in those days either, so the result was that the only way to get out was to climb over the turnstiles. You can imagine how long it took to empty the ground. It was terrible.

The Kop was so packed that everyone just went on to the pitch. What then followed was hilarious. The Kopites started having a giant snowball fight with the Anfield Road End. The Kopites would run up there and hurl snowballs at them and then retreat. In turn, the Anfield Road End came skating up to the Kop and threw snowballs at us. People were making snowmen, and snowball fights were going on everywhere. I don't think we had realised just how bad the snow was until we got out. Everyone was having to dig their cars out of the snow. It was a night to remember, though not for the football.

TOMMY McKINLAY
Kopite

Liverpool v Cologne

The Cologne game was the game that never really happened. When we got to the ground, the crowd was enormous. The queue for the Kop was all the way down the Kemyln Road. There must have been about 10,000 outside, all trying to get in. So we joined the queue, but it didn't look like we had a hope in hell of getting in. The crush was awful, it was really dangerous. A wall collapsed in the street under the sheer weight of the crowd. I thought, 'I'm getting out of here.' So I asked a policeman, and he said, 'Try the turnstile up the other end.' So off we went, and there was no queue up there. We just walked in.

Then the snow came, and the referee had to call the game off. They announced over the tannoy that we could get a pass out that would allow us to come to the game the following evening free of charge. So we then had to queue to get back through the turnstiles. Now the thing about the Kop turnstiles is that they only move one way. So we had to climb over the turnstile and then collect our ticket. You can imagine the chaos. It was a wonder there wasn't a serious accident that night.

CHIEF INSPECTOR IAN THOMSON
Former football liaison officer, Merseyside Police

Liverpool v Cologne

I was on duty the day of the Liverpool–Cologne game. I shall never forget it. It started to snow at about 4 p.m. as we were parading. Everyone was a bit worried, and the club decided not to open the gates until the referee had inspected the pitch at 6 p.m. By then the snow had eased off, and the ref agreed to let the game go ahead. So they opened the gates, and everyone poured into the ground. Then, of course, shortly before kick-off, down came the snow again. In the end, the pitch was completely unplayable, and the ref had to call the match off.

That was when the chaos began. Nobody knew what to do. For a start, nobody had opened the big gates to let the fans out, and everyone was stuck in the stadium. So they all filtered on to the pitch and started throwing snowballs. Then the club decided that they would give out tickets, so that people could get into the replayed game free. Well, that led to even more chaos. The tickets were given to the men on the turnstiles, so you were supposed to go through the turnstiles to get your ticket. But, of course, only about one of the turnstiles was reversible, so people had to climb over the turnstiles, which took an age. Eventually, the gates were opened but, of course, nobody wanted to leave the ground until they had a ticket, so there was further chaos.

In the end, I had a bundle of tickets and I was having to throw people through the main gates and saying, 'Ere are, here's a ticket.' I got away about 11 p.m., and there were still people trying to get out of the Kop. I then had to go back to Anfield at 1:30 a.m., and the last people were just coming out of the ground. Now, as if that wasn't bad enough, the next morning – or rather that same morning – Liverpool were selling tickets for a Cup replay with Leicester. They were due to go on sale at 9:00 a.m. But at 3:00 a.m., people started arriving and began queuing. The snow was terrible, and some of these people had never even bothered going home, let alone going to bed. It was the most chaotic night I've ever known at Anfield.

WEMBLEY STADIUM
(Sung to the tune of 'Tipperary')

It's a long way to Wembley Stadium,
It's a long way to go.
It's a long way to Wembley Stadium,
To see the greatest team I know.
Goodbye, Piccadilly,
Farewell, Leicester Square.
It's a long, long way to Wembley Stadium,
But Liverpool will be there.

JIM HARTLEY
Kopite

FA CUP FINAL, WEMBLEY, 1 MAY 1965

Liverpool 2	Leeds United 1 (aet)
Hunt, St John	*Bremner*

Attendance: 100,000.

Prior to 1965, Liverpool had never won the FA Cup. They'd reached the final in 1914 and 1950, but had been beaten on both occasions. Everton, meanwhile, had won the trophy a couple of times. There used to be a saying in the city that the day Liverpool won the FA Cup, the Liver Bird down the Pier Head would up and fly away. Well, it didn't and, even though we've won it a few more times since we beat Leeds, it still hasn't flown away.

I have to confess that the 1965 Cup final was not the greatest of games, but the occasion was fantastic. Everyone wanted to go, and in those days clubs didn't get as many tickets. I think the thing that I remember was the look of disbelief on the faces of Londoners. Suddenly this great, noisy, red army marched into town and took over. That Saturday night in London was amazing. There were scousers in the fountains, climbing Eros, they were everywhere, and no matter where you went in the centre of London you could hear them singing, 'Ee-aye-addio, we've won the Cup!' I think that day was the first time that song was ever heard. They still sing it after they've won the Cup even today, though nowadays it's sung much faster.

I think that Cup final brought the power of the Kop home to everybody. People knew there was singing up at Anfield, but nobody realised quite how incredible it was until that game, when millions watching on television had their first experience of the Kop choir. It was after that that singing really took off at football grounds. All the papers were full of it, and the commentators were saying that Wembley had never seen or heard anything like it before. It made me feel proud to have been a part of that.

We went down for the weekend, four of us in a mate's car. We had a great time. I don't really remember a lot about the game itself, just the singing and, of course, the celebrating. It was goalless at full-time and then, just a couple of minutes into extra-time, Roger Hunt headed Liverpool into the lead. Wembley erupted, but it wasn't long before we were all feeling miserable as Leeds equalised. Liverpool's winner came with ten minutes remaining, when Ian St John flung himself at a centre. I could hardly watch the rest of the game. And, wow, the excitement when the final whistle went.

The most remarkable thing, of course, was the home-coming. We raced back to Liverpool on the Sunday morning, all hung over. I'd arranged to meet some mates of mine under the Lewis's statue. Well, when I got there I couldn't get anywhere near it. The streets and pavements were jammed solid. I've never seen so many in the centre of Liverpool, or anywhere else for that matter. It was just incredible. You couldn't move. I managed to squeeze up towards Lime Street Station, and we waited. Then out of the station they came in this bus, and the whole city of Liverpool erupted. Everyone was singing. There were these lads all perched on the top of this huge advertising hoarding by the station, and they were banging the hoarding with their heels to the chant of 'Liv-er-pool'. The noise was fantastic.

As the team went past with the Cup, everyone broke ranks and this huge mob of people, thousands of them, followed the coach through the city down to the Town Hall. Well, you could not get to within a quarter of a mile either side of the Town Hall. The crowd was that dense. People were fainting everywhere. Hundreds were treated in hospital. The next day, the papers reckoned half a million people had turned out. It was the greatest homecoming any team has ever had anywhere, and I have never seen anything like it since.

Liverpool: Lawrence, Lawler, Byrne, Strong, Yeats, Stevenson, Callaghan, Hunt, St John, Smith, Thompson.

Leeds United: Sprake, Reaney, Bell, Bremner, Charlton, Hunter, Giles, Storrie, Peacock, Collins, Johanneson.

STEPHEN F. KELLY
Writer

EUROPEAN CUP SEMI-FINAL, FIRST LEG, 4 MAY 1965

Liverpool 3   Inter Milan 1
Hunt, Callaghan, St John   *Mazzola*
Attendance: 54,082.

It was a privilege to be there. It was my first European Cup match, and almost certainly the greatest Anfield has ever seen. Liverpool had won the Cup for the first time in their history on the Saturday, beating Leeds United 2–1 at Wembley. On the Sunday, they had returned home to a tumultuous welcome from something like half a million fans. I had never seen anything like it. Two days later, they were due to play the world club champions and European Cup-holders, Inter Milan, in the first leg of the European Cup semi-final.

Everybody I knew at work wanted to go. The problem was that I was working until 5:30 p.m., and I was a bit worried about my chances of getting in. One of the lads in the office decided to go and ask the boss if he could skip off an hour early. The boss was quite amenable and said yes, but when the word got around everybody was queuing up outside his door. Having said yes to one he had something of a dilemma. When I timidly knocked on his door, he just glared at me and moaned. 'Oh no, not another one,' he said. 'Go on, I suppose so,' he agreed, entering into the spirit that had swept Merseyside those few days. I'll always be grateful to him.

Anyhow, off we all went at 4:30 p.m., leaving the boss and hardly anybody else in the office. We got to the ground about half an hour later and, even by then, the queues and traffic were enormous. They had just opened the gates, and we settled into the crush outside the Kop. We finally got into the Kop at about 5:30 p.m., and it looked fairly full then. The gates were locked some ten minutes later. There were something like 25,000 of us on the Kop that warm May night. The sway was incredible, but we were happy, singing all the time, entertaining ourselves. The main chant was to see the Cup.

At around 7:15 p.m., the Inter Milan players decided to come out early for their kick-about, and as they came out they automatically ran towards the Kop end. They were greeted with a deafening shrill of whistles. But instead of standing their ground they turned and ran for the other end. From that moment on, Inter Milan were beaten men.

Bill Shankly, sitting in the dressing-room, could hear this chant to see the Cup and came up with an inspired idea. When Liverpool took the field they were accompanied by Gerry Byrne and Gordon Milne, who appeared holding the trophy above their heads. The Inter Milan players must have been quaking in their boots, because the noise was phenomenal. Byrne and Milne slowly carried the Cup around the ground and, when it finally reached the Kop, there was a noise which Anfield had never heard before, nor since. It was deafening. People were crying, jumping up and down, singing and swaying. I'll never forget it.

Four minutes later, Roger Hunt had put Liverpool into the lead. Liverpool won 3-1 that night. No team in the world could have lived with them. We stood for something like four hours on the Kop that night, and I finished up at least thirty yards from where I had started. When the ball came down the Kop end, I was lifted off my feet and carried helplessly forward. It was frightening, but what a night.

Liverpool: Lawrence, Lawler, Moran, Strong, Yeats, Stevenson, Callaghan, Hunt, St John, Smith, Thompson.
Inter Milan: Sarti, Burgnich, Facchetti, Tagnin, Guarneri, Picchi, Jair, Mazzola, Peiro, Suarez, Corso.

BILL SHANKLY
Liverpool manager, 1959–74

Liverpool v Inter Milan

Three days after Wembley we thrashed Inter Milan, who were the champions of the world, 3–1 at Anfield in the semi-final of the European Cup. We were without Gerry Byrne as well as Gordon Milne that night, but though they were missing from the team because of injuries they still played their part. I asked Milan to go out early, but they kept hanging about the dressing-room. I said, 'It's time to go now,' and eventually they made a move and went on to the pitch. That's just what I wanted, psychologically, because I then sent out Gordon and Gerry with the FA Cup, followed by the team.

Dear God, what an eruption there was when our supporters caught sight of that Cup. The noise was unbelievable. The people were hysterical.

PHIL THOMPSON
Liverpool player, 1971–85

Liverpool v Inter Milan

My mum got us tickets for the Inter Milan game. I was 11. I always remember we were in the front row of the Kemlyn Road Stand. We'd just won the FA Cup, and Gerry and Gordon came round the ground before the kick-off with the trophy. The Kop was great that night, probably the greatest I've ever seen. The whole night my eyes were fixed on the Kop. I couldn't believe it. I was mesmerised. The steam was rising, and the noise was incredible. 'Go back to It-alee,' they were singing, to the tune of 'Santa Lucia'. I suppose that night more than any other turned me into a Liverpool fanatic.

CHIEF INSPECTOR IAN THOMSON
Former football liaison officer, Merseyside Police

Liverpool v Inter Milan

I was policing the Liverpool–Inter Milan game. What a match. Oh, the atmosphere was just incredible. The place was packed, with the Kop full and the gates shut hours before kick-off. I was on the pitch down the Anfield Road

End most of the evening. The Kop looked unbelievable. The noise was incredible. When that Cup came out, I'll swear the earth was vibrating. I've never experienced a noise like it, your head was just buzzing. We could have beaten anyone that night, including Pele and Brazil.

SHOW THEM THE WAY TO GO HOME

(Sung to the tune of 'Show me the Way to go Home')

Oh,
Show them the way to go home,
They're tired and they wanna go to bed.
Oh, they've had a little game of football
Against the boys in red.
Oh,
Show them the way to go home,
They're tired and they wanna go to bed,
Cos they're only half a football team
Compared to the boys in red.

ROGAN TAYLOR

Kopite and a founder of the Football Supporters'
Association

Liverpool v Inter Milan

The Inter Milan game. For me, that was the first really big game I saw. We had a great side but we were largely unknown. We had been in the second division for a decade and had only been out a couple of seasons. Suddenly, we were taking on the cream of Europe. Nobody from northern Europe had ever won the European Cup, which had to that time been dominated by just three clubs – Real Madrid, Benfica and Inter Milan. And here we were playing Inter Milan, the world club champions. We had won the Cup just days before, and then we humiliated Milan. But the one thing I'll never forget about that night was the look on the faces of the Inter Milan players as they left the pitch. They looked utterly stunned and dejected, no doubt thinking about the rotten tomatoes and eggs that would greet them when they landed back in Milan. I've never seen such looks of anguish before or since.

BOB AZURDIA
Radio Merseyside

EUROPEAN CUP-WINNERS' CUP, SEMI-FINAL, SECOND LEG, 19 APRIL 1966

Liverpool 2   Glasgow Celtic 0
Smith, Strong
Attendance: 54,208

Another great night was the Celtic game. I was there that night as an ordinary punter. We'd lost the first leg 0–1 at Parkhead in front of 80,000 people, and thousands of Celtic fans came down to Liverpool for the return. I hadn't been able to get a ticket and then, late in the afternoon, a friend rang me and said he had a spare ticket for the Anfield Road End. Did I want it? That was where all the Celtic supporters were going to be, but I didn't worry about that. I just grabbed at the opportunity.

Hemmed in the middle of all these Celtic supporters I managed to keep quiet, all the time wishing I was on the Kop as I saw this mighty mass at the other end of the ground, swaying and roaring. Then, when Geoff Strong headed his goal, I automatically leapt into the air. I couldn't stop myself. The entire Anfield Road End was silent and still, except for me punching my arm into the air and letting out a cheer. Someone immediately turned around and punched me in the face, smashing my glasses. But, thankfully, another group of Celtic fans quickly stepped in, pulling me away. They surrounded me and told me to stay there with them and just keep quiet. I was very grateful.

Liverpool: Lawrence, Lawler, Byrne, Milne, Yeats, Stevenson, Callaghan, Strong, St John, Smith, Peter Thompson.
Celtic: Simpson, Young, Gemmell, Murdoch, McNeill, Clark, Lennox, McBride, Chalmers, Auld, Hughes.

CHIEF INSPECTOR IAN THOMSON
Former football liaison officer, Merseyside Police

Liverpool v Glasgow Celtic

I was on duty outside the ground for most of the night. Surprisingly, we didn't have a lot of trouble, although I do remember coming on duty at 7 a.m. and some Celtic supporter had just been arrested for being drunk. How he was drunk at 7 a.m. is beyond me. Drink was the biggest problem that night. All the time I was stopped by Scotsmen asking, 'Hey, Jimmy, where's the nearest off-licence?' Of course, then, you could take drink into the ground. There were binfuls of empty bottles everywhere. Not just beer, but whisky.

The other problem was containment, keeping the Celtic supporters off the pitch. Just towards the end of the game, Celtic were denied a penalty, and dozens of empty bottles came flying on to the pitch. We thought the bottles were going to be followed by fans, but we managed to keep them at bay. And, at the end of the day, surprisingly few people were arrested.

HUGH O'NEILL
St John Ambulance

Liverpool v Glasgow Celtic

The night of the Celtic game was the night everyone thought the Kop was on fire. It had been raining that day, and people had got soaked on their way to the ground. When they got inside the Kop, which was full to capacity, all their damp clothes began to dry off and, as you know, when damp clothes dry they give off steam. Well, all this steam was rising up into the roof of the Kop, and it looked like smoke was pouring out of the Kop. A lot of people thought the Kop was on fire and started panicking. Suddenly, people were pouring on to the pitch trying to get away from this imaginary fire. It took a while to settle things down.

LIVERPOOL DAILY POST AND ECHO
Monday, 2 May 1966

Division One, 30 April 1966

Liverpool 2	Chelsea 1
Hunt 2	*Murray*

Attendance: 53,754.

Manager Bill Shankly is right! There's no football crowd anywhere to compare with the vast Anfield throng for their fervour, their ability to make the most of the occasion, any occasion, great or small, their spontaneous humour and abundant wit. Entirely original, they are not so much part of a scene, as scene-stealers. So it was once again at Anfield on Saturday, when Liverpool took the league title, to which they have been heirs apparent for so long, for the second time in three years.

For all that, there was a sense of relief when it was all over and the prize was theirs, entirely as the result of their own efforts, rather than any fortuitous outside contributions.

With nearly twenty minutes remaining and Liverpool leading 2–1, the Kop exhorted their favourites to 'Show them the way to go home, they are tired and want to go to bed.' There followed the inevitable chant, 'Champions,' and their 'London Bridge is falling down, poor old Chelsea.' With play still in progress as the last moments ticked away, they began their standing, clapping ovation in quick time, and it swept round the ground like a forest fire. Just three minutes remained when out came the inevitable: 'Ee-Aye-Addio, we've won the league.'

I realise that to have brought the league championship trophy to Anfield in anticipation of a Liverpool triumph, may have been tempting providence, but surely it was a chance that should have been taken. Here was the ideal climax, instead of a formal handing over at the annual meeting of the League, where there will be as much enthusiasm as could be expected just now in the board-rooms of clubs like Blackburn and Northampton, con-demned as they are to second-division football. The silver-paper creations provided by the fans were better than nothing, but imagine the scenes that would have accom-panied a presentation in earnest!

It was uproarious enough in all conscience, as the team stood in the centre of the pitch, with hordes of photo-graphers milling round. The call was 'Shankly, Shankly, Shankly,' and out came the manager, for a reception that told him as plainly as actions could that his considerable part in the Anfield success story is both understood and appreciated.

The lap of honour produced a frenzied salute, and I don't think I have ever seen a more colourful spectacle than when they slowed their pace in front of the Kop, which became a throbbing sea of red and white. 'Kings of football,' read one of the multitude of flags, and this could truly be termed a unique coronation ceremony!

Liverpool: Lawrence, Lawler, Byrne, Milne, Yeats, Stevenson, Callaghan, Hunt, St John, Smith, Peter Thompson.
Chelsea: Dunn, Kirkup, R. Harris, Hollins, Hinton, Boyle, Houseman, Tambling, Osgood, Murray, Robson.

INSPECTOR BERNARD SWIFT
Football liaison officer, Merseyside Police

FA CUP, FIFTH ROUND, GOODISON, 11 MARCH 1967

Everton 1   Liverpool 0
Ball

Attendance: 64,851 (Goodison); 40,149 (Anfield).

One of the first games I remember was the Liverpool–
Everton Cup-tie in March 1967. Liverpool had won the
league the season before, and Everton had won the FA
Cup. Both sides were going great guns. Then they got
drawn against each other in the fifth round of the Cup.
The demand for tickets was incredible. Everyone wanted
to go. The game was at Goodison, so Liverpool decided
to install TV screens at Anfield so that those who couldn't
get tickets could at least see it live. I had to queue up for
seven hours to get tickets, just for the TV game!

I sagged off school that day along with thousands of
others. They had these large screens – I think there were
about six of them – on the pitch, and Anfield was packed
with just over 40,000 watching, while at Goodison there
were 64,000. To have 104,000 watching the game, that's
fantastic. It must be one of the largest crowds ever to
watch a match in England. I remember it was a very
windy day, and one of the screens blew down. It was
amazing on the Kop, there would be about 22,000 there,
everyone singing and chanting at a TV screen. Unfortunately, we got beat; Alan Ball scored the only goal. But
the worst problem about watching it at Anfield was that
we had a re-run of the goal. That we could have done
without.

Liverpool: Lawrence, Lawler, Milne, Byrne, Yeats,
Stevenson, Callaghan, Hunt, St John, Smith, Thompson.

Everton: West, Wright, Wilson, Hurst, Labone, Harvey,
Young, Ball, Temple, Husband, Morrissey.

LENNIE WOODS
Kopite

THE FAIRS CUP, SECOND ROUND, SECOND LEG,
26 NOVEMBER 1969

Liverpool 3	Vitoria Setubal 2
Smith (pen), Evans, Hunt	*Vagner (pen), Strong (og)*

Attendance: 41,633.

The Kop has always been very loyal. I remember one ridiculous moment, I think it was 1969. Anyhow, Liverpool were playing Vitoria Setubal, the Portuguese side, at Anfield in the old Fairs Cup. It was the season they introduced the away-goals rule, and nobody was quite certain how it worked. Liverpool had lost 0–1 in Portugal. At Anfield, Vitoria went ahead in the first half and then in the second half got another goal. That made it 3–0 on aggregate to them. But then Liverpool came storming back. Tommy Smith got a penalty and then, in the last two minutes, Liverpool scored twice, first through Alun Evans and then, almost with the last kick of the game, Roger Hunt made it 3–2 on the night.

Now, although they had drawn 3–3 on aggregate, the Portuguese went through because of the away-goal rule. Unfortunately, nobody on the Kop would accept this. Deep down, people knew they had lost but they refused to believe it, and everyone stood their ground waiting for extra-time. We all refused to go home. The players left the pitch, but nobody on the Kop would admit defeat and leave. Finally, they had to put a tannoy message over saying that Liverpool were out of the competition because Setubal had scored two away goals. I guess we all got caught up in the excitement of those last few minutes. It seemed such a shame after that great fightback then to discover that you were out.

Liverpool: Lawrence, Lawler, Strong, Smith, Yeats, Hughes, Callaghan, Peplow (Hunt), Graham (Evans), St John, Thompson.

Vitoria Setubal: Vital, Rebelo, Cardosol Alfredo, Carrico, Tome, JoseMaria, Vagner, Guerreiro (Baptista), Arcanjo (Herculano), Jacinto Joao.

PHIL THOMPSON
Liverpool player, 1971–85

DIVISION ONE, 23 APRIL 1973

Liverpool 2   Leeds United 0
Cormack, Keegan
Attendance: 55,738.

I was only just beginning to get into the team that season. I'd played the previous two matches, and Shankly called me up to play that day. It was right at the end of the season on an Easter Monday, and we had to beat Leeds to be virtually certain of winning the title. The position at the top of the table was desperately close. It was between Leeds and us.

It was an incredible day, the passion everywhere was so intense. There were 55,000 inside Anfield. Peter Cormack put us into the lead just as the second half began, but Leeds kept battling all the time. There was no let-up, it was knife-edge stuff and then, with five minutes to go, Keegan scored down the Kop end. The Kop erupted. The noise was deafening. It was clear that we were the new champions. The game was then played out in carnival atmosphere as the Kop celebrated. They knew we were safe.

I played a stormer that day, and I remember half-way through that second half the Kop chanting my name. It was one of the first times they had ever done that. I was in defence and I must have done something good, and the whole Kop was chanting my name. I felt like a million dollars. It was terrific.

Liverpool: Clemence, Lawler, Thompson, Smith, Lloyd, Hughes, Keegan, Cormack, Hall, Heighway, Callaghan.

Leeds United: Harvey, Reaney, Cherry, Bremner, Ellam, Hunter, Lorimer, Clarke, Jordan, Yorath, Madeley.

LIVERPOOL DAILY POST AND ECHO
Monday, 30 April 1973

DIVISION ONE, 28 APRIL 1973

Liverpool 0   Leicester City 0

Attendance: 56,202.

No crowd in the country can rise to an occasion better than Liverpool's – and they excelled themselves on Saturday when a goalless draw at Anfield against Leicester City was enough to clinch the club's record-equalling eighth title.

For colour, Liverpool's vivid red, of course, fervour, song and sound, this was the day of days. 'Super Liverpool' was their salute, and even if the match was slightly anti-climax, 'Super Liverpool' they remained for the presentation of the trophy by the League's president and the Leicester City chairman, Len Shipman, for the lap of honour and the adulation that did not subside until Bill Shankly, the last club member off the field, had dragged himself clear of doting worshippers.

The first scene-stealer was probably the youngest spectator in the 56,202 crowd. Before the match began, he was lifted out of the Kop by a police officer, with a great sense of the occasion, and carried towards skipper Tommy Smith. He was just a toddler, 2½-year-old Michael Briscoe of Cantril Farm, carrying with him a red and white ball and a cup made of silver paper.

After dutifully handing over the makeshift trophy, he was lifted up and hugged by Smith as the crowd roared their appreciation. Then it was back to the Kop – a face lost in the crowd.

The League trophy was not unveiled to public view until the final, almost triumphant blast of referee Jones's whistle. Then out it came to the players in the centre circle, closely followed by Mr Shankly, whose appearance increased the bedlam to deafening volume. As the swaying Kop stretched their scarves end to end among the 22,000 fans there, moving rhythmically to present a vast, almost dazzling sea of colour, off came the manager's coat to reveal a striking red shirt.

President Shipman might have saved himself the formality of a presentation speech, for I doubt if anybody heard a word. What he said was: 'I congratulate this great club, for in my opinion this is the greatest honour any club can achieve – forty-two matches and eight months of a season. This demands great stamina and fitness. It's a tribute to the city and the players.'

First to congratulate Mr Shankly was Keith Weller, the Leicester captain, scorer of three goals in the earlier game at Leicester. After this Liverpool reverse, way back in August, Weller had said: 'We beat them today, but I fancy them to win the league.'

The club's request to fans not to invade the pitch was broken only by five or six youngsters – and they were driven off by the crowd's 'Off, off, off' chant. Only when the players began their lap of honour was discipline thrown to the winds, with hundreds pouring on to the field.

The parade began with skipper Smith and the youngest player, Phil Thompson, carrying the trophy. As they progressed, it was passed round to every member of the side, with manager Shankly showing that, at 59, he is still fit enough for any lap of honour. Players and manager dallied in front of the hysterical Kop, until it seemed they would never be allowed to go. With the strain and tension of the occasion clearly showing, Mr Shankly was left high and dry by the departing players, with a club scarf, acquired during his tour, tied round his neck.

In front of the Main Stand, someone dropped a red and white scarf to the ground as the manager passed, and a policeman kicked it aside. Quick as a flash, the manager turned, picked up the scarf and carried it with him.

'Nobody can do that with a Liverpool scarf,' he said. 'This was almost sacred property to some kid, and I was delighted when he came round later to ask me for the return of it.'

That's Shankly, the manager with the common touch, ever mindful of the days when he was just another such youngster, caught up in the masses of the Glasgow Rangers fans.

The ground emptied slowly, reluctantly. But the fans were not yet done. 'Super Reds' was their chant as they brought their homeward route to life.

Liverpool: Clemence, Lawler, Lindsay, Smith, Lloyd, Hughes, Keegan, Boersma (Hall), Thompson, Heighway, Callaghan.

Leicester City: Shilton, Whitworth, Manley, Cross, Rofe, Weller, Samuels, Birchenall, Glover, Worthington, Stringfellow.

WHEN THE REDS GO MARCHING IN
(Sung to the tune of 'When the Saints go Marching In')

Oh when the Reds,
Oh when the Reds,
Oh when the Reds go marching in,
I wanna be in that number,
When the Reds go marching in.

EMLYN HUGHES
Liverpool player, 1967–79

EUROPEAN CUP, QUARTER-FINAL, SECOND LEG, 16 MARCH 1977

Liverpool 3   St Étienne 1
Keegan, Kennedy,
Fairclough   *Bathenay*
Attendance: 55,043.

The greatest memory I have of the Kop was the St Étienne game which we played at Anfield. We had to win by two clear goals. We'd lost 0–1 in France. I have never known the Kop so noisy during all my years at Anfield, nor since. They were hungry for success. We felt that if we could beat St Étienne we could go all the way. We knew who we were going to be playing in the semi-final, and we just knew that if we could beat the French we'd not only be in the final but we would win the European Cup as well. We didn't fear any of the teams left in the competition. Zurich were a fourth-division side, and we had the death wish on the Germans. You just had to attack them, and they would collapse. So that night was important. They just sucked David Fairclough into the Kop for his goal. It was an incredible feeling for the Kop, a mixture of relief and anticipation. People were standing on their seats and singing '*Allez les Rouges*'. It was absolutely incredible.

Liverpool: Clemence, Neal, Jones, Smith, Kennedy, Hughes, Keegan, Case, Heighway, Toshack (Fairclough), Callaghan.

St Étienne: Curkovic, Janvion, Farison, Mercahadier, (H. Revelli), Lopez, Bathenay, Rocheteau, Larque, P. Revelli, Synaeghel, Santini.

BILLY WILSON
Kopite

Liverpool v St Étienne

The first time I went to Anfield was for the St Étienne game. I wasn't a Liverpool fan when I went into the Kop that evening, but I was by the time I came out. You could say I'd been converted, and who could blame me? The atmosphere was electric, and the game itself was unbelievable. As a 13-year-old who'd bunked off school that afternoon, I was certainly affected.

Even though I wasn't a Liverpool supporter I knew that this was one of the biggest games in English football for a long time. A friend and I went with two 18-year-olds, who impressed upon us beforehand the fact that the Kop was an exciting and important place where football was taken seriously, and where Liverpool players were worshipped, especially Kevin Keegan. By the time we reached Anfield, I was in a state of barely suppressed excitement. The sound of the Kop, chanting as we waited outside, was unbelievable. The noise was affecting the queue, and everyone was impatient to get inside and join in the singing. When we got in we were advised to go straight to the toilet, as we wouldn't get another chance. Our guide then told us to stick by him for the whole game.

At the top of the Kop I looked along the terracing, and it was a daunting sight. As far as I could see there was no standing room, and I couldn't see anyone standing aside to let us in. 'Come on,' said my mate's big brother as he led us along the Kop until we were directly behind the goal. Then he dived under a crush barrier and started pushing through the crowd. As we followed, I couldn't see anything except coats, jackets and legs, and every now and then my head would clank into a crush barrier. Eventually, we surfaced into the cold night air and, as I straightened, the atmosphere hit me.

The first thing that struck me was how bright everything was, and what a great view of the pitch we had. Beneath us the crowd seemed to slope away right down to the goal-net. On the track at the bottom there appeared to be constant activity, with people being helped away by the St John Ambulance men. We were right in the middle of the Kop. I was amazed when I realised that I could lift my feet off the ground and still be held in position by the tightly packed crowd.

The nearer to kick-off it got, the louder the cheering became. Away to the right-hand side, as we looked, were thousands of St Étienne fans in the Anfield Road End singing, 'Allez les Verts'. It was impossible to stay in one place for more than a couple of seconds before you got caught up in a wave of people swaying. All the time I was straining to keep sight of my friends. When the teams came out, the cheering was so loud the roof nearly came off the Kop.

I remember Keegan's goal going in almost in slow motion. There was a split-second gap, like the Kop couldn't believe it had gone in, before all hell broke loose. The whole Kop went flying forward, and I remember wondering as I went hurtling down the terracing when this massive surge was going to come to a rest. No sooner had it stopped than it seemed to surge backwards up the terracing. I was spun around like a cork on the sea. Even when the surging came to a rest, supporters were jumping up and down on the spot. Total strangers would grab you and give you a kiss, or put their arms around you and go on a mad little jig. Elbows, jaws, heads, ribs, arms, hands, legs: for a couple of minutes the whole lot were just a bony tangle as the Kop totally let itself go.

What a start, and what a roar, as 25,000 voices started singing in unison, 'We love you, Liverpool, we do.' It says a lot for St Étienne that they didn't go totally to pieces trying to play towards this wall of noise. What egged the Kop on to even louder and greater efforts wasn't just the fact that we needed another goal, it was the noise the 5,000 St Étienne fans were making in support of their team. I don't think the noise let up until half-time.

However, the Kop was silenced when Batheney scored. Again, the ball almost seemed to waft in and, from my view on the Kop, it seemed to change direction twice. When Ray Kennedy restored the lead, the Kop really did its utmost to egg the team on to an outright winner.

I never did see the Fairclough goal go in. The Kop had been singing '*Allez les Rouges*' since the Kennedy goal, both to help Liverpool on, and also to throw St Étienne's chant back in their faces. Not long after Fairclough came on he had a chance, and everyone on the Kop seemed alert to the fact that he could do it. When the ball went over the half-way line to put him through, he seemed to hold the ball for an eternity. As he got nearer and nearer to goal with each stride, the Kop roar got louder and louder, poised ready to go mad when the ball went in. All the time, though, there was a St Étienne player hanging on to Fairclough's shoulder. I saw him pull back his foot and shoot, on the run, from just inside the area. The next thing I knew, the crowd was flying forward and you knew he'd scored.

There was pandemonium. I think everyone was in a mad ecstasy, as the Liverpool players dived on to Fairclough. The joy and happiness running through the Kop as they sang, 'Que sera, sera/whatever will be, will be/we're going to Italy/que sera, sera,' will always stick in my memory. In fact, whenever I hear that song, it reminds me of the St Étienne game.

DAVID FAIRCLOUGH
Liverpool player, 1974–82

Liverpool v St Étienne

I came on that night as substitute in place of John Toshack, in an effort to change the pattern of the game. Ray Kennedy had scored to make it 2-2, but we desperately needed to score again. Bob Paisley didn't give me any specific instructions. He just made me feel good and said he simply hoped that I would get my chance. Ray Kennedy started the move for the goal. He lifted a ball over their defence. I battled with the big centre-half knowing that I had to get the ball on target. I was saying to myself: 'Don't make a mess of this!' Thankfully, it went in. I can still remember the euphoria as everyone jumped on top of me, saying: 'We might as well waste a few more minutes.'

Everyone always associates me with the St Étienne game. That and the game against Inter Milan were undoubtedly the greatest nights the Kop ever knew. But, for obvious reasons, the St Étienne game was the greatest of my career, the greatest game I ever saw. The two teams came out together that night, the first time I can ever remember that happening. I had never seen anything like it before. All of us players were looking at each other; 'Geez,' we were saying, 'this is fantastic.'

The whole game had captured the imagination of the public, and I don't think we were really aware of that until we came to the ground that night. I remember the traffic was terrible. Everywhere people seemed to be heading for Anfield. We hadn't really expected it. Inside the ground it was mind-blowing, and so intimidating. I was probably more aware of it than most of the other players as I was sitting in the dug-out. It made me very nervous; you just looked up and . . . WOW! I'm sure there were many more inside the ground than the official attendance. The gates had been rushed, and the gatemen just gave up and let everybody in. It was chock-a-block, and the buzz was amazing.

WE LOVE YOU, LIVERPOOL
(Sung to an original tune)

(*Chorus*)
We love you, Liverpool, we do,
We love you, Liverpool, we do,
We love you, Liverpool, we do,
Oh, Liverpool, we love you.
Shankly is our hero, he showed us how to
    play,

The mighty Reds of Europe are out to win
    today,
He made a team of champions, with every
    man a king,
And every game we love to win, and this is
    what we sing:

(*Chorus*)

Clemence is our goalie, the best there is
    around,

> And Keegan is the greatest that Shankly ever
>   found,
> Heighway is our favourite, the wizard of the
>   game,
> And here's the mighty Toshack to do it once
>   again.
>
> (Chorus)
>
> We've won the league, we've won the cup,
> We're masters of the game,
> And just to prove how good we are,
> We'll do it once again.
> We've got another team to beat and so we've
>   got to try,
> Cos we're the best in all the land, and that's
>   the reason why.
>
> (Chorus)

BILLY WILSON
Kopite

WORLD CUP QUALIFIER, 12 OCTOBER 1977

Scotland 2   Wales 0
Masson (pen), Dalglish

Attendance: 51,000.

I have to be honest and say that one of my most memorable moments on the Kop was standing there for the Scotland v Wales World Cup game in 1977. There was a frenzy there that night unknown even at the St Étienne game. How all the Scotland fans got their tickets when Wales were meant to be at home I'll never know. Scotland more or less took over the place. Somehow they'd got into derelict houses in Walton Breck Road behind the Kop and were leaning out of the upstairs windows waving their flags, or massive sheets with 'Scotland' painted on them.

Traffic on Walton Breck Road came to a standstill, and there was the air of a drunken street party.

As kick-off time approached, minds began to turn to the difficulty of getting in. The more adventurous, or drunk, somehow managed to scale the walls at the back of the Kop, while the police waited to arrest them when they descended. Throughout the evening, the Welsh supporters skulked around the outside of Anfield hoping that they wouldn't be noticed. I saw a few have their tickets 'removed' by Scotland fans. The police seemed to have a 'softly, softly' approach. They sort of stood back and looked on in amusement. The supporters who didn't fancy risking their necks by climbing the Kop wall whilst drunk were attempting to push their way through the turnstiles, ticket or not. Anyone with a ticket for the Kop who'd left it too late had no chance of getting through the mob to the turnstile. Meanwhile, the Kop exit doors were witnessing a scene reminiscent of the storming of a medieval castle. There was a 'thin blue line' of police guarding the gates, which no doubt were well secured on the inside as well. The Scotland mob would gather and charge at the gates. 'Heave,' they'd cry, and the red gates would slowly start to open. A police van would roar along the road at the crowd, who'd disperse, then regroup and start again. Sometimes it seemed that the gates would open and we'd all be through – but they never did.

I was lucky. I got a Kop ticket from a Scotland fan who was so disgruntled that he hadn't been able to get in after half an hour that he was going to tear his ticket up. Luckily, he gave it to me before he stormed off to listen to the game on the radio, or get drunk. It wasn't until half-time that I got in. The first thing that hit me as I looked up the Kop stairs was the number of police lining the steps all the way to the top. Before I had the chance to climb the stairs, a copper said I had to take the stick out of my flag. I was heartbroken, as I'd only bought it that evening and hadn't even had a decent wave in anger.

When I got to the top of the steps I couldn't believe how packed the Kop was. Whereas at Liverpool games there would just be pushing and shoving behind the goals and at each side of that point, this evening there was jostling and shoving right the way back to the steps as fans struggled to get a view of part of the pitch, never mind the whole view. It's the only game at the Kop when I've not been able to filter down to a decent position. The whole game was spent stretching, peering, jostling, and hopping about from foot to foot to follow the ball as it moved around the pitch.

'Oh Flower of Scotland' we sang, as the team went in search of the goal that would secure a place in Argentina. Soon we got a disputed penalty, before one of the greatest goals seen at Anfield, or anywhere else for that matter. Macari and Buchan combined to send the ball over for Kenny to rush in and head home. Scotland were on their way to the World Cup. You should have heard the Scotland fans sing themselves hoarse with delight: 'Kenny, Kenny, we'll walk a million miles for one of your goals, oh Kenny . . .' And that night everyone believed they really would, to help Scotland win. Instead, they merely provided unbelievable support all night. My final memory is of a Scotland fan trying to run off with a piece of the centre circle he'd dug up. But the police were too quick this time.

Scotland: Rough, Jardine (Buchan), Donachie, Masson, McQueen, Forsyth, Dalglish, Hartford, Jordan, Macari, Johnston.
Wales: Davies, R. Thomas, J. Jones, Mahoney, D. Jones, Phillips, Flynn, Sayer, Yorath, Toshack, M. Thomas.

INSPECTOR JOHN JEFFREY
Football liaison officer, Merseyside Police

Scotland v Wales

A lot of reinforcements from St Helens and all over Merseyside were brought in for the Scotland/Wales World Cup clash. We expected a lot of trouble, and I think it's fair to say that everybody was a bit apprehensive. I was on the turnstiles at the back of the Kop checking everyone for drink. I tell you, you've never seen so much drink. They weren't supposed to bring it in but they did – bottles of it, whisky, beer, lager, you name it, they were just swigging it out of the bottle. You'd stop them as they came through the turnstile and say, 'Sorry, you can't take that in,' and they would look at you and say, 'Och aye, officer, have a wee drink yourself.' Sometimes you have to turn a blind eye.

It was a freezing cold night. These poor Scotsmen were all soaking wet and cold; half of them had kilts on or just their Scotland shirts. But the atmosphere was incredible.

You could feel the tension. Potentially, there could have been a major problem but, as it was, it all passed without too much trouble, thanks probably to Kenny Dalglish, who put Scotland into the finals. I dread to think what might have happened if Scotland had lost. But, as it was, it was a great night.

The poor old bobbies from St Helens had never policed a football match before. They had only done rugby. And they had been a bit worried. Half of them had never even been to a football match. But they really enjoyed it. They all said so after the game, how exciting it had been and how wonderful it was on the Kop.

HUGH O'NEILL
St John Ambulance

Scotland v Wales

I was dealing with the Kop the night of the Wales/Scotland World Cup game. I well remember coming out of the first-aid room at the back of the Kop, and there were three bins filled to the top with bottles of booze confiscated by the police. There was a lot of drunkenness. We had one guy pulled out of the Kop with a broken leg. He was so drunk I don't suppose he felt much pain, and he certainly did not want to leave the ground to go to hospital. He was pleading with us to let him stay. In the end, we had to get the police to come and make him go to hospital.

STEPHEN F. KELLY
Writer

MILK CUP FINAL, WEMBLEY, 25 MARCH 1984

Liverpool 0   Everton 0

Attendance: 100,000.

The first ever Liverpool/Everton Wembley final was an astonishing occasion. All the way down the motorway, the entire length from Liverpool to Wembley, you could see nothing but cars, vans and minibuses with fans and scarves hanging out of the windows. But what was amazing was that it was the scarves of both clubs. Some cars even had red *and* blue ribbons tied together on them. Nowhere in the world would you see that.

I remember walking past this particular car trying to park not far from Wembley. There were two elderly people inside. It had blue ribbons and red ribbons all over it. The bloke who was driving got out and was wearing a blue scarf and hat; then his wife climbed out and she was all dressed in red. Fortunately, it was a draw, so they probably didn't argue on the way home.

Then, all the length of Wembley Way, there were Liverpool and Everton supporters marching arm in arm, chatting to each other, having a few beers together, laughing and joking in the pouring rain. There was absolutely no hint of violence. And inside the ground there was no segregation. The two teams had been allotted separate ends, but all the tickets inevitably had got mixed up. I was standing with a bunch of Everton supporters, but there was never an angry word. But the one thing that made me feel proud that day was the chant of 'Mer-sey-side, Mer-sey-side, Mer-sey-side' which went up before and after the game. It was so loud, so moving.

Liverpool: Grobbelaar, Neal, Kennedy, Lawrenson, Whelan, Hansen, Dalglish, Lee, Rush, Johnston (Robinson), Souness.

Everton: Southall, Stevens, Bailey, Ratcliffe, Mountfield, Reid, Irvine, Heath, Sharp, Richardson, Sheedy (Harper).

JIM GARDINER
Kopite

DIVISION ONE, 26 MAY 1989

Liverpool 0   Arsenal 2
                           Smith, Thomas

Attendance: 41,783.

The night I shall never forget was when Arsenal stole the double from us. You would have staked your mortgage on Liverpool winning. They'd won the FA Cup the previous Saturday, beating Everton in the final at Wembley. That had come after all the trauma of Hillsborough. Then, on the Tuesday evening, they beat West Ham 5-1. That meant that Arsenal needed to win by two clear goals, but Liverpool had gone twenty-four games without defeat. It seemed inconceivable to us that Arsenal could stop Liverpool from pulling off a unique second double.

Arsenal went ahead in the second half through a controversial free-kick, but we still didn't feel threatened. Just one minute to go. I can still see Steve McMahon holding up one finger to us, as if to say just one minute. Then Michael Thomas races on to a ball in the area, and bang. I've never known anything like it. We just couldn't believe it. At the end of that game there was silence, sheer silence, on the Kop. There was a look of disbelief on everyone's faces. Even now, when I watch Michael Thomas playing for Liverpool I can still see him nipping into the penalty area to score that goal. I still haven't watched that game on video, and I've only ever seen the goal once.

And yet at the end of that game, when Tony Adams brought the Arsenal team up to the Kop, they got a standing ovation. People say it was the same when Leeds won the title at Anfield one time, and Billy Bremner brought them up to the Kop after the game. Everyone on the Kop stayed behind and applauded Arsenal. They can be so appreciative, so generous. And yes, at the end of the day, Arsenal deserved to win the title. As Arsenal finally trooped off the pitch, people were sitting all over the Kop. They didn't have the motivation to move. They were so stunned, they still couldn't believe it. That was another turning-point. It was the night Liverpool's invincibility started to go.

Liverpool: Grobbelaar, Ablett, Staunton, Nicol, Whelan, Hansen, Houghton, Aldridge, Rush (Beardsley), Barnes, McMahon.

Arsenal: Lukic, Dixon, Winterburn, Thomas, O'Leary, Adams, Rocastle, Richardson, Smith, Bould, Merson.

LONDON BRIDGE
(Sung to the tune of 'London Bridge Is Falling Down')

London Bridge is falling down,
Falling down,
Falling down.
London Bridge is falling down,
Poor old Chelsea.
Build it up in red and white,
Red and white,
Red and white.
Build it up in red and white,
Poor old Chelsea.

Six

LOVE AND DEATH ON THE KOP

You'll Never Walk Alone

YOU'LL NEVER WALK ALONE
(from *Carousel* by Richard Rodgers and
   Oscar Hammerstein II)

When you walk through a storm,
Hold your head up high,
And don't be afraid of the dark.
At the end of the storm,
There's a golden sky
And the sweet silver song of the lark.
Walk on through the wind,
Walk on through the rain,
Though your dreams be tossed and blown,
Walk on, walk on,
With hope in your heart,
And you'll never walk alone,
You'll never walk alone.
Walk on, walk on,
With hope in your heart,
And you'll never walk alone,
You'll never walk alone.

STEPHEN F. KELLY
Writer

Hillsborough, 15 April 1989

Death inevitably brings with it many forms of ritual. From

the perfumed smouldering pyres of Varanasi to traditional Mexican villages, where villagers pay their respects by laying food, candles and water at the door of the dead. In Liverpool, they adopted a ritual of their own. On that Saturday night, the scallies sneaked up to Anfield and furtively tied their red scarves to the Shankly Gates. It was their ritual, and the dead would have been impressed by it. It was reported on the local radio stations and, as Sunday wore on, more scarves, hats and flowers were added. By Monday, the Shankly Gates had been turned into a shrine, as pile upon pile of flowers, wreaths, scarves and hats hung proudly and sadly from the railings.

Then someone asked if they could lay flowers on the Kop. 'Of course,' said the club, and the gates were obligingly thrown open. By the end of the week, half a million had filed past the Kop, laid their flowers, wrapped their scarves to the railings, paid their respects. They came from far afield to join in the pilgrimage. The mightiest in the land. Crown princes, politicians, local dignitaries, footballers, supporters, ordinary folk, some who had never even seen a football match, let alone Liverpool. I threw my scarf on the Kop.

Gradually the wreaths spread, extending from the back of the goal to cover the goalmouth, then to hide the penalty area. By the time they closed the gates a week later, half the pitch was shrouded in flowers. They said that, in the early morning, the fragrance and the gentle rustle of cellophane in the Mersey breeze was enough to make any grown man weep.

In Liverpool that Saturday night, life came to a standstill. The pubs, normally a hubbub of clinking glasses and chattering foursomes, lay deserted, the cinemas empty, the clubs silent, the music switched off. By midnight, the death toll was in the nineties. And the next day, as the news began to sink in, Liverpool turned into a ghost town. Its inhabitants remained indoors, sifting tearfully through their Sunday newspapers, listening to the local radio stations, hoping it was all a nightmare. It was how Manchester must have felt after Munich.

In the evening, there was a hurriedly-prepared mass at the Catholic cathedral. A white-faced Kenny Dalglish clung to his wife; Bruce Grobbelaar, so often the clown of Anfield, his voice now shaking as he bravely read the lesson; John Aldridge shamelessly brushing aside his tears; the other players looking as if they had not slept that night. And outside thousands, listening, praying, sharing their grief. Footballers and fans, so often accused of frivolity, now dignified as they mourned. And you could hear the nation's tears.

BILLY WILSON
Kopite

Events just seemed to grind on . . . outside human direction, but with a life of their own . . . there was a shuttle service now of supporters carrying the dead and injured to the half-way line . . . then the sun started to set, and it was still happening . . . the Wednesday Kop was empty . . . all around was clearing . . . eventually we knew we had to go and face whatever news there was . . . two things stick in my mind as we left the ground . . . Archie Gemmill down on the touchline, which seemed surprising as football was so peripheral now . . . and the other was seeing a St John Ambulance man giving a Liverpool supporter the kiss of life, and the lad's friends urging the man on like he was a star player, almost chanting or singing for him, and then the ambulance man gesturing like he had scored and he'd saved the boy – YES! – before his expression changed a split-second later, and he realised the supporter was now dying . . . I can still see him hurling his cap into the grass in an expression of anger, anguish, futility. He couldn't loiter, though . . . he had to go and help others . . . the lad's friends stood around bemused . . . this wasn't like the films . . . no one died in close-up or a blaze of glory that day . . . events happened in slow motion . . . people clutched their chests or did nothing . . . they just lay down like they wanted a nap in the warm April sunshine . . . it goes hazy here.

The next thing I know, we're out in the streets and nearly back at the pub where the furniture van is parked ... flash like a scene from a film ... we're at a phone box, and the queue is stretching back for about a mile, but everyone is orderly, there is no talking, there's no pushing, shoving or anything, fans are standing there like bright red statues, no one is in tears ... there is just stunned silence. The first person I saw when we got back to the van was Martin, we hugged each other like we were long-lost brothers, he was grinning ... he'd been in the Leppings Lane End and was no doubt glad to be alive ... he hadn't seen the others, or had he? 'I think I saw Keith ... he's all right ...' but he wasn't sure. We opened the van and for some reason put the radio on ... it's now I realise we thought that they were going to tell us, somewhere along the line, that our mates were OK. 'And here's a message for the lads in the furniture van: Rob is OK.' One by one they all came back ... and everyone had the same sheepish grin on their face, but no one said a thing about what had gone on ... meanwhile Martin was leaning against the side of the van vomiting ... and grinning at us ... it was handshakes and hugs all round ... some of us had only met that day ... then we wearily climbed into the van and thought about heading home ... there was no fighting for places on the wheel hubs this time ... no one was surprised that none of us was injured or worse ... as they'd come back one by one, it had somehow seemed inevitable that they would ... so now here we all were in the back of the van, just like you'd expect ... although subdued, no one speaking, except generalisations like 'I don't believe it ...' and 'They'll have to replay it ...' It was only when we started on the last of the cans that bits and pieces came out ... 'I was hanging on to a crash barrier ... They came thundering past me like a herd of elephants ... I saw you in there ... I moved to the side ... I was standing all over people to stay up ... Stop the van ...' and someone would be sick ...

We got back to the pub and we got drunker than we've ever been before, and everyone was so glad we'd all made it, and the pub stayed open all night, and total strangers shook our hands . . . and we did the same all over again the next day.

On Monday, we all hung around the pub avoiding work or college or having to watch the telly or read the nonsense in the papers, until someone decided to hire a taxi to take us to Anfield. We bought a bouquet and stood queuing to get in, and the feeling of solidarity among the fans was unbelievable. A foreign TV crew stuck their camera in our faces, but we couldn't be bothered. We all knew it would take away some of the pain and anger and anguish if we could pay tribute, however small, to those fans who died. When we got in we laid the bouquet on the spot where we usually stood, to the right in the Kop, to the side of one of the pillars. It was great to see so many other fans laying bouquets on their parts of the Kop. We stood for a few minutes in our own thoughts, and thought about the dead. We put the bouquet there as a mark of respect from everyone who'd gone up in the van that day. Then we quietly left the ground, not wishing to stay over long, and went round the corner to the pub for a quiet pint, and talked about how we were going to pick up our everyday routines the following day. But what happened that April day will always stay with us.

STEVE SHAKESHAFT
Photographer, Liverpool Daily Post and Echo

On the Sunday morning, I went up to Anfield. There were already a few scarves hanging from the Shankly Gates and, as the morning passed, more and more people were arriving and tying their colours to the gates. By the afternoon, there were so many people there that the club just spontaneously opened the gates and let everyone into the ground.

I went in with them, and what was astonishing was that everyone walked slowly around the ground and made straight for the Kop. It was just automatic. It was as if they knew and had decided that the Kop would be their shrine. Then they all started tying their scarves to the goalpost, and others climbed into the Kop and put their scarves on the barriers, maybe the same barrier they stood behind week after week. There were a lot of typical Liverpool scallies who had small bunches of flowers which they'd obviously taken from their gardens, and they laid them on the Kop. Other people just went and sat silently on the Kop.

I felt that I was imposing. I had to take my photographs, and yet I didn't want to. I felt as if I was exploiting the situation. But nobody said anything. A Salvation Army band had followed us into the ground, and they grouped themselves in a small circle inside the penalty area and then began playing 'Abide With Me'. It was so spontaneous. We were all in tears. Suddenly, I had a different perspective on the Kop and all those who stand on it. It had become a shrine, their shrine.

MICK GRAHAM
Kopite

I have to admit the Kop came between my wife and me. In the end, we finished up getting divorced. She was never that keen on football. I think she just went along with it when we were courting, though she did come on the Kop a few times, but I don't remember her actually enjoying it.

After we got married, I continued going to matches. It wasn't so bad if they were at Anfield, it was when I used to follow them away that it began to cause a problem. I don't even think it was the amount of time that I was away that caused the problem, but the money. It got to be a bit expensive, and money was tight at the time. I wasn't working at one point. But I have to say that we often went by car, me and my mates, or sometimes managed to get a free ride on the train.

Anyhow, she resented it, especially when they started doing well in Europe and I was going to see them in Rome and Paris. That cost quite a bit. We didn't have a holiday one year either. That brought it all to a head. She went off with somebody else in the end. I think he was an Evertonian. Serves her right.

JACK PAYNE
Kopite

It's not just Kopites who are football-mad. Everyone in this city is a little bit football-barmy. My wife comes from a family of Evertonians, every one of them a true blue. They were so mad about football that the day her father got married – which was in 1928 – they had the ceremony in the morning. It was a Saturday, and after that they went back to the house for the do. They had spent all the money on the do, so about 2 p.m. the father – that's the bridegroom – starts going around and asking each of the guests if anyone had a couple of bob he could borrow. He wanted to go to the match that afternoon. Anyway, someone eventually gave him two shillings, and off he went, leaving his new bride and everyone else at the reception.

PHIL ASPINALL
Kopite

I first met my wife, Debbie, in the Chaser pub in Fazakerley. She'd just come back from Canada. I'd had a few drinks, and we got chatting. I asked her if she'd like to go out one day. 'Where are you going to take me?' she asked. 'On the Kop,' I replied. I mean, where else would you take a girl! She was a bit worried about that, but I told her she'd be OK. Anyhow, I took her.

It was Liverpool against Wimbledon. I got there at the usual spot, and all my mates are saying, 'Hey, Assy, I didn't know you had a daughter.' Ha, ha. The only problem was when everybody started peeing, but they all tried to turn away and be subtle about it. She liked John

Barnes's legs, though. After the game we went to The Albert. She said she really enjoyed it all, and that being on the Kop made her realise how much she loved the city of Liverpool and its people. She was supposed to be going back to Canada, but in the end she decided to stay, and we got married. All thanks to the Kop, I suppose.

ROMEO AND JULIET
(Sung to a traditional tune of that name. The
   new words are by Stan Kelly)

(Chorus)
Two clubs alike in dignity,
In Liverpool where we set our scene,
And Juliet's dad was Everton-mad
While Romeo's followed Bill Shankly's
   team.

As she was going to Goodison Park,
It being on a derby day,
He passed her on the way to the match
And pretended that he'd lost his way.
'Ello dere, Jill, can you help me,
I'm sweating cobs cos it's ten to three.
If I don't find that Goodison Road,
I'm bound to miss Hunt's opening goal.'

(Chorus)

She flashed her saucy eyes at him,
And, oh, but they were Kendall-blue,
She answered him quite modestly,
'I'd sooner be dead than a Red like you.
'I'm a Catterick maverick through and
   through,
'And I would die for the lads in blue,
'But I'll guide you to the holy ground,
'Lest you miss Alan scoring two.'

(Chorus)

He arched his back against the bar,
To save her from the swaying fans.
They sang 'You'll never walk alone',
And they left Goodison hand in hand.
Well, Juliet's dad was raving mad,
And Romeo's nearly went berserk,
But over a black-and-tan that night,
They agreed mixed marriages never work.
So while the moon was shining bright,
Our star-struck lovers eloped one night,
On the midnight ferry they crossed over,
Now they're both supporting Tranmere
  Rovers.

(*Chorus*)

GEORGE SHANNON
Kopite

I felt a terrible shame after Heysel. The date I shall never forget: May 29 1985. I'd been supporting Liverpool for years and never really seen any trouble, and then all those lives. I just felt awful. I wanted to be sick. Suddenly, it was a disgrace to be a Liverpool supporter; you didn't want to call yourself a Kopite any more. Before that, we'd been so proud of ourselves. I'm glad it came at the end of the season, because I couldn't have gone to a match a few days later. It took me a while to get over it. I suppose we did get over it, although at the time I thought I'd never go again.

I was there at the beginning of the following season. It was such a difficult game, that first match. I didn't know whether to cheer or not. I think everybody felt the same. It was a strange feeling on the Kop. Nobody wanted to sing before the game but, once Liverpool scored, it seemed to release a pressure valve.

But I tell you what, something began to go out of Liverpool after Heysel. The terraces, and the Kop, changed. It was never quite the same again. Then, after Hillsborough, it changed totally. I know they're going to seat the Kop and I don't particularly like it, but after Hillsborough we have no option, not Liverpool. And, anyhow, the days of the 1960s and those huge, singing crowds on the Kop are long gone. The past is the past, we have to look to the future.

REV. JACKIE WATERMAN
St Columba's, Anfield

I recently officiated for a family who were scattering the ashes of their mother at Anfield. The seven daughters all came up to Liverpool for the brief ceremony. Their mother had been born in Liverpool but had moved south. She had always been a Liverpool fan and had continued to follow their fortunes even though she had been living away from the city for some years. She used to send birthday cards to the players and, after the Hillsborough disaster, had sent one of her daughters up to Anfield to lay a wreath on the Kop. Anyhow, after she died, her family thought it would be appropriate to scatter her ashes on the ground, and I was asked to conduct a service. She may even have asked for it in her will, I'm not sure.

The daughters were all in awe as we came through the players' tunnel and on to the pitch. Their faces when they saw the Kop! It was like a pilgrimage for them. The funeral had actually taken place in September, and this was November, so they had all managed to arrange for a day in Liverpool. Anyhow, we walked on to the pitch, me and the seven daughters, with the groundsman showing us where to go. It must have been a strange sight to see us, eight women there scattering the ashes of another woman on the pitch. The groundsman had dug a small plot for us to put the ashes in. What usually happens is that the ashes are left in a small urn and then buried in the ground but, in this case, the daughters simply wanted to throw the ashes on to the grass.

So we stood there, with the groundsman keeping a respectful distance, and I conducted a short service from the Church of England Alternative Service Book which is designed for such occasions, although I don't imagine those who wrote it ever thought it would be used for the scattering of ashes at a football ground. During the service, we took the mother's ashes from the casket – it was a sort of small coffin – and then scattered them on the ground and into the hole, and I have to confess that, while the groundsman wasn't looking, we put some of the Anfield soil into the casket. They were really thrilled about that. The groundsman told us to make a note of where the ashes were, in case they might want to lay flowers there in the future.

It was the first time I had done such a service, and it was nice. I felt that we were not just ministering to the dead, but also helping the living to come to terms with their grief. To them, this was a secular shrine. People should be allowed to grieve as they wish and to work through things to help them. The Kop and Anfield had meant a lot to their mother; it was her Mecca.

STEVE SHAKESHAFT
Photographer, Liverpool Daily Post and Echo

I got a phone-call one day from someone who asked me if I would come and take some photographs. His family were scattering the ashes of a relative on the Kop, and they wanted it in the paper. So I went.

Anyhow, when I got there, Bill Shankly had joined the family on the Kop, and a small service was about to take place. Shankly got very upset. 'You've nae right to be here, son,' he said. 'Yer intruding on people's privacy.' Fortunately, the family explained that they wanted me there to take some pictures, and he cooled down.

It was a strange scene, so quiet, the family just standing there. Football stadiums are eerie places when there is nobody in them. No shouting, no singing, no tension. Just silence.

HUGH O'NEILL
St John Ambulance

I think the worst game we ever had to deal with was the 1970 derby against Everton. Liverpool were losing 0–2 at one stage but went on to win 3–2. It was in November, and people had probably come to the ground wearing too many clothes. There were 53,000 in Anfield, and we almost had another Hillsborough that day. There were casualties everywhere. The pitch was littered with them. We had every conceivable injury. It was dreadful in the Kop. We had to bring reinforcements up from the Anfield Road End. People were lying on stretchers all over the place, and all the ambulances were in constant use. Luckily, nobody died.

But one thing I will always remember about that game was a girl who was pulled out of the Kop. She was an Evertonian, and had fainted and was unconscious. Me and a policeman struggled to get her out. As we dragged her out, I suddenly realised that everyone was whistling. Then I looked and saw what it was. The poor girl's knickers had come right down as we had been carrying her, and she had achieved every Evertonian's ambition by showing her backside to the Kop!

JOHN FRANK
Kopite

Liverpool girls seem to have a natural understanding of football. They know the rules, they know which is which team and who are the star players. I guess that some weeks they find themselves going out with a Liverpool supporter, and then the next it might be an Evertonian. They have to learn to adjust, swearing blind that they have always supported his team. Secretly, they probably don't give a damn about football, but they have to feign appreciation and commitment, otherwise it might limit their chances of finding a boyfriend in this city. You won't find many lads here who aren't interested in soccer. They have to be in order to survive. You can spot lots of girls at Anfield, which is nice, and you see plenty of them on the Kop as well. It's good that they feel safe enough to go on the Kop.

Liverpool girls know how to look after themselves. I'm telling you all this because I once took a girl from the south on the Kop. I was living in London at the time, and I was going out with this very middle-class girl. I brought her home one weekend and, of course, you can't come to Liverpool without going to a game. So I took her to Anfield, and not having a lot of money I took her on the Kop. We got a decent spec, though we were quite a way back. Anyhow, at half-time, the score was 0–0. It had been a fairly exciting first half, with Liverpool kicking towards the Kop. They won a few corners, but nothing more. But the astonishing thing was that, as the half-time whistle went and the players were trooping off the field, this girl turns round to me and says, 'They're doing all right, aren't they, 2–0 up already?' I couldn't believe it. She thought they had scored two goals. I think it was the surge forward at the corner-kicks that had confused her.

It marked the end of our relationship. It was never the same after that. I mean, how can you take anyone seriously who doesn't know when a goal has been scored? She finished up marrying a Tory councillor in London. She's probably running the country now.

HUGH O'NEILL
St John Ambulance

There was this wonderful woman who used to go to every match. She was a real character. She was getting on a bit but she was always there in the Kop, never missed a match. She always wore dark glasses. I don't know what her name was, we used to call her 'Ma'. She used to give the players some stick, she'd call them for everything. She died a few years ago, but she continued going on the Kop right to the end. She had cancer but she'd still be there. Some weeks she could barely stand, so we used to let her sit on our stretcher. She was a true Kopite, a wonderful character.

I've dealt with every imaginable illness at Anfield, but the one that has to be the best was the woman who gave birth. She was a fanatical Liverpool supporter and insisted on going to every Liverpool game and standing on the Kop, even though she was pregnant. Anyhow, it was a Boxing Day in the early 1970s. Midway through the second half, we got a call to see this woman. She said she was feeling ill. It was quite clear she was pregnant, so I asked her when the baby was due. 'This week,' she replied. Well, it was obvious why she was feeling ill. So we thought we had better take her to the first-aid room at the Anfield Road End. Before we could get her there, she went into labour. Eventually, we managed to get her there, and fortunately we had someone who was a midwife with us that week, so she was able to deliver the baby in the first-aid room at Anfield. I think it was probably the first and only birth at the ground. What a nice place to be born.

LINDA WINROW
Kopite

Love certainly blossomed on the Kop for me. I suppose it all began about twenty-six years ago. My mother and sister used to go on the Kop, and I was always the one left at home to baby-sit. Then one day my mother couldn't go, so I went instead. I was hooked from the word go, and I've been coming ever since. So that's how I started.

I then began to go to the away games, and I met my husband-to-be on an away trip to Watford. I next saw him at the supporters' club, and we started going to matches together. He had always stood at the back of the Kop with his mates and, when we went to matches, that's where he continued to go. I had always gone near the front where I could see and I stayed there, but after a while I decided to join him at the back.

It was Liverpool Football Club that brought us together and, after twenty-four years of married life, here we are still going to the match together. He's gone for a drink with his mates down town as usual this afternoon, and I'm here at the supporters' club having a drink with my pals. And we'll all meet up at the usual spot on the Kop later.

People do wonder if being a girl might lead to problems on the Kop. But I can tell you I've never had any problems. Anyrate, Liverpool women are pretty street-wise and know how to deal with these things. If somebody starts pushing up a bit too close for comfort, you just shove them away. You soon learn how to deal with it.

I kept coming on the Kop when I was pregnant and never thought twice about it. In fact, I was coming here when I was six months pregnant. After that, I thought I had better stop. And now I go on the Kop not just with my husband, but with grown-up children as well.

STEPHEN F. KELLY
Writer

The day Liverpool clinched the double in 1986 has to be one of the greatest moments in the club's history. But, for me, it was to pose just about the worst dilemma any man can ever face.

I had gone to the game with my girlfriend, Judith, and we had found ourselves a good spot up on the Wembley terraces behind the goal. I'll swear there were more than 110,000 in the ground that day. The crush was terrible. Getting into the ground had been a nightmare as well. Outside, the crowd had been frightening. Fans were climbing up the walls, and the gatemen were being slipped fivers to let people in. A number of gatemen were later prosecuted. I've been to Wembley countless times but never before, nor since, have I known it to be so crushed.

Anyhow, things settled down once the match had kicked off. Liverpool began badly, and Everton were by far the better team for all but twenty minutes. After half an hour, Liverpool were trailing by a goal, and it really was not looking good for them. They seemed ragged at the back and were dragging their tired limbs around Wembley.

Then suddenly, fifteen minutes into the second half, out of nowhere they struck. It was 1–1 and, with the scent of the double in their nostrils, Liverpool now began to play like champions. Molby was swinging the ball from one flank to the other, and Rush was starting to make his sprints into the box.

The tension was fantastic, and the Liverpool crowd were beginning to sense that the double really was on. Then, suddenly, Judith turned round to me and whispered the immortal words: 'I think I'm going to faint.'

'Yeah, it's certainly getting exciting,' I replied above the din.

'No, seriously, I feel ill, I'm going to faint. I'm going to have to go,' she said.

Now here was my dilemma. Liverpool were about to strike again. But what was I to do? Do I escort her out of the ground, or do I say, 'See you after the match?' Of course, there was only one thing I could do.

'See you after the match,' I replied.

So off she went, staggering through the bemused crowd, white-faced and with sweat glistening on her brow. Somebody asked if she was an Everton supporter beating a quick retreat. Then I thought, but where on earth will I see her? Wembley is a big place and, with at least 100,000 people here, there isn't a hope in hell of finding her again. But suddenly Liverpool scored, and Judith was forgotten. Within minutes, bedlam had been let loose. Then Liverpool sneaked a third goal, and the double was won. Everyone was bouncing up and down.

That's the other thing I remember. The terraces were literally moving up and down as we all bounced. I had visions of that entire Wembley terrace collapsing. For a moment it was frightening, although a civil engineer later assured me that there was enough of a built-in factor to compensate for that kind of movement.

Anyhow, the final whistle went and, just as I was beginning to wonder what to do about Judith, she appeared at my side, a huge smile across her face. No, she hadn't been out of the ground. She had gone further up the terracing where the air was clearer, and had recuperated, hastened no doubt by a couple of Liverpool goals. How she ever found me again I shall never know. Astonishingly, she later agreed to marry me. But she could never say that she did not know where my first loyalty lay.

FOOTBALL-CRAZY
(Sung to the tune of 'Football-Crazy')

Oh, he's football-crazy,
He's football-bloody-mad,
And football it has robbed him,
Of the little bit of sense he had.
And it would take a dozen skivvies,
His clothes to rub and scrub,
Since Jack became a member of that
     Liverpool Football Club.

And his wife says she'll divorce him,
If Jackie doesn't keep
Away from football-kicking,
At night when he's asleep.
Well, he calls her Ian Callaghan
And other things so droll.
Last night he kicked her out of bed,
And shouted, 'It's a goal!'

Oh, he's football-crazy,
He's football-bloody-mad,
And football it has robbed him,
Of that little bit of sense he had.

> *And it would take a dozen skivvies,*
> *His clothes to rub and scrub,*
> *Since jack became a member of that*
> *Liverpool Football Club.'*

WENDY DOIG
Kopite

It would be very difficult to forget the day I got engaged.
It was the day Liverpool won the FA Cup for the first
time. It was 1 May 1965. My boyfriend, John, had been
to Wembley and had seen them beat Leeds in extra-time.
He came home that evening and came straight to the
Blundellsands Hotel in Crosby, where I was working as a
receptionist. Everybody in the hotel was having a wild
time. Well, John came in and, of course, he was drunk,
totally drunk. 'Right,' he said, 'that's it. We're getting
engaged.' I'd only known him six months, but I accepted.
I suppose you could say I knew what I was letting myself
in for.

JUDITH JONES
Kopite

Having an interest in football is something I can remember from childhood – maybe that's just the way it is in
Liverpool. To start with, I supported Everton. I think it
had something to do with the way they came back against
Sheffield Wednesday in the 1966 FA Cup final. But
Liverpool soon became the more successful of the two
Liverpudlian clubs and, probably in the era of the Beatles,
the more glamorous. So at the tender age of nine I
switched allegiances and never looked back.

My dad took me to my first football match around the
age of 10 but, anxious to protect the tender sensibilities of
his daughter, insisted that we went in the Anfield Road
End, from where I could only watch in wonder at the
Kop. I can't recall too much of that first visit, but I do

have vivid memories of going down into the centre of Liverpool in years to come to welcome home Cup-winning sides. I was even once in a lift with Ian Callaghan and Gerry Byrne, but was too dumbstruck to ask for their autographs.

Whilst studying French I had to spend several months working in the north of France. Fortunately, I was working alongside a fanatical Kevin Keegan supporter, so we could discuss football and I'm sure my accounts of the Kop helped European understanding. Marie-Claire invited me to watch her local team, Lens, and the contrast between that match and what I was used to at Anfield only reinforced my homesickness. (It is an all-too-common phenomenon that scousers do not travel well!) There was none of the bustle, the singing, the humour of the Kop – rather the French supporters sat down on the terraces tucking into their baguettes stuffed with cheese and pâté, while a youth match served as a prelude to the main feature. And even the arrival of the home side didn't seem to arouse much enthusiasm in the crowd.

In later years, my choice of where to live and work was seriously influenced by whether they had a team in the first division, and whether I could get to see the Reds. Well, why else would you want to live in Wolverhampton? Finally, I saw the error of my ways and returned to live in Liverpool. Those were the glory years. Liverpool had known nothing but success for almost as long as I could remember. The city may have been dying on its feet, but at least we could still be proud of our football team. As a woman I never felt intimidated on the Kop; I may have been teased but never harassed. My one moment of fear actually came at Wembley following the 1977 Cup final against Manchester United. Leaving the ground after the match, I felt concerned at the number of people all pushing to get out and had almost a premonition of what should happen if someone fell.

The years passed, and boyfriends came and went, until I found a man with a spare season ticket. Our first date was supposed to be a home match against Stoke, but I was playing hard to get and missed a 5–1 victory and a Kenny Dalglish hat-trick. That was surely a sign. I accepted the next invitation, and we never looked back. A few years later we were married. I suppose you could say that was going to extremes just to get hold of a season ticket.

It seemed like Liverpool's success would go on for ever, and then came Heysel. I could never feel quite the same about the club after that – somehow all the pride I had felt at being a Liverpudlian was tainted and, rather than boasting of it, I sometimes felt more ashamed. It was like the end of a dream; real life had broken in. Memories of Hillsborough can still reduce me to tears. My son's first visit to the Kop was not the event I had anticipated with such excitement: it was to the shrine it had become in the days which followed the tragedy. It would never be the same.

Seven

THE KOP ON TOUR

Allez Les Rouges

LIVERPOOL FOOTBALL ECHO
25 April 1914

1914 CUP FINAL, LIVERPOOL v BURNLEY

Something like 20,000 excited, shouting people left Liverpool for London last evening, and the enthusiasm bubbled over into the morning and filled one of the biggest trains on record. For the early 'football special' which left Lime Street at 7:40 this morning carried over 1,200 people. Eighteen coaches and a half had to be used to transfer the population of a 'village' from Liverpool to London in one swoop.

And the travelling 'village' from Merseyside was very happy. They did not seem to mind the crush, although in many places they were packed in like cigars in a box. But that generally was their own fault. They came in parties and refused to be separated; so if fifteen or sixteen came together they crammed into one compartment, preferring to suffer the discomfort of standing or sitting on one another's knees to the cruel alternative of splitting up and being unable to discuss the possibilities of the match together.

BILLY O'DONNELL
Kopite

I went to my first away match in the 1930s after I had started working. There were special trains, much like there are today. They were cheap, and we used to have a good day out. I remember some of my mates were going to Wolverhampton to see Liverpool. They'd queued up half the night for a ticket and then had to queue to get a train ticket. Well, I hadn't bothered. I was in the pub with them on the Friday night. They were all laughing cos I didn't have a ticket. I said: 'Well, I'll come down to the station with you in the morning and see you off.' So, at 8 a.m. the next morning, I'm down the station when someone says, 'Hey, there's some tickets left for the train over at the kiosk.' So I thought I'll take a chance. So I bought a ticket.

Anyhow, when we got to the ground, there was someone outside with bundles of tickets for the game. There was no problem getting in. So I went to the game without having had to queue all night. My mates were furious. I remember going to Molineux for another match during the 1950s. We were beaten 1–3 that day. But, with ten minutes to go, an announcement comes over the tannoy: 'For the benefit of all Liverpool supporters, the pubs will be opened immediately after the game ends.' Can you imagine that today!

BOB AZURDIA
Radio Merseyside

Since the 1970s, I've been to just about every game Liverpool have played, usually working. I've commentated from all over Europe. And the thing that has always amazed me is that, no matter where Liverpool play, the Kop turns up. Wherever you go in the world you will find Kopites. I don't know how they managed to get to some of the places, or even how they afforded it, but somehow they would get there. They even succeeded in getting behind the Iron Curtain and to the remotest of places, like Petrolul in Romania or Trabzonspur in Turkey.

Shankly had this wonderful relationship with them. He would always go and chat with them if he saw them around, acknowledging that they had made such efforts to follow the team. You'd see him standing there outside the ground clutching a bundle of tickets. 'Any of you lads without tickets?' he'd be asking as he doled out the tickets. He was a great believer in the ordinary punter.

PHIL ASPINALL
Kopite

We went to Ipswich on the train once. It was about 1975, and in those days you could take as much ale on the train as you wanted. So we had quite a lot. There was this lad, Billy, with us and he managed to drink a whole bottle of Martini during the journey, as well as a few beers. He was pretty drunk. So, just as the train is getting close to Ipswich, he says, 'I don't feel very well, I'm just going to the toilet.' So off he went.

Anyhow, the train gets into Ipswich, and somehow or other we all forgot about Billy. We probably assumed he was somewhere with another bunch of lads on the train. What they do at Ipswich is to put the train in a siding, and everyone gets off and goes to the match, and they leave the train in the siding until after the game. Well, we're all at the ground, and someone says, 'Hey, where's Billy?' Nobody knew, but we didn't think too much about it. Anyhow, after the game we go back to the station, and they pull the train out of the siding and we're all climbing on, when someone shouts, 'Hey, dere's Billy.'

'All right,' says Billy. 'Da was quick. Are we all ready for the game, den?'

'Warra y'mean,' I says. 'Der game's over. We drew 2–2.'

'Ah, go way,' says Billy. 'C'mon, les go.'

Well, he wouldn't believe us. He was half-way home before he was convinced. He'd gone into the toilet and just flaked out and then woke up as they started shunting the train back to the platform after the game. He'd been unconscious the whole time.

JOHN TOSHACK
(Sung to the tune of 'Men of Harlech')

John Toshack is always scoring,
John Toshack is always scoring,
Then you hear the Kopites roaring,
Toshack is our king.

JIM GARDINER
Kopite

I was born and brought up in Edinburgh, and as a youngster I went to watch the Hibs. Then, in December 1970, Liverpool came to play Hibs in the old Fairs Cup. I always remember that night. Toshack scored, and Liverpool won 1–0. I was only 12 at the time. The atmosphere that night was also remarkable because Liverpool had brought two or three thousand supporters with them. Most Scottish football fans also supported an English side, so after that game I decided to support Liverpool.

The next thing I remember was hopping over the border to watch the 1971 Cup final against Arsenal. We didn't get that game on Scottish television, but I didn't have too far to travel to find an English set where I could watch. I then started going to see Liverpool when they played anywhere near Scotland. I went to see my first game at Anfield during the 1973–74 season. They were playing QPR and won 2–1. There were 50,000 at Anfield that day, and I only just got into the ground. Naturally, I went on the Kop. I was in there at about 2 p.m., and it felt great. It still felt great at 3 p.m., but by half-time I had been knocked around a bit. I wasn't able to move most of the time. It was also hot, very hot, and there was a lot of swaying every time Liverpool attacked. But the atmosphere was great.

I think the other thing I liked about Liverpool, and English soccer generally, is that there is none of the religious bigotry that afflicts Scottish football. People occasionally mention that Liverpool used to be a Protestant team but, if they ever were – and I don't think there is much evidence to support that theory – it's all been lost in the mists of time. I was at an age when I was beginning to realise and understand the influence of religion in Scottish football, and I did not like it.

Anyrate, I enjoyed the occasion so much that, from then on, I started saving all my money and coming down to Liverpool. I couldn't afford to come to every game but I got to quite a few. Sometimes I'd persuade mates to come down, and we'd go in their cars; other times I would hitch-hike or go on the train. I even travelled in the guard's van a few times trying to avoid the ticket inspector. I'd always go in the same spot, and I got to know the people around me. We became friends, and many of them are still good pals. I felt that I was part of something. When Liverpool won, you felt that you too had played a role in the victory. It was all to do with Shanks. He was the man of the people.

By this time, I was working for the civil service. I was earning more money and I was able to go to more games. Eventually, I was watching them in all games, home and away. I was also going to all the European matches and on the pre-season tours. I think I've been to virtually every game in this country since the late 1970s. You could count the ones I've missed on one hand. And I've been to almost all the European games as well.

About three years ago, I finished up getting a job in Liverpool, but that was a coincidence. I had been transferred around the country a few times. In the civil service you go where they ask you to. I'd worked in Glasgow, Leighton Buzzard, Worthing, but I never let on very much to my superiors about my football activities. Then, one day, the boss called me into the office and told me that they wanted me to do a new job. It was a promotion. The only problem, he said, was that I would have to move . . . to the north-west, to Liverpool. How did I feel about that? I told him I'd go away and give it a little thought! I can tell you, it was like winning the pools. I wouldn't move from here now for anything.

How much does it all cost me? I dread to think. In fact, it's the kind of thing you deliberately don't calculate, but it's certainly a lot of money. I've only missed a couple of games in the last ten years. I'm not married, I have my mortgage and I enjoy a pint, and all the rest goes on following Liverpool. It's become a way of life and, whatever the expense, it has been worthwhile. I once had to sell my car. It wasn't much of a car, mind you. That was for the 1984 European Cup final in Rome. I was about 26 or 27. I'd just bought my first flat, and there was no way I could afford to go to the final, so I sold the car. It was an old Chrysler Alpine. I didn't get much of a price for it either, but it was worth it.

People might think it odd, but I've seen countries that many of them have never been to. I'm not extravagant when I travel. I always go the cheapest way. I'll stay in youth hostels if necessary. The pre-season tours are the most expensive. Once upon a time, there would be a couple of thousand going on those pre-season tours, but now there's only half a dozen of us.

Last summer, Liverpool were playing up near the Arctic Circle, and we had to get four flights from Oslo to get there. It was the cheapest way. We arrived in this place – there were only four of us – for the last game of the tour. It was a Saturday night, and we went to this bar for a drink. We didn't have much money and, with a pint of lager costing about £3, we just about had enough for a round. Anyhow, I went to the bar and ordered the drinks; then the bar-man called this girl over and started talking to her about something. Then she says, 'Oh, are you from Liverpool?' Here we go, I thought, we're going to be kicked out as football hooligans. I said, 'Yes, is that a problem?' She says, 'No, the drinks are all free for you players.' Well, me a Liverpool player! I'm 20 stone. Who did she think I was, Jan Molby! Anyhow, we weren't going to question it. To cut a long story short, it turned out that the Liverpool players were coming in later that night. That was at eight o'clock; we were there until four in the morning. Now I don't normally associate with the players. I think they like a bit of privacy, and that should be respected; I'm not one of the hangers-on. I think the players respect you more for it. Anyhow, I put my principles aside that night, and we had a good few drinks. The players eventually arrived, and we had a great time together.

My best memories are of that 1984 European Cup final. But there was a lot of trouble after the game. When we left the stadium we came through this underpass, and suddenly everything was being thrown down at us by the Roma supporters. Bottles, stones, they had knives as well. I don't mind admitting that I was frightened. We just ran as fast as we could and jumped on the first coaches we could spot. There was also trouble when Liverpool played Juventus in the Super Cup. That was quite nasty. I actually got a lift on the press coach to the stadium that night, and all sorts of things were being thrown at us.

You could sense there was something fermenting before Heysel. It was appallingly policed there that night. But that's not to excuse what happened. I knew there had been deaths, I had walked around the back of that terrace and had seen the bodies covered in sheets. I just wanted to get out of the ground. I walked away and went back to the coach, but the police told me I would be safer inside the ground. So I went back to the stadium and stood at the back of the crowd, but I wasn't really watching. I didn't want to see the game, although it was probably right for it to go ahead because, had it not been played, I dread to think what might have happened outside the ground as they let the two sets of fans out. It would have been terrible.

Something went out of Liverpool Football Club that night. Some of the magic disappeared. A lot of people never went on the Kop again after Heysel. I said the same when I got back home but, after the summer, I felt different and I returned. I could understand what

Grobbelaar felt when he said he wanted to quit the game. Fortunately, there was a long summer break, which gave people time to reflect. But there was no doubt that things have never been the same since Heysel.

I love the Liverpool fans. That Cup final against Wimbledon summed them up. They had just lost the second double, and they were still smiling. It was so silly that they had lost, a joke. I went to Alan Hansen's testimonial a few days later, and more than 30,000 turned up – and that was after losing the Cup. There was a banner there, I always remember it, it said: 'Shankly gave us all the dream; Paisley built the greatest team; Fagan won the famous treble; now Kenny's got the double double.' And they had crossed out the last 'double' on the banner. I thought that was nice. Anywhere else, they would have crucified the manager or the players, but not the Kop. That was the Kop at its best.

Of course, it has to be seated. But it will never be the same, though having said that it hasn't been the same for some years now. They don't cheer or sing anything like they used to. Liverpool fans were the first to do everything. The first to chant, the first to sing, the first with banners. The sight of the Kop with all those banners, that's my memory.

But after Heysel and Hillsborough, something went out of Liverpool. And the night Arsenal won here, something else went. And now something further will go when the Kop's seated. I'd love it to stay as it is. But I would feel uncomfortable if we were still standing after all those people had died. The Kop has been something very special. But now we must build something new. It won't be easy.

BARRY WILFORD
Kopite

It was the Everton/Liverpool derby of the 1982–83 season, the game Liverpool won 5–0 at Goodison. I'd come down from Scotland and went with a few Scottish friends who lived down here and supported Liverpool. We were in the Main Stand at Goodison, that huge triple-decker effort. Anyhow, we were in the middle tier right up towards the Bullens Road End, where all the Kopites were massed behind the goal. The part of the stand that we were in was also full of Liverpool supporters. It was an amazing game, because Ian Rush hit four goals and Everton were thrashed on their own territory.

We were aware of these three girls a row or so in front of us. They were young and quite attractive and were squawking and screaming every time Liverpool scored. And when Ian Rush hit his hat-trick, they went mad, standing up and waving their arms to the Kopites behind the goal. I think at that point everybody noticed them.

Anyhow, ten minutes or so later, Rush hits his fourth goal and Liverpool's fifth. You can imagine, everyone went crazy, especially these girls, who suddenly pulled their jumpers up and bared their naked breasts to the Kopites and started bouncing their tits around. Suddenly, the entire Bullens Road End stopped cheering Rush and turned to look at these lassies. Everyone was looking at them. There was bedlam. Behind us people were shouting, 'Hey, this way too, lerrus have a look as well.' There was a mini-stampede going on. The Kopites were going bananas.

Finally, we all sat down and started praying for another goal, wondering what kind of celebration that might produce. Then the Kopites all started chanting at these girls, 'Give us another look, give us another look.' Then the Evertonians joined in as well. 'Warra bout us, warra bout us!' they were singing. Unfortunately, no sixth goal ever came.

PHIL ASPINALL
Kopite

We were going to St Étienne. We didn't have much cash, so before we left I went to Asda and I bought a whole pile of tins of baked beans and sausages. I had this rucksack full of these tins, and I also had a small Primus stove and a load of paper plates. I didn't have a train ticket for the journey, but we got on anyhow. Well, there we were on the train going from London to Dover, and we're all starting to feel a bit hungry. There's fifteen of us scousers in this train compartment, and someone says, 'Eh, I feel a bit peckish.'

So I gets the stove out and the tins of beans and says, 'Ere are, I'll cook us up some beans.' So I'm sitting there with the stove on the shelf by the window, and I'm heating up these beans in the tin when the ticket inspector comes in.

'Ay,' he shouts, 'you can't have a fire in here. Come on, put that out.'

'Ah, come on,' we says, 'we're starving, we just want something to eat.'

'No,' he says. 'You can't do that on British Rail. It's not allowed. You might start a fire. Put it out.'

Well, this goes on for a little while and, in the end, he finally persuaded us to put it out. He was so thankful. I think he was a bit worried. 'Thanks, lads,' he says. 'I've seen everything on this train, but I've never seen fifteen scousers cooking tins of beans on a stove before.'

And with that he went. And totally forgot to ask us for our tickets.

PHIL ASPINALL
Kopite

It was 1976. I hadn't planned to go to Barcelona, but I went to Anfield on the Saturday before the Barcelona game and started to wish that I was going. We were in the pub after the match, and we'd had a few ales and we were feeling pretty good, and everyone was talking about how well we'd do against Barcelona. So suddenly I decided, I'm going. So I just says to everyone, 'I'm going, I've decided.'

'How are you going to get there?' they all asked.

'I'll hitch,' I said. Then one of my mates says, 'Ere, I'll come with you.' So after closing time I said, 'Hang on, cos I'm just going home to get me banner.'

So I dashed home, got my banner, and half an hour later I met Billy, and we made our way to the East Lancs Road and started hitching. Anyrate, it was dark and it was raining, and after a while the ale was beginning to wear off. We finally got a lift at 3 a.m. in the morning, and he took us a mile down the road and dropped us off. So we started hitching again. By 4 a.m., we were very wet, and the ale had worn off completely. So I said to Billy, 'Come ed, I'm going home.' So we went home.

JOHNNY KENNEDY
Radio City DJ

I used to go away to all the matches, both in Europe and other grounds, with the same group of me mates. We all drank in a pub called The Cannon, which was on the corner of Cannon Road in Liverpool. We all travelled together, and there are pubs all over the country – we were the Kopites on tour – pubs all over Britain where we were so welcome year in, year out.

There was a pub called the Dearne Grove Inn, near Barnsley. This, again, is an example of Liverpool wit. We'd been to see Liverpool versus Arsenal at Hillsborough, and we were in a transit van, twelve or fifteen of us, and we found this pub. Immediately across the road there was some waste ground that we parked on and, as we were walking across the road, Billy Edwards, one of the lads, looked at the name of the pub and said, 'This'll do us, the Daren't Go In.' So that became the name of the pub for us.

But we did go in. It was empty, of course – it was only about six o'clock – not a soul in, and suddenly fifteen scousers are through the door. Anyhow, the landlady's name was Mary. She was a nice woman, a little bit guarded at first with fifteen scousers coming in. We ordered a load of ale and, of course, everybody paid for the ale, no problem there. We'd been shouting all afternoon, so the pints disappeared in quick time, so we're back again for fifteen more pints, black-and-tans, brown mixed and all that. So she's already taken more money than she's taken all day and, of course, the lads were laughing and joking, and she was laughing with us. She was a really nice woman and she took a shine to us. In the first hour we had spent a fortune. She's thrilled to bits; it's not seven o'clock yet, and she's quids in the till. Anyhow, she said, 'Why don't you stay the evening,' so we decided we would. We'd had a few ales by this time and we always had the guitars, and everybody agreed later it was the greatest night out we'd ever had in a pub.

We went back subsequently on a few occasions and had great times. But it was a magical night that first night. She went upstairs and made us food, brought a tape recorder down and asked us to sing 'Scouser Tommy'. She loved it. And top of all that, much to our surprise, one of our lads opened the *Echo* one night, and there's a letter from her saying what great ambassadors we had been for the city of Liverpool.

SONS OF THE KOP
(Sung to the tune of 'The Soldier's Song')

Sons of the Kop,
Liverpudlians are we.
We will travel anywhere
For Liverpool to see.
We will go to Hampden Park
And to Europe too,
Because you can't beat the boys from the
Spion Kop
That made old Liverpool's name.

Loyalists are we,
Whose lives are pledged to Liverpool.

We have come (where from?)
From the mighty Spion Kop.
Sworn to be red,
We're loyal Liverpudlians,
We'll follow our team
Throughout the land,
Tonight we'll raise the red flag high for
   Liverpool,
We'll live and die,
And as we march, eternal light,
We will chant the loyal song:
Liverpool-Liverpool-Liverpool.

PHIL ASPINALL
Kopite

When Liverpool got into the semi-finals of the European Cup in 1977, I was out of work. I'd spent all my cash in going to see Liverpool play in St Étienne and I hardly had anything left. I didn't think I was going to be able to go. Then I got an idea.

You know those silk scarves they sell around the ground? Well, I thought, I'll buy some of them and sell them in Zurich, see if I can finance the trip. So I went to Anfield and I bought thirty of these silk scarves at 30p each. Anyhow, when I got to Switzerland I sold the lot at £10 each. Couldn't get rid of them quick enough. The Swiss fans just wanted anything that had Liverpool's name on it.

I'd gone with a mate of mine, and he'd only bought ten cos he didn't think we'd get shot of them. Anyhow, it turned out he didn't have the heart to sell them for £10. He thought it was exploitation. So I says to him, 'Ere, I'll buy them off you for £5,' so he says, 'OK.' Couldn't understand that. He wouldn't sell them to the Swiss for a tenner, but he'd sell them to me for a fiver.

Anyhow, I had no trouble getting rid of his lot at £10 a go as well. So I finished up having four days in a hotel, paying for my tickets, my train fare, and as much ale and food as I could take, and I came home with £4 more than I'd started.

JOHN CULL
Chief programme seller

EUROPEAN CUP-WINNERS' CUP FINAL, HAMPDEN PARK, GLASGOW, 5 MAY 1966

Borussia Dortmund 2	Liverpool 1 (aet)
Held, Libuda	*Hunt*

Attendance: 41,657.

We left Liverpool by car at about 9 a.m. It was already raining then. It poured the entire journey to Glasgow. It took us ages, because the M6 only went as far as Carnforth in those days. We got there about 3 p.m., and all afternoon it rained. We were like drowned cats wandering around Glasgow, looking for shelter. Everywhere there were Liverpool supporters all soaking wet. Then, at night, it just threw it down. Hampden didn't have any cover in those days, the terraces were open, and we got drenched. The water was cascading down the terraces like a waterfall. It was terrible.

And the game wasn't much better, either. We lost in extra-time. Liverpool never really looked like winning. The Germans went ahead in the second half, but we equalised. Then, in extra time, Libuda blasted a shot from way out, and Tommy Lawrence was left stranded. Roger Hunt missed a good opportunity towards the end, but it just wasn't to be our day. The rain said it all.

We had expected about 110,000 at the game, but in the end only 40,000 braved the conditions. We finally got home about 4 a.m. in the morning. Coming down the East Lancs Road, the police had erected a check-point and were stopping everybody. Some cars had been stolen in Glasgow, and they were checking all the vehicles. It was a long hold-up. We were very weary when we eventually arrived back at the house.

Liverpool: Lawrence, Lawler, Byrne, Milne, Yeats, Stevenson, Callaghan, Hunt, St John, Smith, Thompson.

Borussia Dortmund: Tilkowski, Cyliax, Redder, Kurrat, Paul, Assauer, Libuda, Schmidt, Held, Sturm, Emmerich.

STEPHEN F. KELLY
Writer

DIVISION ONE, 8 MAY 1972

Arsenal 0   Liverpool 0

Attendance: 39,289.

It's not just the great moments you remember, but the tears as well. And, with me, it's always Arsenal who seem to have brought so much heartache. Although the obvious game to talk about is that epic final match of the 1988-89 season at Anfield, when Michael Thomas scored in injury-time, I have other appalling memories of Arsenal.

I always remember being at Highbury for the last game of the 1971–72 season. It was all very complicated. Derby County were top of the table, but had finished all their fixtures and had gone away on holiday. Leeds and Liverpool had one game left. Leeds were favourites to win the title as they had only to play Wolves at home. I think a draw would have been good enough for them. Anyhow, Liverpool's last game was away to Arsenal. Nobody really reckoned they had much chance, as it meant Leeds had to lose and Liverpool had to win to take the title. Of the three contenders, Leeds were favourites with Derby second favourites, and Liverpool some way off the reckoning.

The game was at night, and I parked myself at the Clock End at Highbury among all the Liverpool supporters, most of whom, like me, were exiled scousers. I was right behind the goal. Late into the second half, the news came over on someone's radio that Wolves had taken the lead against Leeds. Liverpool were still drawing 0–0. So we all started chanting, 'Wolverhampton Wanderers, Wolverhampton Wanderers!' I think the Liverpool players soon got the message because they began to throw everything at Arsenal. They were kicking down towards the Clock End where all us scousers were standing, and it was getting really frantic. Just one goal, but the minutes were ticking away.

I always remember this. I was getting really anxious and I didn't think we were going to make it. 'We're not going to do it,' I shouted out to some bloke next to me. I don't know who he was, but I always remember what he said. 'Don't worry, son,' he replied, 'we'll make it.' His optimism was astonishing. It was a typical Kopite response. We're not finished. A minute later, John Toshack put the ball in the back of the net and we all went berserk but, just as we came back to earth, the referee was pointing for a free-kick. Toshack was offside. To this day, I refuse to believe that Toshack was offside. I know he wasn't.

And so it was gone, another league title hope dashed. Only one goal, and Liverpool would have been champions. In the end, Derby County, sitting in some Spanish hotel, heard on the radio that they were league champions. I was living in north London then, and I couldn't bear to catch the bus home with all those gleeful Arsenal fans. So I walked the two miles through the wet and lonely streets, feeling so sorry for myself. And all I could think about was how the Gunners had robbed us again. I could barely bring myself to speak when I got home. I just wanted to be alone.

Arsenal: Barnett, Rice (Roberts), Nelson, Storey, McLintock, Ball, Simpson, Armstrong, Radford, Kennedy, Graham.
Liverpool: Clemence, Lawler, Lindsay, Smith, Lloyd, Hughes, Keegan, Heighway, Toshack, Callaghan, Hall.

PHIL THOMPSON
Liverpool player, 1971–85

EUROPEAN CUP FINAL, ROME, 25 MAY 1977

Liverpool 3   Borussia Moenchengladbach 1
McDermott, Smith,
Neal (pen)   *Simonsen*

Attendance: 57,000.

I was injured for the 1977 European Cup final and didn't play, but I went with the lads nevertheless. Half an hour or so before kick-off, we all decided to go on the pitch and have a walk around. We came out of one end of the Olympic Stadium, and what a sight. The entire Kop had been shifted from Anfield to Rome. The atmosphere was electric. It was like everyone was having a holiday. There were so many chequered flags and banners, it seemed that everybody had one. I always remember the eyes of our players. They were transfixed. We just walked towards them. Nobody said anything. We were gobsmacked. Looking at them gave us such a kick to go out and win that match. No way could we lose that night. That was the best without a shadow of a doubt.

Liverpool: Clemence, Neal, Jones, Smith, Kennedy, Hughes, Keegan, Case, Heighway, Callaghan, McDermott.

Borussia Moenchengladbach: Kneib, Vogts, Klinkhammer, Wittkamp, Bonhof, Wohlers (Hannes), Simonsen, Wimmer (Kulik), Stielike, Schaffer, Heynckes.

BRIAN JAMES
Sportswriter

Liverpool v Borussia Moenchengladbach

At Rome airport, then at the team's hotel, we ran into the advance guard of the red army of Liverpool fans. Eventually, there were to be an astonishing 26,000 of them,

drawn up like some monstrous legion in the eternal city
... someone did his sums and worked out that they'd
spent £1 million on travel alone, just to get there. Some
had left by car or coach straight from Wembley last
Saturday; others had had a nightmare three-day journey
by train with a five-hour wait at one point with no heat,
light or water in the carriage. Their clothes were ruined,
their faces looked wrecked, but at the sight of Hughes, or
Jones, or Paisley, they broke into instant cheering. And
their enthusiasm, like the journey's laughter, only increased my own pessimism.

By nightfall, in a hotel so packed with non-residents in
red it became a struggle to get a coffee or your room-key,
I was convinced Liverpool had thrown away their European Cup chance: they were in the wrong hotel, at the
wrong time, had arrived there the wrong way and in the
wrong frame of mind. Travelling with their wives and
their rowdy mates seemed a mistake. Staying in the city
instead of in the cooler hills outside was surely another.
Being so available to the TV crews, radio mikes and
reporters' notebooks was a clear error; being in a position
to be pestered by fans four-deep wherever they walked
seemed a disaster. Most other British teams, and *every*
continental side, would have isolated a team in Liverpool's position as if they had the plague. They would have
flown last Sunday to a tranquil pub in a forest somewhere,
with security men to ration reporters' access. That would
have been the *professional* approach to this game –
this was a *package-tour* preparation, for which I was
convinced Liverpool players would have to meet the bill.

Listening to coach Joe Fagan in a bedroom corridor on
our way to breakfast next morning did not remove all
doubts: 'Lose today? Forget it,' he insisted. 'Last Saturday
our attitude was all wrong. Going to the match it was just
another Cup final. If that sounds daft remember we had
been playing games as important as that for weeks ...
seventeen of them in three weeks to be exact. But today's
different ... I've already been round most of the rooms.

They're tingling . . . anxious to be at it . . . want to get out there and make them Germans have a bit of it . . .' He made a punch-up gesture with his fist by way of farewell at the lift.

Nevertheless, the day lasted an age. It was a relief to reach the stadium an hour earlier than necessary, to feel that at last the end was beginning. (Reporters get butterflies, too, at these big matches. Like the players they are performers in that what they say, and how they say it, with only seconds to compose their phrase and arguments, will be judged next day by literally millions of readers, and compared by self-elected juries of their professional peers. 'He had a bad European Cup/World Cup,' is a dismissive judgement that a sports journalist can take years to live down.) We spent the time playing Spot the German.

But the Olympic Stadium clearly belonged to Liverpool . . . a singing, dancing, flaunting horde that seemed to fill the bowl. The only unit of identifiable Gladbach fans was represented by a small square of green figures high up opposite the Main Stand – they looked like a patch of moss and were to wither and disappear long before the end.

Someone nearby looked deep into this scene of Hogarthian revelry and said: 'I think the foreigners' idea that every Englishman looks like David Niven is destroyed for ever tonight.' It was a nice remark, but wrong. For just then Liverpool's team appeared – and in the next two hours they reincarnated the ideal of the foppishly-cool, elegantly-deadly, effortlessly-precise, innately-gracious English Milord – with their football. They stepped straight on to the pitch, slung aside with their tracksuit tops all the misery of Saturday, all the distracting bonhomie of the days since, and even their homeland reputation for ploughing through games like some machine. The stuff they played now was of a different style entirely; from that endless larder of Liverpool resources they reached to a seldom-touched shelf and produced a game-plan that was all about containing, patient, probing attacks pressed home with wit and invention. And when repulsed, they simply went back and built another.

They scored a goal in twenty-seven minutes: Callaghan to Heighway, Heighway forward and then, as Callaghan, Case and Kennedy all made decoy runs as though taking part in some Merseyland morris dance, Heighway through for McDermott to slide past Kneib. It took a rare mistake by Case to give Simonsen an equaliser after an hour ('the noise you heard at that moment which sounded like thunder,' Hughes insisted later, 'was just my jaw dropping').

It took brilliant saves by Clemence, from Heynckes and Simonsen, to prevent a setback growing into calamity. But Liverpool supremacy was so overwhelming they were merely setting the stage for the final heroics. First Tommy Smith, whose final match before retirement this was to be, came racing to a corner to score with his head. Then Kevin Keegan, whose farewell match before transfer this was to be, completed a ninety-minute job of destruction on the West German captain Vogts – by provoking a penalty. Phil Neal tucked it away . . . 3–1. And finis.

The Kop-in-Exile went predictably berserk behind a barricade of barbed wire and barking police dogs, but the Kop's representative in the team, Joey Jones, festooned himself with caps, scarves, badges and bowler and led his cart-wheeling team-mates in lap after lap of honour. From that helicopter overhead it must have been like looking down into a strange sort of Hades . . . where every mouth was open to sing, shout or laugh.

Then back to the hotel for the party. It would probably be easier to detail every shot of a civil war than to convey a complete picture of this celebration; I can only give glimpses. Like seeing a fan creep into the banqueting room, run to the table to kiss the cup, and back reverently out, or another supporter who sought out every player in turn and knelt before him, explaining, 'Dey's royalty . . . dat's why' . . . or a third Kopite of ferocious mien and stupendously drunk, swaying in front of the Minister of Sport, Denis Howell: 'We are going to have the greatest booze-up ever . . . but don't worry, Mister, we ain't Leeds . . . and we ain't Manchester United . . . we'll behave. Dat's a promise.' (A promise absolutely kept – Italian papers next day praised Liverpool's football *and* lavishly apologised for the harsh things they'd predicted about the supporters.)

At first, the fans were kept outside. But Emlyn Hughes (who managed the feat of ending the year as a footballer of fabulous achievement and still a very nice man) kept spotting faces above the policemen's helmets – and making a dash for the door with a fresh bottle of champagne. Eventually, though, the cordon broke . . . the mob burst in, took turns at being pictured with the players, or swigging from the cup. At one time, the huge trophy vanished: 'Never fret,' said a Liverpool official. 'It's outside being trooped around the grounds by the fans. Scared? Listen, if we forget it, it'll turn up at Anfield in two days . . . unmarked and polished like new.'

Next morning around dawn, weary waiters cleared away 385 empty champagne bottles, and tireless players tossed passing reporters into the pool, and gardeners prodded bushes and Liverpool fans fell blinking into the sunlight, and every hill in view from the roof of the hotel had little knots of red figures lurching around asking each other, 'What happened to the last coach back to Kirkby?' and it was all over.

EMLYN HUGHES
Liverpool player, 1967–79

Liverpool v Borussia Moenchengladbach

The buffet that we had after the final was the best that I have ever seen. It was miles and miles long. We were all there, the players, wives, club officials and so on. We were so euphoric we just picked at it. Then Bob Paisley, seeing all these Liverpool fans who had discovered our hide-out banging at the doors, said, 'Why don't we let the lads in?' So in these Kopites piled and, within five minutes of these hordes coming in, the buffet was gone, completely gone. You've seen a turkey picked clean. It was like that. It was ravaged. It was like ants had crawled all over it. There must have been a thousand supporters got in to that do. It was a fabulous night, the best ever.

PHIL THOMPSON
Liverpool player, 1971–85

EUROPEAN CUP FINAL, PARIS, 27 MAY 1981

Liverpool 1   Real Madrid 0
A. Kennedy

Attendance: 48,360.

I was captain of the side that won the European Cup in Paris in 1981. When I went up the steps to receive the trophy, the first thing I did was to lift it up and show it to all me mates from The Falcon pub in Kirkby. I had a football team which I helped run there. They'd all come over for the game, and I knew exactly where they were cos they had all these banners and Union Jacks with Kirkby written on them. I wanted to show it to them first cos they were the lads who went on the Kop.

It was a great night, possibly the greatest moment of my career. The crowd was wonderful. Then we went back to Liverpool and, after the tour of the city on the bus, the cup was handed back to me as captain. I had responsibility for looking after it. I had arranged to go down to The Falcon pub after the tour. We were going to have a great party. Anyhow, I took the cup with me and, when I walked in with the European Cup, everyone went mad. We decided to put it behind the bar along with the trophies which the pub team had won. And it stood there all night. We all got a bit plastered. Anyhow, the word got around that the European Cup was on view behind the

bar of The Falcon, and hundreds started descending on
the pub. What a night.

Liverpool: Clemence, Neal, A. Kennedy, Thompson, R.
  Kennedy, Hansen, Dalglish (Case), Lee, Johnson,
  McDermott, Souness.
Real Madrid: Augustin, Garcia Cortes (Pineda),
  Camacho, Sabido, Stielike, Navajas, Del Bosque, Angel,
  Juanito, Santillana, Cunningham.

JOHNNY KENNEDY
Radio City DJ

Liverpool v Real Madrid

The best European Cup final I ever went to was in Paris.
The same lads again. The game itself was not as good as
the other games. We were behind the goal, sitting down,
when 'Barney' scored. We went berserk.

We went celebrating after the game. We'd had a
brilliant time in Paris. We never stopped laughing from
the moment we got there. We went in this little bar
mid-afternoon. These lads were OK, they were boisterous,
singing and all that, but they never caused any bother, no
fighting or anything like that.

We've been in there about an hour, and around about
late afternoon this old French bloke comes in, very
dignified-looking, probably 70-something. He was on his
way home and he called in every night for one drink.
Well, this particular day he saw all us and must have
wondered what was happening to his bar. Anyhow, the
lads bought him a drink and said how nice it was to be in
Paris, and he was delighted. And he sat down with us and,
instead of having his one usual drink, he probably had
about three or four. In the end, he said, 'I must go now,
I've stayed much longer than I normally stay.' And it was
a great moment, this. I can see him now. He stood up, and
he was very slim and nicely dressed, grey hair. He stood
up and said, 'Au revoir', and started to walk out, and as

one man – talking about the Kop on tour – everybody, all of us lads, stood up and started humming the *Marseillaise*. The old fellow was in tears, trickling down his cheeks. That's the kind of lads they were.

After the game we were staying in the Novotel. This particular one was a few miles out of the centre of Paris. The coach driver said, if you're going celebrating after the game I can't be waiting all night for you. I'm going back to the hotel. You can either find your own way back or come back to the hotel, and we can celebrate there. So most of us did that. We met after the game and went straight back to the Novo. Anyrate, when we get there, because there's Real Madrid supporters staying in the hotel as well, the manager had closed the bar. So there was no ale.

We immediately leave the hotel and start looking for a bar. Couldn't find one. It was a very quiet place where we were. Anyhow, we go down this lane, a big gang of us, thirty fellows. And suddenly we saw this chink of light fall across the road. A door opened, a fellow came out and got on a bike. So we ran to the door, and it was a bar. The fellow on the other side of the door said, 'Closed, *fermi.*' We said, 'From Liverpool, just one drink, a little celebration.' So he said, 'How many of you?' Well, there were only a few of us, the rest were straddled out behind us still coming down the lane. So we said, 'Just us,' and went in. But suddenly the place was full. All the lads had legged it down the road.

'Just one drink, sir,' we said. So Sid, who's the sort of leader of us lads, says, 'Quieten down, boys, we're going to mass. Not a word out of anybody.' So the barman says, 'One drink, pay now.' We all had a drink and kept nice and quiet, smiled at him. We got a little bit of rapport going with him, talked about the game and smiled a lot. So he relents a bit, and then we asked for another drink. 'Would you like a drink as well, sir,' we asked him. 'Martini?' 'Oh, thank you very much,' he says. So we gets two out of him. By this time he's warming to us – good lads, these. 'How about the same again, sir, and one yourself?' Anyhow, the next thing is, he's on the phone, ordering food. Well, we're there all night, aren't we? The next thing is, he's cutting loaves in half. A whole loaf sliced in half with ham. Delicious. That was a memorable night. We left in the early hours of the morning.

THE PRIDE OF ALL EUROPE
(Sung to a traditional tune)

We are the pride of all Europe,
The cock of the north,
We hate United and Cockneys, of course,
We only drink whisky,
And bottles of brown,
The Liverpool boys are in town.
Oh, oh, oh,
(Repeat)

Eight

AS OTHERS SEE US

If You Come to Anfield, We'll be Running After You

GEORGE COURTNEY
Former Football League referee

When the letter used to arrive at my home telling me that I was booked to referee at Anfield, I would feel really excited. There was a sense of expectation, because you get that quiver of excitement when you go there. There is nothing bigger in club football than to referee at Liverpool. Professionally, it was a big bonus for me to go there. I didn't even have to get psyched up or do anything to get the adrenalin going. It was automatically done for me simply by being there.

I always looked forward to my two or three visits every season. It was an inspirational place, even for referees. When you referee at Anfield you have to be totally in charge. I would never let the Kop sway me, although I have to admit that it's impossible to gauge how much they can influence you subconsciously. The thing about refereeing at Anfield is that the stage actually enhances your performance. It's a bit like being an actor: the bigger the stage, the better the performance and, as I say, there is no stage bigger than Anfield in club football.

I like their football as well, they just knock the ball about, and it's delightful to watch. It suits me, because I like to keep the game going. The only problem was that sometimes the pace of the game there was a bit knackering.

One reads of referees being intimidated at Anfield and of managers accusing referees but, in my experience, it can be the very opposite. Your awareness is that much greater, and that can work against Liverpool. I used always to give my best performances there. You certainly can't afford to make mistakes, or the Kop will crucify you. When you're concentrating you don't always pick up on what the Kop are yelling but, when there's a lull or an injury, you hear them. I remember once they had been having a particularly difficult time, nothing was going their way, and then I awarded them a penalty. Up came the cry from the Kop, 'Who's the scouser in the black?'

I used to get some abuse from the Kop, but only verbal. Generally I found them very good-humoured. But I was never a great favourite of the Kop by virtue of a few decisions I gave against them at Wembley. But then I did referee that Liverpool/Man. United League Cup final when Grobbelaar might have got his marching orders, and I did give them a penalty when John Barnes went over in the Charity Shield against United. So perhaps they shouldn't have been so begrudging.

Anfield for me was Ronnie Moran and Roy Evans, whom I've known for years, in the dug-out. They were the barometer. I didn't look at the Kop, I looked at the dug-out. And, of course, they were never short of a bit of advice. I always allowed Ronnie to have his say, and I never had to talk to him once. I would just smile across at him, and that seemed to placate him. But it wasn't quite so with Graeme Souness. I've had to speak to him on a couple of occasions, But never with Ronnie. He was always good-humoured and a good barometer of my performance. At the end of a game, I always got a good slap of the hand from him.

I have to say that I've not had too many difficult times at Anfield. I've never sent anyone off there, though I do remember giving a penalty against Liverpool down at the Kop end. It was for Chelsea about five or six years ago. I can't recall the reception I got, but I do remember not standing too close to the byline. I think one of my most memorable games was when Wimbledon came to Anfield and had the audacity to win. I always remember the Kop applauded them off the field at the end.

SANDY ROSS
Television producer

Back in the early 1980s, I was producing an adaptation of Alan Bleasdale's *Scully* for Granada Television. If you remember, Kenny Dalglish is Scully's great hero, and Scully dreams of one day running on to the pitch in Kenny's shirt and playing for Liverpool.

Well, just to be authentic, we decided to film at Anfield. We got the players to agree to run on to the pitch one Saturday twenty minutes before the game kicked off. Scully was going to come on to the pitch with them, wearing Kenny's No. 7 shirt. Kenny, of course, would not be there. So all was agreed. There was a bit of publicity in the papers about it, and I think there was something in the programme. We didn't really expect anything dramatic to happen, we were just letting the crowd know what we were up to. So bang on the dot, at 2:40 p.m., Liverpool came running out on to the pitch and towards the Kop. The Kop was packed. Souness was leading them out, and there at the back was Drew Schofield, the actor who was playing Scully, in Franny's No. 7 shirt.

Well, you should have heard it. The entire Kop suddenly began singing, 'One Franny Scully, there's only one Franny Scully.' It was astonishing, we had never expected anything like that. They all kicked the ball about in front of goal, with Scully knocking a few past the 'keeper. And all the time the Kop is chanting his name, as if he really is the world's greatest player. It was like having an unpaid cast of thousands. In fact, it's probably the largest unpaid cast in the history of British television. It was so good that we used it for our opening titles every week.

GORDON BANKS
Leicester City, Stoke City and England goalkeeper,
1958–72

I played my last ever game at Anfield. But that wasn't intentional. I played there on the Saturday, and then I was involved in the car crash the following day that eventually led to my retirement. Ironically, Stoke's first game of the following season was at Anfield. By then, I was helping out on the coaching side at Stoke, and Bill Shankly, knowing this, very kindly invited me to Anfield as a guest of the club for the day. They made a special presentation to me on the pitch before the match, and then Shankly and I did a lap of honour. Shanks gave me a Liverpool scarf, and I wrapped it around my neck. The Kop gave me a wonderful reception, and it was a very moving and emotional moment. I don't mind admitting that I was tearful. They're lovely people.

I always enjoyed playing in front of the Kop. They were, and still are, a wonderful crowd. I think they realise the volume of noise that they create, and they know that they can undermine goalkeepers. So they put it to good use. But it can also inspire you and, as I always loved playing in front of big crowds, the Kop was always something of an inspiration to me. I was usually very busy there. It was certainly an awesome sight. When you come out, there is this sea of faces. I'm told there could be as many as 25,000 people on the Kop. That's amazing, it's bigger than most clubs can attract to their entire ground.

The thing to me was that they were always very sporting. They obviously wanted their own team to win, but it never stopped them appreciating things which the opposition might do. If they saw something special or a good goal, they would applaud it. And, with me, it was a case of appreciating my goalkeeping. I'd go down and make a save and sometimes I'd find myself lying on the ground looking up at the Kop, and this great crowd would be tumbling down towards me. It was a bit like a wind blowing across a field of corn, with all the corn bending in the breeze. And the look on their faces, a look of anguish and disappointment that I had saved what seemed to them a certain goal.

JOHN MAPSON
Sunderland goalkeeper, 1935–52

I played at Anfield many times during the 1930s and 1940s. I vividly remember getting carried off there once. I collided with Jack Balmer in front of the Kop goal. I got up and I had a swelling the size of an egg on my leg, and they had to carry me off. I think I probably had my first game there in 1935, but we never seemed to do very well at Anfield. Sunderland were a great team in those days, we were the best in the country. The Kop was just the same then as it is now, very vociferous. It was always a great crowd and very appreciative.

Liverpool folk are like north-easterners, they understand their football. They know when they see good play, and they know good players. They just want to see good football being played. It was just the same then for goalkeepers at the Kop end. You'd get applauded when you came running down towards them.

Football was the working man's sport in the 1930s and 1940s, not like it is today. And the Kop was where the working man used to stand. Our games with Liverpool were always competitive. Liverpool had some fine players like Matt Busby, Jackie Balmer, Gordon Hodgson – he was a big bloke – and then, later on, they had Billy Liddell.

I wouldn't say that the Kop particularly inspired me to great feats. You always do your best wherever you are. It's a job just like any other, and you have to get on with it. Mind you, I always enjoyed playing in front of the Kop, but it didn't affect me. I was probably used to big crowds at Sunderland. But the Kop was very noisy; it spiced the game up, got the adrenalin going.

Another thing I used to like about Anfield was that, in a way, I was coming home. I was born in Birkenhead and I had lots of relations there. So I would go to see them on the Saturday morning and take them some tickets for the match. It made for a nice weekend, going to Liverpool.

CHARLIE MITTEN
Manchester United player, 1945–50

I once had the rare distinction of scoring a goal for Manchester United in front of the Kop. Now that was very unusual. It certainly shut them up, for a while anyhow. I remember they had been very noisy before that. It was just after the war. I played there many times during that post-war period before I went to South America. I remember after I'd scored, Bill Jones, the Liverpool centre-half, caught hold of me. 'That was a bit of a fluke,' he said. 'Not half it was,' I replied. You see, we used to talk to each other in those days. It was a much fairer game.

Playing Liverpool at Anfield was one of the highlights of our season, especially if we could beat them, which we didn't do very often. The Kop always got behind their team. They were worth a goal start. They were always so good-humoured, so sporting. That's the thing that sticks out for me. I was really impressed by their sportsmanship. Even if they lost they would applaud the other team off the field. It was a different kind of spectator in those days. They were much more appreciative of the game, more knowledgeable, more sporting. They were also more orderly. There were no problems, and kids would be sitting on their dad's shoulders. Things like that.

The Kop could be very witty. You'd hear their wise-cracks when you were down that end and hear them all laughing. They used to sing as well, all the popular songs of the period, and sometimes they would put different words to them, you know, something to do with that day's game. But they weren't singing altogether as they do now. It was just sections of the crowd. Oddly enough, I never found Anfield intimidating. They were so fair. Their sportsmanship, that's what I always remember about the Kop.

DENIS LAW
Huddersfield, Manchester City, Torino and Manchester United player, 1956–74

I once had a nightmare. I think it must have been just before we were supposed to be playing Liverpool. I dreamt that I had fallen into the Kop, and all that came out of the Kop were my shorts and socks. Don't ask me why. But that was all that came out. I don't think I came out even. Anyhow, I suddenly woke up in a cold sweat. I was rather glad to realise it was all just a dream. It's true, honest. I was really worried for a while.

Magnificent. That's the word for the Kop. The thing about the Kop is that they appreciate good football. They give the applause to whoever plays well, whether it's their own team or the visitors. They obviously want their own side to win, but even if they lose they can be fair. I just loved playing there. It was a big stadium, always a packed house when United went. We had a great rivalry in the 1960s, and you knew that whoever got the upper hand in our games would probably go on and win the league title. It was like that for about four seasons in the 1960s, with the league championship resting on our games. So I've always got fond memories of Anfield and the Kop.

I used to love running out there. You knew you were in for a hard time, but it was great fun. But I never got too much stick off the Liverpool fans. I had a great affinity with the people of Liverpool because of Bill Shankly. He had been my manager at Huddersfield. It was lovely to go there and see the great man again. Shanks, like Busby, always encouraged good football. We played at the loveliest time when there were such great players on both sides. The rivalry was intense, but it was never bitter.

When you're a player you thrive on playing in front of places like the Kop. The atmosphere was wonderful, all the singing and chanting. It never got to me as it might have done to some players. I just loved it. I always got on well with Liverpudlians. I think they liked me because of the Shankly connection. And, you know, I might well have become a Liverpool player. There was a time when I always thought that I would follow Shankly and, when he went to Liverpool, I fully expected to be joining him. I know Shankly wanted to buy me, but the board said they couldn't afford it. I think Huddersfield wanted £40,000 or £50,000, which was a lot of money in those days. But the Liverpool board said no. I would have loved to have played there, and I know I would have enjoyed it. I would have thrived on the Kop atmosphere. But it was not to be.

KEITH RICHARDS
Kopite

I was a Newport supporter originally but, when they folded, a whole lot of us decided to support Liverpool. I've only been to one game on the Kop. That was the Arsenal game in 1988 when we won 2–0, and I didn't see either of the goals. We were stuck in the middle of the Kop and I couldn't move. Mind you, there were 45,000 there. It was the first time I had come up from Newport to Anfield.

First of all, I had to queue up at twelve o'clock, and there's me who likes a few quiet pints before the game. Then when I got in I couldn't get to the toilets or the coffee hut, it was that packed. But the atmosphere was great, it was brilliant. I'd never known anything like it. But for me it just wasn't an agreeable day.

I used to go to Newport when you could walk all the way around the ground. I just wasn't used to something like the Kop, the swaying, the chanting, the lot. There was nothing I could do. If the crowd went forward, I had to go forward. Then they started to carry people out! I'd never go in there again, but it was one hell of an experience.

ANDREI KISSELEV
Moscow Spartak supporter

I came over from Russia for the Liverpool v. Moscow Spartak game in November 1992, and I thought the atmosphere at Anfield was so wonderful that I decided to stay on, just so that I could go on the Kop. I went on the Kop today for the match against Middlesbrough, and it was really marvellous. I enjoyed the singing so much the other night and all the chanting. It made the game that much more exciting. We have nothing like this in Russia. The ground is so much further away from the terraces that you feel alienated, but here at Anfield it feels as if the Kop is almost on top of the pitch. Also in Russia the grounds do not get full, except for very important games. Our stadium holds 100,000, but it is never full. But here the Kop is full even for a game against Middlesbrough. I clapped and shouted for Liverpool a lot this afternoon. The people on the Kop were very lovely people, they are so warm. They have all been so kind to me.

Everyone in Russia knows about the Kop, it is famous throughout the world. How could I possibly come to Liverpool and not stand on the Kop? It is inconceivable. That was why I stayed behind. For many years in Russia, there was a black market in Liverpool videos. For a price you could buy the latest Liverpool matches. The videos were smuggled into the country, and then someone would buy them and secretly invite all his friends around to his house, and we would all watch Liverpool and wonder at the Kop swaying and singing. And now I have been there and stood on the Kop itself. I was very proud.

PAT JENNINGS
Tottenham Hotspur, Arsenal and Northern Ireland goalkeeper, 1963–84

I always enjoyed playing at Anfield, even though I don't think I have ever been on the winning side there. They

were great to goalkeepers. When you came down the Kop
end, they would give you a wonderful ovation. It was just
like playing at home. You got a great lift from it, your
confidence went soaring. But if they spotted you had a
weakness, they would go for it and give you a terrible
time. I got on well with the Kop, they liked me and I liked
them. Maybe it was the Irish connection, and the fact that
I was a goalkeeper. They do have a special affection for
goalkeepers.

Of course, the day I shall always remember was the
game I saved two penalties at Anfield, one of them in front
of the Kop. I was playing for Spurs at the time, and the
game was played on a Saturday morning (31 March 1973)
because it was Grand National day. Kevin Keegan took
the first one. It was in the first half, and I guessed which
way it was going to go, so I dived and saved it. The noise
as Keegan ran up was deafening. I was really pleased.

Then late in the second half they got another penalty.
This time Tommy Smith grabbed the ball. He and Keegan
then started having a bit of an argument over who was
going to take it. But Smithy took it, and shot in the
opposite direction. I guessed right again: two penalties
saved! There's a picture of me with my fist in the air. I
was overjoyed. Meanwhile, Smithy and Keegan were
yelling at each other. Even the referee was having a smile
to himself. I had already made five or six great saves that
day, from close-range. I was on a good run. The Kop was
stunned. But they were very appreciative. We even got a
draw, 1-1, that day. At the end of the game, the Kop gave
me a great ovation. That afternoon I went to the Grand
National and I won. It was clearly my lucky day.

ANFIELD BUBBLES
(Sung to the tune of 'We're forever blowing
Bubbles')

We're forever blowing bubbles,
Pretty bubbles in the air,

They fly so high,
They reach the sky,
Like West Ham they fade and die.
Tottenham's always running,
Chelsea's running too,
And if you come to Anfield,
We'll be running after you.
LIV-ER-POOL.

BILLY BUTLER
Radio Merseyside

Being an Evertonian, I decided on April Fool's Day 1977 to take the mickey out of the Liverpool supporters. I was DJ-ing on Radio Merseyside that day, so when I came on that morning at 9:00 a.m. I announced that the Kop was on fire. Then every ten minutes or so I kept updating the story with further bulletins, like there was smoke pouring from the Kop and the fire engines were on the way and so on.

Well, the entire city went into a panic. People started streaming towards Anfield to see this imaginary fire. There was chaos. People were heartbroken and were ringing up, dockers were pouring out of the docks, and everybody was making for Anfield. Then, at 10:00 a.m., I announced that they had discovered the cause of the fire. It was an old pair of Tommy Smith's shorts that were on fire.

Well, the joke didn't go down too well in some quarters. 'What A Silly Billy' was the headline in the *Liverpool Echo* that night. And Radio Merseyside banned me from doing a programme on April Fool's Day for the next three years. Anyhow, Tommy Smith got his own back. I played in his testimonial a few months later at Anfield and, when we came out on to the pitch, all the players grabbed me while Smithy threw buckets of water over me.

DUNCAN McKENZIE
Chelsea, Notts Forest, Leeds Utd, Anderlecht and Everton player, 1969–80

Playing in front of the Kop was an incredible experience. I've played on many great football stages in the world, and only once can I remember an atmosphere that was more electric, and that, strangely enough, was in Turkey when I was playing for Anderlecht. But the Kop was so vociferous. You'd come out for one of those derby matches, and first of all you have to go down the tunnel, and there is that sign just above you which Shankly cleverly had put up, reading 'THIS IS ANFIELD'. And then you'd come out into the daylight, and there would be 50,000 packed inside the ground. The Kop was so big, and it would be jammed tight and swaying. It was worth a goal start to Liverpool. We used to have this talk in the dressing-room, and we always said that if we won the toss we'd get Liverpool to kick into the Kop first-half, otherwise you'd be up against it. Liverpool playing into the Kop in the second half was unbelievable, and to be avoided at all costs.

Yet, although the Kop was so vociferous, I never found it intimidating. I used to go along with it. Being an Evertonian and a bit of a character as well, I used to get all the dog's abuse. They used to sing about Duncan McKenzie being a spastic, so I'd limp down the pitch and give them a wave. So it was not so much intimidating. It was usually good-humoured and always appreciative. You couldn't help but hear the chants going on throughout the game. They were impossible to ignore, and sometimes you'd find yourself smiling along at their wit.

I remember going there along with a young Chelsea side once, and we were beaten 0–2. After the game, our chairman, Brian Mears, came down to the dressing-room and was shaking everybody's hand as if we had won. He even wanted us to go out and do a lap of honour. He thought we had done so well to keep the score down to just two when he had expected us to lose about 0–6. I think he and other chairmen felt like that. They all expected a drubbing at Anfield, and if they didn't get it they could hold their heads up with some pride when confronting the Liverpool directors. The Kop is like a breeding-ground, fathers and sons. The fathers take their sons, and when they get older they get a season ticket in the stands, and their sons start going with their children. And so it goes on.

I never had problems playing in front of the Kop. I used to love it. It was the Liverpool-born players in the Everton side who had the most problems. Lads like Darracott, Jones, Lyons, Kenyon. Half that side were Liverpool-born. To them, the derby at Anfield was a battle of pride. If they won they could go out with their families and friends that night. If they lost they had to hide for a few weeks. They felt it and suffered the most. It was staggering watching them cope. They would run out on to the pitch, and the adrenalin would be at fever-pitch. It wasn't so much the winning, it was the fear of losing.

BRIAN LABONE
Everton player, 1957–72

The Kop? Frightening, that's the word! I don't remember the exact date, but I do remember the occasion when I first played in front of the Kop. Liverpool had just come up from the second division. The noise was incredible. It was a cauldron of sound, it was a concentrated sound. Sitting in the away dressing-room at Anfield you could hear the noise. There was a small window out on to what was then the Paddock, and you could hear the noise filtering through. And then going out on to the pitch was like going out at Wembley, the noise suddenly rising to a crescendo, and then hitting you. It was frightening.

The Kop could suck the ball into the penalty area. You'd have your backs against the Kop, and you couldn't get the ball away. All the time it was coming at you. Once the game gets under way, you're concentrating and you're not aware of the chants and humour so much but, as soon as the game stops, you look up at the Kop, and wow . . . it's nerve-wracking. That's when it gets you. Eventually you get used to it, and later in my career it didn't worry me, but that first time was frightening.

I'd stood on the Kop as well when I was a schoolboy. I went to the Liverpool Collegiate School, and I used to go along at three-quarter time and get in free. One week I'd go to Anfield and the next week up to Goodison. This was in the 1950s. The first time I went on the Kop I was in my school blazer and I had my sandwiches in my pocket. Well, the crowd was so big I couldn't move; I was just a small schoolboy. I couldn't even get my hand in my pocket to take out my sandwiches, it was that crushed. When I got home, the sandwiches were all squashed up, flattened.

The Kop never really took the mickey out of me, but they used to love having a go at our goalkeeper, Gordon West. He was a bit of a Bruce Grobbelaar-type character and would always respond. They used to sing, 'Hey there, Gordon West, you're the biggest queer since Georgie Best.' Imagine standing in the Kop goal with 25,000 people behind you singing that. And when George Best came, they used to sing, 'Hey there, Georgie Best, you're the biggest queer since Gordon West.' One day, someone came running out of the Kop and gave Gordon a handbag. But he took it all in good spirit. There was no doubting his genes, I can tell you.

DAM BUSTERS
(Sung to the tune of 'The Dambusters' march)

We hate Nottingham Forest,
We hate Everton too.
We hate Man. United,

But Liverpool we love you.
All together now ...
(Repeat)

BILLY BUTLER
Radio Merseyside

I was saying on Radio Merseyside one day how it was that Bruce Grobbelaar rarely saved a penalty. And it was true. Neither he, nor Ray Clemence for that matter, ever saved many penalties. Anyhow, I was making out that Bruce wasn't much good and that even I could put a penalty past him. Phil Thompson heard me say this and he got in touch with me. He asked me to go and play in his testimonial at Anfield and said, let's have a little wager on the side for £100 with the money to go to a charity. All right, I said, and we agreed a bet that I couldn't put seven out of ten penalties past Grobbelaar.

Anyhow, the night of the match, we had our competition at half-time. I took the first five down the Anfield Road End, and I put the first four straight into the back of the net, then I missed the fifth. The next five I took up the other end in front of the Kop. Well, you should have heard the noise. It was terrible. They all started singing, 'You're going to miss this one, Billy, miss this one, Billy ...' And, of course, I did miss the first one, then I missed the second; and the noise was getting worse. I put the next two away, and that left me with just one more shot to win the bet. God, the noise was even worse, but somehow I managed to put it away and I won my bet. But, to be fair to the Kop, they gave me a great roar when I scored.

DAVID FAIRCLOUGH
Former Liverpool player; with Oldham, 1985–86

I once had to play in front of the Kop when I was with Oldham, and it gave a totally different perspective. It was a League Cup-tie in 1985, and Oldham were then in the second division. I was more aware of the Kop that night than ever I was playing for Liverpool. During the second half, we were penned down in our own area. And we just couldn't get out of the shadow of the Kop. It was almost claustrophobic. It was so intimidating. You think everything is against you. You've got Liverpool powering down from every angle and direction. Then you've got the Kop, and this almighty sound droning down on top of you. You get totally overpowered.

All the Oldham players that night were overpowered, and at the end of the game we were drained. We lost 0–3. When you look back on it, it's amazing that Inter Milan and St Étienne didn't allow themselves to be totally overawed, they didn't cave in. A lot of foreign teams do fold, particularly the Scandinavians, who have never seen anything like it.

SANDY ROSS
Television producer

The thing that has always amazed me about the Kop is their generosity. They are always prepared to be charitable. If they've been fairly beaten they'll applaud the visitors, while opposition goalkeepers always get a good hand, no matter who they are. I can think of no other set of supporters and no other ground where the home supporters are so big-hearted.

But the thing that really astonishes me is how civilised the games are against Everton. Coming from the hotbed of Scottish football, I've always been accustomed to bitter rivalry and hatred between the likes of Celtic and Rangers, or Hearts and Hibs. No way could the two sets of supporters mingle together as they do at Anfield. Yet there they are on derby day, Liverpool and Everton supporters, massed together on the Kop without a barrier or policeman to keep them apart. It would be unthinkable in Glasgow. But on the Kop it's taken for granted, and there's not a sign of violence.

Nine

THE KOP TODAY

Ring of Fire

WILLIAM MACINTYRE
Kopite

The 1990s on the Kop were a totally different ball game from the experiences of the 1970s and 1980s. The 1970s had been a surging, swelling roller-coaster of a ride and, despite the safety cuts in capacity during the 1980s, there were still some fantastic atmospheres – and the moments of humour were all still there too. However towards the late 1980s a certain 'crisis of expectation' had set in and if teams were not being drubbed 4–0 or 4–1 there would be slight grumblings.

After Kenny left and Souness took over the atmosphere changed again and there was a sort of willing-them-on attitude, often tinged with desperation at some of the performances. However, you had the feeling that now was the time to get behind the team and try to push them to what we saw as their rightful position. However during this time I don't think I ever saw so much bemused head-shaking at some of the players' performances – except this time it was no laughing matter, unlike some of the eccentricities we used to see from a Joey Jones.

The best atmosphere of the Souness era I felt was in the 3–3 draw with Manchester United in January 1994 after being 0–3 down. There was a real frenzy on the Kop that night. However it was a moment to savour as it seemed as the atmosphere got flatter and flatter during the mid-1990s. There was a period from 1995 to about 1998 when the team would flatter to deceive and you just new that they would flunk it when it came to the crunch. Every season a bright start fizzled away into the ether.

To be honest going to the Kop could be a bit of a chore during this flat period, not because of the play necessarily, but because the level of grumbling really seemed to increase. And whereas players used to be affectionately encouraged by their first names, I noticed it was more 'c'mon Collymore,' 'c'mon Babb'.

Having said that, we did seem to be signing more players who never fulfilled their potential. Whereas you might previously have the odd 'Alun Evans'-type buy, increasingly it seemed that players did not improve or step up to that extra level needed with Liverpool. During this time you would occasionally get more atmosphere at the FA Sunday Cup semis which were played at Anfield, than at some of our mundane home games.

Going back to the Kop atmosphere, I also noticed a growing increase in the number of southern accents, and how hard it was to get any coherent chanting going at some games.

But with the full-time appointment of Houllier the optimism barometer on the Kop seemed to go up again, and no-one who was on the Kop can forget the night of his return from his heart problems for the game against Roma in March 2002. That was like a European night of old, the ground full well in advance, the crackling atmosphere of anticipation, the banners, the Italian opposition, and of course his emotional return to the touchline for the first time since October 2001.

What a masterstroke that was – it compared with the parading of the FA Cup before the European Cup semi against Inter in 1965. The Kop was going wild chanting his name and gave the extra verve and passion needed to win. However, he was never the same after his heart attack, and it was something of a relief when he left and was replaced by Rafa.

GERARD HOULLIER
(To the tune of 'No Limit')

Allez allez, (Allez allez)
Allez allez, (Allez allez)
Gerard Houllier
Allez allez, (Allez allez)
Allez allez, (Allez allez)
Gerard Houllier

ROGER WEBSTER
Third-Generation Kopite

The first time I went in the Kop was in the sixties. I was still at school then. Although I was born and bred in Liverpool at that point I was not actually living in the city. I think it was early September and I had come up to Liverpool and was staying with friends. It was my first time in the Kop. I'd been told all those stories about rolled up *Liverpool Echo*'s and to avoid them. But what I hadn't been told about was the heat. I went there wearing a big coat and as the game wore on I became hotter and hotter. The Kop was so packed that I couldn't get it off. And it just got worse. It got so hot that at one point I passed out. When I came to I was still standing up. The crowd was so densely packed that it had actually been impossible for me to drop down to the floor. I must have been unconscious for a few minutes and all that time I had remained standing. It was very frightening.

In our family we now have four generations of Liverpool fans. There's my grandfather, my father, myself, and now my son Duncan. My grandfather was from Prescot. He left home when he was quite young and got a job as a cub reporter on the *Liverpool Echo* and one of his jobs was to report on the football from Liverpool. He used to tell me that in those days they had carrier pigeons – I guess this must have been the early days of the twentieth century – and they used to put the scores and reports on to a sheet of paper and then put it on a ring on the pigeon's leg. They'd do this every ten minutes or so. The pigeon would then be released and would fly straight back to the *Echo*'s office. That was how they used to get the results in so quickly because they didn't have telephones, radios and so forth in those days.

My father always used to tell the tale of the first time he went to Anfield and his first memories of the Kop. He must have been eight or nine. It was when the Kop had just had its roof put on, in 1928, and one of the games arranged to celebrate this was an England v. Ireland international friendly. My grandfather took him. He told me that they stood in the paddock, which would have been down towards the bottom of what is now the Main Stand. In goal for Ireland was the great Liverpool goalkeeper Elisha Scott while England had Everton's Dixie Dean at centre forward. Anyhow, at one point England were awarded a penalty in front of the newly roofed Kop and up steps Dean to take it. Most of the Irish supporters were packed on the Kop and when Scott saved the penalty, all the Irish supporters went mad, throwing all their hats into the air. My father still has this very vivid memory of hats being tossed high into the air. It was something they used to do in those days. He says that for the next ten minutes everyone was scrabbling about trying to find their hats.

As for me, I think the new Kop is better in many ways. After Hillsborough we could never have continued with standing. You certainly get a better view now but that huge collective whirlpool of passion is not the same. Of course there are less people on the Kop now – maybe half the number that used to be allowed – and that reduction in crowd size inevitably makes a difference. Nonetheless I took some friends from Paris to Anfield not so long ago and they were really impressed by the Kop with all its flags and banners and singing. So there's still a very powerful atmosphere, enough to impress many people.

JOE MURRAY
Kopite

The new Kop is obviously not the same but in a lot of respects it is similar. Firstly, it is a single tier structure instead of two. I think that was a conscious decision when they built it. Secondly, it's still the area of the ground where the songs begin. But it's not the same. I don't think it ever can be when you're sitting in seats as opposed to standing up. When you stood on the Kop you always went to the same place and saw the same people. That's forced on you now because you're always in the same seat. And there are a lot of season ticket holders in there. But you still get the flag that goes up at the beginning, it still goes up at the same time, same place and there's a lot of ritual about it.

It's not as noisy as it used to be but there's not as many people. I think there were twenty odd thousand or more in the old Kop but there's only 12,000 or so now. But more of the ground sing now than they used to, a lot more of the crowd are involved. The St Étienne game was the first game I ever went to where the stands were even singing but that happens more at big games now than it used to. Maybe that's because when the Kop was being rebuilt people moved to different parts of the ground, maybe liked it, and stayed there.

The thing that used to get me about the old Kop was how low the roof was. If you were standing at the back, in particular, you couldn't see the rest of the ground. You could see the pitch okay but you couldn't see the rest of the ground because the roof was so low. In the new Kop the roof isn't as low but it is still imposing because it's one single stretch of seats without any tiers or second layer or anything. It's still an imposing sight but it's much more ordered. There was a general disorder about the old Kop because of the swaying and movement. When you can only see necks and faces as opposed to chest, necks and faces that you see now, it's diluted.

I think football clubs have changed in general because your average working man has been priced out of the game. Twenty years ago your working man could probably take his two lads to the game and buy them a programme and a pie and a coke. It can't happen now, not with the prices as they are. Football fans have changed too. It's more upmarket, less spontaneous. It's all-ticket now, you can't just turn up and go to the game. I think there are the same ethics, they still clap the opposing goalkeeper at half time. I don't know if that happens at other grounds, I suspect it doesn't, but it still happens at the Kop. Past players – there's still a bit of banter with past players when they come back. There's still comedy there. It's still the same as it was but it's more diluted.

There's more women go to the game generally now and so there's obviously more women on the Kop. It was perceived as a place where you wouldn't go behind the goal in the Kop if you were a little lad, but you can sit anywhere in the Kop now. The first game I went to was when my brother was home on leave from the navy and I was about thirteen. I was on a barrier behind the goal and I was swept twenty yards when the first goal went in. It was the only game I've ever been to when I didn't want Liverpool to score again cos I was scared stiff.

In big games I think the new Kop does begin to rival the old Kop, but I think it's really the whole stadium. But people look to the Kop first. In big games once the Kop starts the rest of the ground comes in. That never really used to happen. The other people were a bit lazy and they used to rely on the Kop for all the banter and singing but now more people join in around the ground.

The Kop is still imposing because of its size. There may not be as many people on it but it's still very imposing. At the time it was the single largest structure in Europe. They could have fitted more people in by building a second tier but they deliberately kept it as a single tier and kept the atmosphere of the Kop. Obviously there are more facilities, you can get a McDonalds on the way in and then there's the superstore. Some people like that. The old Kop did lack many of those basic facilities, like toilets. But it was easy to get in and out of.

It's lost the raw charm. It's diluted now, more sanitised. I know you always look back through rose-coloured spectacles; you think ah yes, look at the Kop, but it wasn't a pleasant place really. The steps were too small, if you weren't tall you couldn't see, the facilities were no good, it was too packed. I'd say it's probably better now but it's a Kop for the 21st century. In the modern game of football the old Kop hasn't got a place, it's just too Dickensian. It had seen its time and it was time for change.

ALEX FINLASON
Kopite

As an architect myself, I think that the Kop – as a building – doesn't really impress. It doesn't have an identity; it could be any building, any stadium, anywhere in any country. It could have had a very, very strong identity as a separate piece of the stadium but instead, it's faceless really. The previous building had a presence to it. It wasn't an architectural presence, but it had a presence in the sense that it conveyed an almost religious space the way the structure overhung the terrace. It was a cavernous space. My enduring visual memory is always of those large, square windows at the back of the Kop that gave some daylight to it and the entrances which gave larger pieces of daylight as a backdrop to the crowd. Today there is no penetration, no perspective to it.

On a cold day the Old Kop used to steam. If it was a slightly wet day, you could actually see the steam coming off people, rising. That was amazing. I've never been in a space that created such an impression. It was almost like a cattle market, a mixture of sweat from people's clothing, rain water drying out, urine trickling down the steps. My overriding view of the place was one of steam.

243

The facilities in the new Kop are adequate. You're given hospitality like you weren't before. But it's anywheresville, it's McDonalds, its adequate, its samey. You wouldn't know where you were, it could be any ground in the country. There's nothing to distinguish it from anywhere else, and that's the whole thing about the new Kop: it isn't a building that stands out at all.

Of course the facilities are better, you don't wee on the steps anymore and there are all sorts of modern convenience – sandwich bars, drinks, hot sausages rolls – they were bound to provide those facilities but they were all done at the lowest common denominator.

I used to find the Old Kop a bit intimidating. The movement was like a sea. You could pick your legs up and you could end up anywhere. It was not somewhere I felt that I could go on my own as a young teenager. At thirteen or fourteen, people might put you to sit on a rail but once you got a bit older you were on your own. I used to go in the Paddock as a result and used to watch the Kop. I loved watching it and you were a lot safer. When I was older and bigger I went back in, I could push and shove a bit more then.

I don't think there's that much difference in atmosphere. The Kop as an entity responds to the football on the pitch. It acts collectively. When I look at the Kop I look at the people, the flags, where the chants start. That still happens now as it did then. Nowadays I'm in the Main Stand and while obviously I'm watching the football, plenty of the time I'm also watching the Kop; the colour, the vibrancy of it all. It could easily be 30 years before, it reacts just the same. There's perhaps less humour, but maybe that's me getting older. I think it was noisier in the past but that was against a background of less people in other areas singing and chanting. I think these days people are chanting and singing in all those other areas of the ground, which never used to happen. From where I sit now the Kop is still a very powerful element, last season particularly. But the Kopites have spread out. They've grown up and moved out to other parts of the ground and that gives a more vocal support as a totality.

The other thing is that I don't remember many women ever going on the Kop. It was characterised by old blokes. There's more women and kids now. I would never have dreamed of taking my kids on the Kop. But I've taken the two young lads – William and Aidan – they were twelve and eight. You wouldn't have done that in the past. They knew about the history behind Anfield, and the Kop. For a lad of eight who's a fanatical Liverpool supporter it's fantastic to be able to go in a place like that and be a part of it. There were lots of women when we went in, lots of other kids and lots of foreigners. That's another thing, I can never remember there being lots of foreigners. Today, there's Japanese and lots of Scandinavians who come over very regularly, big groups of them. It's a far more diverse community. It's not that indigenous, working class, Merseyside community any longer, it's almost European. Travel is cheap, it's achievable to get there. New people will also react differently to the event and the circumstances of being there. It's bound to change, to move on, it's not the same fellowship. It's now open to others, it gets watered down but that's no bad thing. It should be open to all.

FIELDS OF ANFIELD ROAD

All round the Fields of Anfield Road
Where once we watched the King kenny play
   (and he could play)
We had Heighway on the wing
We had dreams and songs to sing
Of the glory round the Fields of Anfield
   Road

ANDREW CASHIN
Toronto-based Red

In December 2004, my wife Maeve and I had the pleasure of being Ron & Ann Yeats's guests at the LFC Former Players' Association Christmas Dinner at the Holiday Inn in Liverpool. After our defeat at Goodison earlier in the day, my Evertonian Uncle took pleasure in dropping us off at the hotel proudly displaying his Everton flags. Phil Neal greeted us at the door and just shook his head.

After spending several hours in the company of greatness, it was time to head back across the Mersey. In thanking our hosts, I asked Ron if he would like to join Maeve, my Uncle Ron (yes the same one who dropped us off) and me for the game on the following Tuesday night – we had tickets on the Kop. To my surprise Ron accepted with great enthusiasm, telling us that he'd never been on the Kop. 'Wow,' I said to myself. 'What an honour.'

Signed in 1961, and aside from a few stints elsewhere as his career wound down, Ron has always been at Liverpool and now holds the role as Chief Scout – and he had never sat on the Kop. I was going to be sitting on the Kop, not only with my wife (her first ever game at Anfield), my Everton supporting beloved Uncle, but also with Ron Yeats, 'The Colossus' – not only a legend, but also a great man and cherished ambassador for Liverpool Football Club.

Prior to the game, my Uncle Ron, Maeve and I had decided to pop into my Grandad's old local in Greasby for a few beers, to honour his memory. To our surprise the landlord was also off to the match – who was, coincidentally, Barrie Mitchell, Ron's first signing when Ron took over as manager at Tranmere Rovers. It seemed as if all the stars were lining up for a great night.

Over at Anfield we met up with Ron at the entrance behind the Main Stand and made our way around to the Kop. I can tell you there were more than a few stares. I felt so proud to be walking with this legend, not only because of his status with the club, but because Ron was my friend; an idol yes, but more importantly, also a friend. As we entered the turnstile, the ticket collector was a tad stunned as Ron presented his ticket. I entered behind Ron and the ticket collector said, 'Do you know who that was?' I just smiled and nodded.

As we made our way into the bowels of the Kop, the first phrase Ron uttered, was 'Wow, this is the Kop? It's nice isn't it?' It was around this time that a buzz started to circulate about the crowd as they lined up for a bet, a programme, the toilet and a beer. You could hear people whispering, 'Is that Ron Yeats?' 'I'm sure that's big Ron.' One bloke came over and said, 'Ron, my daughter just pointed you out to me, so I had to come over and say hello and thanks for the memories.' We looked over and his daughter must have on been in her teens, born much after Ron had hung up his boots, but it was a testament to Ron's legacy. As the fervour grew, Ron became mobbed, though he remained gracious throughout. We managed our way to our seats, in the middle of the Kop, to the left of the goal. We stood as fellow Reds continued to welcome Ron – shouts of 'Lace up your boots mate!' seemed to be the most common.

Ron sang 'You'll Never Walk Alone' with the same passion as the collective of which he was now a part – hands in the air as well. He loved the vantage point of the Kop and enjoyed the singing and shouting, often agreeing with some of the more critical taunts applied to Reds not playing for the shirt. I sat next to Ron on my left and, as you know, sitting in the Kop for a big lad is not necessarily the most comfortable couple of hours. But hey we are not there to sit, we are there to support. I'm about the same size as Ron, so two big lads sitting next to each other, plus my Uncle on Ron's other side, made for a tight squeeze. I can tell you that Ron kicked, headed and ran for every ball during that game. Somehow the earlier shouts for Ron to lace up his boots were not far off the mark. He was forlorn. We parted company and Ron returned to his car for his drive home, a mellow ending to a remarkable day.

KENNY DALGLISH
Player, Manager

The memory which stands in my mind more than any other is walking through the Kop after the Hillsborough disaster and seeing the hundreds of tributes to those who had died.

I was with my son Paul and daughter Kelly, on a Friday night after most of the people had left the ground.

That was the only time I had stood on the Kop. I will never forget it.

There were odd times when we were two goals behind and attacking the Kop end. Those supporters helped players all the time, but they were invaluable when the team was trailing. They knew we needed them and they realised their importance. So did we.

ROY EVANS
Player, Manager

The 68 bus from Bootle to Stanley Park was full to capacity as it was match day at Anfield. I was seven years old and in the charge of my elder brother Malcolm. He was about to introduce me to the Kop.

Excited? I couldn't hide it. Like everybody else aboard I was gripped by the passion, the atmosphere and the expectancy. I'd never been to Anfield before. I was decked out in red, of course, and I carried a heavy wooden rattle which would be classed as a dangerous object today. Once inside the boys' pen, I remember staring in bewilderment at the thousands who congregated under that famous roof. Their feelings for Liverpool were ultimate and their humour was unbeatable.

There was the place where we stood too. A little piece of concrete that we felt was our own personal property. I still look at the spot which was mine.

Then came Bill Shankly and the greatest of all manager-supporter relationships began. It will never be equalled.

The common bond and honest expression was unique. Fans and manager were inseparable.

GILL HOLROYD
Ex-Kopite

I started to like football when I was about eight years old. I remember my dad, who always went to work in a three-piece suit, kissing the telly in 1965 when Liverpool beat Leeds to win the FA Cup for the first time. I always remember that. The next day he took me to see the cup coming home. It was an amazing experience. We were just on the corner outside Reece's and I sat on his shoulders. I've never seen so many people. And from that moment on I became a supporter.

He used to take me to games. Most of the time we went in the Paddock but once or twice we went in the Kop. I always remember how he used to protect me from the police horses as well. One of them stood on his foot once.

I was only a wee girl of eight or nine so it was a bit difficult going in the Kop. But when I was a teenager I started going in the Kop with my pals. I went for years, not every match, but I'd go to plenty of games a season. We'd get into the ground an hour or an hour and a half before kick off so that we could get our regular spot. We used to stand about half-way down and to the right; never in the middle as that was too crushed. I always remember how we'd leave the ground and all these men would be weeing and we'd be averting our eyes like good girls. A bit like a blinkered horse in the National; head down, blinkers on, not looking right or left. I'd probably be about fourteen by then. I did that for about ten years.

It wasn't always easy being in the Kop, but people were helpful. You'd get knocked over in the sway but people would pick you up and be helpful, make sure you were okay. You never saw many girls in the Kop in those days but I never had any problem with any men. I don't even remember being offended by the language either. No, I never had any problem, never got my bottom pinched or anything like that.

These days you see plenty of women at football, not just going in the Kop but in all parts of the ground. Where I sit these days in the Main Stand, I'm surrounded by women, dozens of them. I think the audience has changed. It's not a working class audience any more. There's more money, more women, more black people. And I also have to say that in the Kop there are so many foreign accents. When you're outside the Kop you hear so many different accents. There are people coming to Liverpool from abroad for a weekend. easyJet and Ryanair have made coming to Anfield a real prospect for many people in Europe.

But it was the camaraderie in the Kop that I really loved. The singing and chanting. And the noise. It was so noisy. I used to go to a lot of rock concerts in those days but it was even noisier on the Kop. It was a real community as well. I always liked Emlyn Hughes because he showed such passion and commitment. He was one of us and he passed that passion and commitment on to all those standing on the Kop.

GARETH ROBERTS
Kopite

My first memory of standing on the Kop was a cup tie against Crewe – we won 5–1. I'd actually 'sneaked' to the match as there was no-one in my family who was really into footy like me, and my Mum and Dad didn't like the idea of me going without an adult. But I just had to go and it didn't disappoint. I can still remember getting to the top of the steps and seeing the inside of the ground for the first time 'for real'. It was great, I had butterflies in my stomach – I can still picture the Annie Road without the second tier and the Wonderfuel Gas advert on the top of the stand.

From there on I was hooked and I got to as many games as my money would allow. Myself and a couple of friends from school in Huyton stood in the same spot for years and we'd see the same fellas week in week out. We were soon up to speed on the rules – how to avoid the crush barriers, how to be aware of the fellas just out of the alehouse who'd soon be dying for the toilet and wouldn't think twice of aiming their piss down a rolled up *Echo* and into your pocket.

We followed the same routine before every Saturday home game – visiting my mate's Grandad near the ground before and avoiding his dodgy scones (the same ones were put on a plate week after week). Then there was my 'nan sweets' – a bag of éclairs my nan gave me before every game which I dished out to my mates at half-time.

Back then everyone would pile in the ground hours before kick-off – I stood on the Kop as early as 12.30 for some of the big Saturday games. But it was all part of it: booing the opposition as they came out for a first look at the pitch, studying the warm-ups, baiting the away fans and so on . . .

We used to dare each other to shout things; if you got it wrong you could almost hear thousands of people scowling at once. I got it right once, someone threw a bog roll at Nottingham Forest keeper Steve Sutton and on my own I shouted 'wipe yer arse Stevie'. He did, and I'm sure he gave us a little wink. I was buzzing – everyone was grinning at me – for that moment I was the funniest lad on the Kop.

The Kop also influenced my love life. My comprehensive school crush asked me to take her to the match but her Dad didn't want her standing on the Kop. So we watched from the Anfield Road. As the Kop cheered every home player's name, I sulked. It wasn't right sitting here. 'What's up?' she said. 'What's different about the Kop?'

'Well they cheer the names for a start,' I said.

'We can do that here,' she said before proceeding to cheer at the announcement of the much-maligned Barry Venison. 'Ar, eh love, you don't like *him*, do yer? Where'd you get her from, lad?' boomed a burly bloke in front. The shame. That was it, the next date was the Kop no matter what her old fella said!

Outside our school at twelve I'd told her – it was Spurs, the last game of the season and bound to be a sell-out. One o'clock she turned up – we didn't get in and a tout wanted £70 for a ticket. That was it, back to Huyton, not a word to her, other than to snub her offer of watching a video at hers. And that was that – we never went out again – she'd got between me and the Kop.

I always remember a derby on the Kop when it was standing. Just as the game kicked off I spotted a Bluenose I knew. 'What you doing here,' I shouted, to which he responded by chanting 'EVER-TON' and raising his arms in triumph. With that we took the lead, David Burrows I think it was banging one in after just a few seconds. 1–0! I'll never forget his face, it was priceless. How to silence a Bluenose in one easy step . . .

Since those days, I've sat in every stand at Anfield but I still find myself studying the Kop when 'You'll Never Walk Alone' kicks off – it's not the same anywhere else – I'm not sure half of them know the words in the Main Stand. I make sure I'm back on the Kop for the big European nights and for me Chelsea was the best ever. That's the loudest crowd I've ever been a part of in seventeen years of going to Anfield. It was unbelievable. Everyone sung, everyone stood and everyone was every-one else's best mate; I was hugging strangers left, right and centre on the final whistle like I'd known these people all my life. No-one wanted to leave. We were in the European Cup final. The stadium announcer had to tell us all to get off in the end, almost half an hour after the final whistle.

Istanbul was just as impressive. It was like a home game, we had that many fans there. Out of everyone I could have sat in front of I sat in front of the biggest pain in the arse in the world. Nearly 40,000 Liverpool fans were standing on their seats before the game, waving flags, showing off their banners, but this man wanted me to get down off my seat, emphasising his point by pushing me off my seat. Needless to say it was close to a scrap but my mate sensibly advised they wouldn't let me watch the game in a Turkish prison.

3–0 down, 3–3, win on penalties, the rest is history. But as we celebrated and created a huge pile of Reds I found myself hugging a stranger again, both our faces contorted with delight – then I realised, it was the man who wanted me to get down off my seat . . .

HARRY LEATHER
Kopite

At times I think we have a rosy view of what the Kop was like. Yeah, back in the sixties and seventies it was fantastic. Every game the atmosphere was amazing. Singing and chanting all the time. But in the eighties it got very quiet and complacent. We'd been winning everything for so many years that when the fans turned up they didn't think they had to cheer any more. They just expected us to win and usually we did. You didn't need to cheer. So it wasn't always as people tell you.

The facilities were appalling as well. The toilets were dreadful and they were miles away. When you were stuck in the middle of the Kop you couldn't possibly get out to get to the toilets. So, of course, everybody just weed where they were. There was little food as well. There used to be a small tea-bar up in the corner of the Kop and that was about it. You couldn't see very well either. You'd be standing for hours because you had to get there early in order to get in and to get a good spot, so you might be there for three hours.

You were also looking at the game from an odd angle and worst of all you were shoving and swaying and having to hoist yourself up on someone's shoulders every time the ball came anywhere near the penalty area. Sure, it could be great fun, but it wasn't really the ideal way to watch football. So, let's not get carried away with thinking that everything about the Kop was amazing.

Having said all that there was something about being on the Kop. You were among a great community and, as Shankly said, it was Liverpool's twelfth man. You felt that you were playing a vital role, as much as any of the players. You were making your contribution to the side.

So, what's it like now? Well, it's a lot more civilised. There's no weeing in the gangways. If you did that today you'd get thrown out, never be let in again and everyone around you would complain as well. There are plenty of decent toilets, lots of places to grab food or drinks and you also get a good view. No bobbing up and down all the time or getting crushed. And also, I'd forgotten this, there are no stanchions in the way. It's a clear view of the game. The atmosphere is certainly not as good as it was in the sixties and seventies but then, as I've said, it wasn't much on the old Kop in the eighties either. Plus, there's not as many fans on the new Kop, so it goes without saying that it's going to be less noisy.

These days I think you might just as well be in the Main Stand or the Centenary. You get a better view from there as well, the pitch is sideways on and that gives you a much better perspective of the game. I tend to go there these days but sometimes I'll go in the new Kop, especially for the big European games. The atmosphere is so much better for European matches. And although generally it's a lot quieter than it used to be, there have been some big European games here when the atmosphere in the new Kop has been every bit as good as it was in the old days – Roma, Barcelona, Celtic, Juventus, Chelsea; they were all fantastic nights with an amazing atmosphere.

The other thing is that the fans in the Main Stand and the other stands all make a noise these days which they never used to. In the old days it was only the Kop and the Annie road. Now everybody's singing, well at least for those big European games.

DAVE WOODS
Radio Five Live Commentator

When I'm commentating on games I sit on the gantry which is high above the Centenary Stand. You get a bird's eye view and the visual aspect lends to the noise aspect as well. It's a terrific sight and a terrific sound, even at the most ordinary game. I think the most moving aspect when you're covering a game at Liverpool is when they start singing 'You'll Never Walk Alone' and every single fan on the Kop seems to have a scarf or some kind of representation of their support for Liverpool.

I think the most awe-inspiring occasion when I've been there was a few seasons ago when they were playing Barcelona. On those European nights I think the whole of Anfield sizzles even more than it does for a regular domestic game. On this particular night it was a cracking atmosphere and the teams came out to 'You'll Never Walk Alone' and it was just sensational, it really was sensational. I led the commentary that night and I was first on doing the commentary as Alan Green insisted that he went last. When they handed over from the studio I think my first words were along the lines of, 'I can't think of anywhere I'd rather be than here at this moment.' All that singing just lent to the whole occasion. It was a phenomenal atmosphere and of course it's the Kop which drives that atmosphere.

It is one of the most atmospheric stands in football. In fact I'd certainly put Anfield in the top five grounds for atmosphere anywhere in the world. Not necessarily from just walking into the ground as some grounds can do even when empty, such as the Nou Camp. I was lucky enough to do a Barcelona v. Real Madrid game from there and that was frightening. Celtic Park now that it has been completed, especially for an Old Firm game. The San Siro for a big Italian game is pretty special too. That actually vibrated – you could feel it. Those grounds do have that ability to stir you when empty. But Anfield just has a special, almost unique, atmosphere that is provided only when it's full. There aren't many grounds that provide that same kind of intensity of atmosphere that the Kop does. And it is essentially the Kop that does that because that's where the greatest passion and knowledge and the greatest desire comes from.

When people talk about the Kop being Liverpool's twelfth man, I'm sure there is something in that. I've spoken to sport's people about the intimidatory factor, about going in an arena where there are 40,000 fans against you and bellowing against you. It can either crush an opponent or it can inspire. But to be able to play with the knowledge that all those fans are fanatically behind you must, must, make you grow an extra leg. Going back to that Barcelona night; if you were walking out of the tunnel in a Liverpool shirt you would have felt that it wasn't just you and your ten team-mates but that there was also someone else playing on your side.

STEVE HEIGHWAY
Player

My first experience of the Kop was in May 1970. I was still a student at Warwick University, but had decided to sign professional for Liverpool on completing my degree in June. As a student I was quite surprised to be called by Mr Bill Shankly who invited me to play in Gerry Byrne's testimonial for a Celebrity XI against the Liverpool side.

Not only was it my first visit to Anfield, but it was also, at the age of 22, my first visit to Liverpool itself. It was a filthy night with rain and sleet, but I recall that about 50,000 people were there.

The two teams walked side by side to the centre of the pitch and I stood next to an ex-Everton fullback who was playing in the Celebrity team. With total honesty and complete naivety, I quietly said to him, 'which end is the Kop?' He looked at me as if I had come from another planet and pointed to the bulging end rather than just the full end.

That was my first experience and, of course, there were many more opportunities to play in front of what was obviously the fanatical end. I had good games and bad games through my eleven years, but I feel extremely fortunate that at no time did I ever feel animosity from the Kop. I would have found that very difficult to live with and I am extremely grateful that the Kop always seemed to recognise that I was doing my best.

JOHN WILLIAMS
Kopite and Director of the Centre for the Sociology of Sport

There is no doubt that the new Kop is different. It is certainly safer, which is a good thing, and maybe we, more than any fans, have to be especially mindful of the dangers of mass standing, especially given the favoured 'intense' styles of support here. Of course some fans have been excluded – younger teenagers, the poorer fans, some of the singers, and so on. But others have come on board – more women, certainly more black and Asian fans. And we have to be *told* now when to bring our flags, and when to get excited: I think things could be much more relaxed here and we could get a lot more colour on the Kop.

Our major impacts are still on the great European nights – as it always has been – and now also through the fan mosaics. The latter would have been impossible on the old Kop and, though they are less spontaneous, they are part of the new mythologies. The atmosphere? Well, it's more sedate, certainly more willing to wait for things to happen. But we also forget the old days when the Kop was quiet. The Champions' League match with Chelsea was as good as any I have ever been to – the Kop was electric that night.

And yes, there is still wit, most definitely. Liverpool people still say the best things at matches and sometimes collectively the Kop still gets to it. The verbal outpourings – on flags in Europe – is amazing. There is a fantastic oral culture here and you still hear something to make you smile almost every game.

There is however now also an exclusion by technology, as people use credit cards and the net to buy tickets. No-one even believes you can buy on the day anymore and this is part of the problem. Mid-week games you can still often get in and the club have tried to make League Cup matches and early European matches better by price. This also means a more local and louder crowd, and one that is less cynical, so the atmosphere is better. But the club also want to tap into its regular customers, hence the various new loyalty schemes, so lots of fans are still left outside.

I think the facilities are better. It's certainly more comfortable. No-one pisses on walls anymore – though we often have to do when playing away from home, for example at Portsmouth this season! You can get a drink at half-time, but they haven't put any tellies in the foyers, which is right. Half-time should be for deep talking about the match, not watching on the screen. There are plenty of football heads on the Kop. I think they could dress up the foyers a little: where is the roll of honour, the huge pictures of the great past Liverpool players, past triumphs? These would inspire fans and give them a sense of connection with past glories. We could learn a little from abroad here.

There are a few other things as well. Every time Liverpool attack the Kop or get a corner people stand up. Everyone pretty much stands up. This is fine with me, a sign of the crowd moving with the match. For big European matches everyone stands up all the time; a link with the past and a signal of the crowd's role in urging the team on. The club – very sensibly – have stopped trying to get people to sit down on these nights. It's a fair compromise, I think.

You also get to know the people you sit with and you become a 'community'. We have a group of forty-something Liverpool fellas in front of us, who we talk to or argue with; some St Helens guys behind, the same. We row with people five rows in front who don't like what we shout. You can still move your season ticket if you want to and these groups around you evolve. I do think the crowd is getting older though.

The Roma game was incredible because of the return of Houllier: I don't think any club's fans bond with its managers like this one. Who else ever sings their name? Juve was difficult for me. I wasn't happy with the, 'Well we have offered our banner, let's get on with the game' approach. I don't blame the Juve ultras at all for turning their backs at Anfield. I might have done the same. Olympiakos and Chelsea was near hysteria, close to being frightened by just how much people had invested in those matches. The first Newcastle 4–3 was also fabulous. Outside the ground afterwards everyone was silent: people were just exhausted, drained.

As an 'odd' memory I would also point to Porto in 2001. It was our first match back in the European Cup but it was also on the night of September 11, so there was a really odd sensation around the ground and on the Kop. People were numbed, uncertain about the world and their future, wondering why we were playing football at all. So the atmosphere was flat for what should have been a great Liverpool football night on the Kop.

STEVE MORGAN
Ex-Kopite

My first time on the Kop I went in the Boys' Pen. I can't remember how old I was exactly but it was myself and a couple of lads from school. I used to go to St Francis of Assisi in Garston. We'd go in the Boys' Pen and be in there five minutes, then we'd climb over the top and onto the Kop, which was a pretty stupid thing to do because you could hardly see anything. You just hoped that someone would pick you up and put you on a barrier so you could see. I used to always go to the opposite end in the far corner. Why I went there I've no idea. I think I tried everywhere else to get a decent view and when you're only pint size it's hard to find a good view. I used to find that if you went on the opposite side – the Kemlyn Road side – you could actually get a view and see about 20 per cent of the match. This was in the early 1960s.

Leyton Orient, in the second division, was the first game I saw. I remember us being promoted. I'd never seen Liverpool lose and then I saw Sheffield Wednesday in the first division. That was in the days of Peter Swan and Bronco Lane. They absolutely ripped us to bits. We lost 2–0. I remember another game in that first season. Spurs were the top team in those days and they came to Anfield on Good Friday and we won 5–2. Nobody could believe it. Then on the Easter Monday we went to Tottenham and we lost 7–2. It was a big reality check. Those were my early memories.

I probably didn't become a regular on the Kop – in the sense of never missing a match – until I was about thirteen. Funnily enough we had moved to North Wales then and I used to travel from North Wales and went to more matches than when I lived in Liverpool. I think this was because I got in with some mad keen Liverpool fans and we used to go as a group. We used to bunk on the trains. I used to buy a platform ticket at Colwyn Bay. They got wise to me eventually because I was buying the ticket at ten in the morning and then I was coming off with the same platform ticket at seven in the evening. So I then had to start buying a day return to Abergele, which was fairly near and cheap, then you came off with a proper ticket at Colwyn Bay. I did that from the age of thirteen until I learnt to drive at seventeen. I used to go all over the country, bunking the trains; down to London, Southampton, Norwich, always bunking the trains with this day return ticket to Abergele.

My heydays in the Kop were in the late sixties and seventies. I think it was the humour I liked. I always remembered tales when Gary Sprake [ex-Leeds goal-keeper] hurled the ball into the back of his own net. Des

O'Connor had a record in the charts called 'Careless Hands'. Within seconds 25,000 people were singing 'Careless Hands'. It was things like that. It also coincided with the peak of hooliganism and there were always scraps, especially at the away games, but sometimes at the home games as well. I remember we'd gone to Old Trafford one season and had basically taken over the Stretford End and there was a right punch up. The following season at Anfield about 500 United supporters came up. There were no tickets in those days, you just queued up and came in. About 500 United fans came into the Kop and took over the centre of the Kop. They must have come in about one o'clock because we came in about half past. By this time the United fans were completely encircled by the Scousers, the Kopites. There was a lot of argy-bargy going on, then all of a sudden somebody shouts 'charge!' And these United fans just scarpered everywhere. They were on the pitch, all over the place; they got battered. Very few of the 500 United fans left Anfield without getting bloodied noses. They got a right good tonking. You never saw a United fan in the Kop after that.

It used to be quite scary going to the away games because you would frequently get ambushed by mobs. There used to be a bunch of head cases called London United. You'd go down to Euston and you'd have all the Arsenal, Chelsea, West Ham fans come together just to beat up the Scousers. Because I was that age myself, you were always up for it. It was part of the culture really. It was the way it was. You almost expected a scrap when you went to an away match. But that in itself almost bred camaraderie. We used to hitch-hike down to the away matches and you'd meet up with the same lads at the Motorway service areas and we'd say meet you at Watford Gap or the Hilton services. You'd start off at three or four in the morning and you'd hitch through the night. I'd leave Colwyn Bay on my own and by the time I got to London there'd be ten or twelve of us. That sense of camaraderie, having a few drinks before the game and so on, was terrific. We used to sing so hard you'd have a migraine by the end of the day. That went on for years. It became a part of my life.

I think the Kop is definitely different today. The Kop was always evolving. As I say, when I was a kid I'd go in the corner because that's where I got the best view and you didn't get crushed on the barriers. But then when you're fourteen, fifteen, through to your early twenties there is only one place you want to be and that's right in the middle of it, right where the action is. Being crushed when they scored a goal was just part of the fun. But then when you get into your mid-twenties you graduate out of there. You get to a point where you don't want to have your ribs crushed against a bar. There was always an evolvement. The centre of the Kop was always packed with teenagers and blokes in their early twenties. Then as people got older they moved away. But today, because the Kop is season ticket, people have the same seats all the time. So all that happens is that you get in the centre of the Kop and you just get older. And as you get older you're not quite up to shouting your head off all the time. That's my theory any rate.

But then you get nights like the Chelsea game when the Kop has never, ever, been better. I don't think in all the hundreds and hundreds of games I've been to at Anfield I've ever heard the crowd – and not just the Kop – make a noise like that. And I've been to them all – St Étienne, Inter Milan, Roma, all the great games. There's been nothing quite like that night. It completely intimidated Chelsea. We really were the twelfth man. If there was a man of the match award it should have gone to the crowd that night. They were outstanding. The hairs on the back of your neck just stood up.

The difference today is that you get the singing coming from every corner of the ground. You even get it from the Director's Box – well you certainly do from my end! It's normally quite subdued in the Director's Box but for that

Chelsea match I shouted my head off. After the game I had one of those bursting headaches from just shouting.

It was the same in Istanbul. A group of eight of us went there, including Ian Rush. We went down the day before and had a great time. Everywhere we went Rush was mobbed. But it was fantastic. We had a wonderful lunch but then it took forever to get to the ground. This ground was like it was right out on the moon, some kind of lunar landscape. But once we got there and got in and only about twenty minutes before kick off it was amazing. At 3-0 down we were in despair. We were all just hoping we weren't going to get such a hammering that we would be humiliated. We just did not play well and they were awesome. But once Stevie G got that first goal you felt that something was going to happen and that we might nick it. I think the singing of 'You'll Never Walk Alone' at half time was another example of the twelfth man. It left a lump in the throat. We all sang it. It was an act of defiance 'Stuff you. Come on lads!' It was a phenomenal rendition. You could not help but be uplifted by it. It was the best rendition ever. It said to the players you've got to go and do it for the lads. They've come out here and spent all this money. It was fantastic. I'd like to know from the players whether they thought it played a part because I certainly thought it did. It took me four days to get my voice back after Istanbul. Three days to get rid of my hangover and four days to get my voice back.

The Kop is obviously safer now. I know everybody was sad to see the old Kop demolished and make way for an all-seater stand. There are people who go on there now who never even saw the old Kop, let alone stood on it. It's hard to explain to them what it used to be like. But I think it had to be done after Hillsborough. I don't think there was any choice. It was unsafe, we've all been there when you've been taken by surprise. There was a skill in riding the Kop but just occasionally you'd get caught. There would be a surge that you weren't expecting and when you got that and your ribs were up against it, it was scary.

There's been a few quite hairy times when you thought your lungs and your ribs were going to burst, so in this day and age it was the right thing to do, but it's still tinged with sadness that it's all gone.

When it went to seats it was inevitable that you weren't going to get that evolution of younger people going into the centre. When I was thirteen, fourteen, through to my mid-twenties you just shouted your head off every single game. Now as you get older you tend not to do that as much, so if the centre of the Kop gets occupied by older people you're never going to get the same level of noise. On the other hand, the travelling Kop is always better than the Kop at Anfield. It's because those who travel are the more enthusiastic and younger ones. They congregate together and that's why they are frequently better. You see it at Anfield when the away fans come. They shout their heads off but when you go to their ground, you never hear them.

You get more women going to matches as well and on the Kop and that's good. You also get more families. We could do with – if we ever have a larger stadium – having more seats for families. It's expensive taking a family of four to a game – £100 or more – so it would be nice to encourage more families to come.

WAYNE GORDON
Kopite

Stories started to filter through that it was taking ages to get to the stadium, so myself and a couple of mates, Jonesy and Andy, decided to head for the ground. The journey itself was another crazy taxi ride. It's hard to describe, but if you have ever seen *The Italian Job* with all the minis, well, it was like that except for yellow cabs. There was an endless entourage of these cabs snaking their way round the winding roads to the stadium, with the odd bus thrown in. There was even singing from the taxis and the whole place was rocking.

When we got to the vicinity of the stadium, we had to get out of the cab and trek down a big hill to get to the ground. When we got to the stadium itself and turned back the sight was one of the most bizarre I've ever seen. Thousands and thousands of Reds walking over a hill and down the other side. It was like *Braveheart*. Thousands of Reds with banners, singing and chanting, coming over the hill. At one stage they were singing 'The Reds are coming up the hill, boys' and I suppose this was it. The Reds were literally coming up the hill. In their thousands! It was almost biblical.

The sparse facilities at the stadium meant that no programmes, drinks or food were readily available, so we just stood around in groups talking about the game, singing and invading a stage, much to the horror of the organisers. They had some poor soul trying to get a couple of thousand Scousers off a stage by screaming that it would collapse and the stadium was now open.

Anyway, about an hour before kick off, we made for our seats. I was trying to take it all in. This was the European Cup Final; this was it. I was there. A lifetime's ambition fulfilled.

Then Maldini scored. Fifty seconds into the game.

The 45,000 or so Reds in the ground rallied; we tried to get behind the team, make ourselves heard. And then it was two. Crespo. I couldn't believe it. This couldn't be happening, this wasn't in the script. I sat there shell-shocked. And then it was three, right before half-time. I sat down, head in my hands, I felt like crying. The text messages started coming in from my Manc supporting mates. I almost bounced my mobile off the ground. I could just imagine it back home, how we were disgracing English football, how we should never have been in the competition, never mind the final.

And then something happened, something magical, something mythical, and I think only the people who were there will ever truly appreciate it. The first few bars of 'You'll Never Walk Alone' started. It gathered momentum. By the time it got to 'Don't be afraid of the dark' it was a crescendo of noise echoing around the Ataturk. It was an arms aloft and fists clenched, an act of pure defiance from the Reds. It was a battle cry.

We have always prided ourselves on being the best fans in the world. Well, at half-time we not only showed our team what we were about, we showed the world what Liverpool fans are all about. The Kop might have been uprooted and transported to the Turkish wilderness, but it was still the Kop.

When the team came out you would have thought we were three up rather than three down.

Then it happened. We scored. And we were still celebrating when we scored again. And then the penalty. I couldn't watch. But I couldn't not watch either. Who would take it? Xabi. Okay, he should score. But no the keeper's saved it, Xabi to the rebound, and absolute pandemonium. Someone fell down the steps beside me. I was hugging strangers, I almost cried. The rest of the game I just sang myself hoarse. My heart was in my mouth every time Milan had the ball.

Extra-time, I couldn't take much more, our players looked shattered. We had to hold on, then the ball fell to Shevchenko, he must score, and Dudek somehow saved it. I sat back in my seat. This was unreal. When the ref blew for penalties I was relieved. We looked shattered, we were on the back foot, and we always win on penalties, don't we?

Anyway, I was at my wits end. If we lost, at least we had our pride back, but we couldn't lose now surely, not after that!

Milan were up first. I said a small prayer. It must have worked, as the penalty went high into the Turkish night sky. I looked at my watch. It was half an hour past midnight. This must have been the first European Cup Final played over two days.

Hamann stepped up.

No, not Hamann, not him!

Scored! Never doubted him! Great pen.

Their second taker walked up. Dudek handed him the ball. I remember thinking that was great by Dudek, eyeball him. And then he saved it. Get in! A roar went up around the ground.

Cissé. He had to score hadn't he. And he did.

We were two up with three to go. Surely we couldn't lose now.

They scored.

We missed. And Riise's pen was the best of the night too!

They scored again. 2–2.

Then Smicer. Dear God no, not *Smicer*!

Scored! Never doubted him. Great pen.

Shevchenko next. If we score our next, we win. I couldn't believe it.

Shevchenko ran up. Dudek saved it.

For a split second nothing, no one moved. Then we collectively realised that that was it. There was pandemonium in the stands. We had won, we were European Champions. I couldn't believe it. We had won the greatest final ever!

That night was the best night of my life. I was there. I witnessed it. Even the thirteen-hour journey home didn't matter now. We were champions of Europe. I was part of it. I was there, and I still can't quite believe it.

RAFA BENITEZ
(To the tune of 'La Bamba')

Ra Fa Benitez
Ra Fa Benitez
Xabi Alonso, Garcia and Nunez
Ra Fa Benitez
Ra Fa Benitez

HARRY LEATHER
Kopite

There have been times when the atmosphere has been just as good as it was in the past. Take the Chelsea game for example. I reckon that was as good as any game I've ever been to at Anfield. And I was there for the Inter Milan game and the St Etienne one which most people always reckon were the best ever. Well the Chelsea semi-final was every bit as good as either of those.

When I arrived at Anfield and walked in, the Kop was a sea of red. I've not seen it so red for years. And when the sides came out the noise was deafening. There were flags and banners everywhere. It was just fantastic. Before the game the Chelsea manager José Mourinho had been saying that his team would not be frightened by the noise. Well, I can tell you that they were: they were terrified. It had been the same with the Bayer Leverkeusen game and then the Juventus game. Both of those sides froze when they arrived on the pitch cos the noise was just frightening. It was like we had been rehearsing. First with Olympiakos, then Leverkeusen, then Juventus, then Chelsea.

The fantastic thing about the Chelsea game was that the noise did not stop from start to finish. And when we scored, it was like, shit, we can really win this. I've never heard it so noisy. There was chanting and singing for a full ninety minutes. And the last twenty minutes were sensational. Everyone was on their feet. Now I've never seen that since St Etienne. In the Kop we always stand for the big European games, and we'd stood for the whole of that Chelsea game, but in the Main Stand, Anfield Road and the Centenary Stand you could see that they were all on their feet. I haven't seen that for thirty years. Some were even standing on their seats. Everyone was just urging them on.

Shankly used to say that the Kop was the twelfth man. Well it was that night, just as it had been against Olympiakos, Bayer Leverkeusen and Juventus. Then when the final whistle went against Chelsea there was bedlam, we went berserk. Just amazing. I reckon that's why we won the European Cup cos the Kop and all the fans really got behind the team like they used to in the old days. I'm convinced that's what did it. It was the same in Istanbul. If we were like that for every league game we'd win the Premiership, no trouble. But of course we're not. We only do it for European games. Maybe next season . . .

WAYNE GORDON
Kopite

I never actually got onto the old Kop until I was quite old, sixteen or seventeen. I was never really allowed on it – it was too dangerous. The swaying, you'd see it surge forward. When I was a kid on the old Kemlyn Road stand or at the Anfield Road end, you just wanted to be a part of the Kop because that was where all the noise was coming from. You wanted to be in there singing but you were so small you probably wouldn't see anything. But when I did get onto the Kop, clicking through the turnstiles for the first time was like my dream. My dream wasn't to be winning the cup or whatever, it was just to be on the Kop at Anfield watching the team play towards me. It was the biggest buzz in the world. I remember when 'You'll Never Walk Alone' started, the hairs on the back of my neck just stood up and it's still the same today. I've heard it hundreds of times now, but you make the effort even now to be there ten minutes before the start of the game to sing that song. I think there's something absolutely magical and unique to Anfield when it plays. It just gets everybody in that part of the ground standing and singing.

I think to an extent there is less atmosphere in the new Kop. That's because in the old Kop you could go and stand with your mates. Maybe fifteen or twenty of you could go together. Maybe you didn't turn up at the same time but you always met at the same spot; whether it was behind a crush barrier, in a corner or in some certain spot, you always congregated there. So if you wanted to start a song or a chant there were fifteen or twenty of you and so you stood more of a chance of getting it going. Now it's seated, my friends are scattered everywhere around the ground – and not solely on the Kop – while the guys who are on the Kop are often blocks away. So it's harder to get the atmosphere going, but, saying that, you do sit with the same people every week and you do have the characters. I know there's guys who've stood on the spot where they now sit. They're all in their sixties and seventies and the stories they tell! They've seen it all. Some of them get very bitter when they see the players coming, knowing how much they're earning. They're used to seeing Jimmy Case or Graeme Souness or Kenny Dalglish giving their all, and sometimes they see players who don't want to be there, or don't seem to try, so there is a bit more venom towards the team. They don't seem to give the players as much time now cos they're used to seeing the legends.

I think there's a different type of person who goes on the Kop now. You get a lot of families whereas before it was unheard of to see mum, dad and the two kids with the jester hats and the plastic bags. Now you do see that. In some ways it takes the atmosphere away because the Kop was the working man's club. I remember at a cup match a few years ago against Bolton, someone stood up and someone actually asked them to sit down – they were about two rows behind. And I just thought that if that had happened ten years ago you would have got a smack in the mouth. On another occasion someone about two rows behind me swore and the guy who was sitting beside him asked him not to swear in front of his kid. I was just thinking, this is the Kop for God's sake, you can't tell someone not to swear. These guys have been working in a factory or an office from nine to five all week and they're just venting their anger. Those are two moments when I thought, this place has changed for good.

But then you get nights like Chelsea in the European Cup semi-final or Juventus in the quarter-final or the Newcastle games in the league and the spirit is still there. The people may have changed slightly and they may be more spread around but when that stand gets going it really is something very, very unique.

The Chelsea game for me was probably the greatest experience I've ever had at Anfield. I was lucky enough to be there when Houllier came back from his heart surgery – and it was special because Houllier meant a lot to many of the fans. But the Chelsea game ... I remember the Chelsea manager saying that he'd been to Anfield on New Year's Day and he wasn't put off by the Kop. I think he dissed the myth of this twelfth man. But Mourinho didn't take into account that the Chelsea game was 12 o'clock on New Year's Day when most of the fans had not slept, or were hungover or were topping up from the night before. The atmosphere was a little bit flat and the game itself – well we probably should have won and there was a little bit of dissatisfaction at the end. But the night of the Chelsea match there was so much build up. It was the romantic tie because Chelsea had all the money and they had bought their way to where they were. We had the history and the soul and we are a romantic club. I was nervous all week just thinking of the game. Usually at a league match I'll get in my seat twenty minutes before kick-off, but at this match I was in the Kop an hour before kick-off and the place was three quarters full. The players had come out on the pitch to just walk around. The place was bouncing a good hour before kick-off. It was what I would imagine the old European nights were like on the Kop, everyone wanted to be there.

The great thing about cup matches is that it's not like league matches – you can get seats with your friends. That night for me – surrounded by my friends, and watching the team do something I never thought I would see again – was the most magical experience. Up until the final itself. I came out of the Kop high on adrenaline. I couldn't sleep that night. I couldn't sleep the night before either because I was nervous. But the night that we got to the European Cup final, I came out and went to the Oakfield bar and had four or five pints. I went home and thought

I'll go home now and get some sleep. I was emotionally shattered. The adrenaline kept going. I just sat watching Sky Sports over and over again.

To be on the Kop that night, to hear the noise and the humour even when people couldn't bear to watch it, to have been there that night . . . I'll be able to tell my kids. That was probably my generation's St Etienne, my generation's Inter Milan. I can look back and say I was one of the 12,000 people stood on the Kop that night. I've got my ticket. I never buy a programme but I've got a programme from that night and that ticket. It's a memory that will stay with me forever. The absolute passion that people felt. There were grown men crying. The noise, the shaking, especially when 'You'll Never Walk Alone' came up at the end of the match. You heard the first bar and it just took off. There was this noise reverberating around the whole ground and you could see the looks on the players' faces. They were stunned. Every single person, whether you were in the actual Kop or elsewhere, was singing. That was what the Kop was all about. That was the night when we really were the twelfth man. It happens every now and then and when it does it's magical. It's hard to describe but that's what it's really like.

The fans stand more at European games. The steward-ing policy seems to be a little more relaxed. I think a lot of it is down to the fact that because it's a mid-week match there are a lot more Liverpudlians at the match. I know it's strange, me being Irish, and saying that, but living over here I can see that the type of people who go to mid-week games are different. You don't get the day-tripping fan from Cornwall or Norway – no disrespect as they have every right to be there – but I think on European nights, and Cup matches especially, you can get your tickets near your friends. You can't do that for league matches. You're sometime sat on your own surrounded by a family of four from Devon and two Norwegians. Sure you can be sat next to the same guys every week but you don't know them; you don't meet them outside after the match. When you're with your friends it's a lot easier with the songs. It seems to be a better atmosphere for European games. There's a tradition. People are aware that we've been there, we've done it.

Anfield is revered all over Europe. I'm lucky to be able to travel to the European games and everywhere you go, you might not be able to speak the language, but they will know the Kop. I don't think, say, any Aston Villa fan could go away and mention the Holte End, or any Manchester United fan could say Stretford End in Rome and they'd know what they were talking about. But if you say Kop, they know straight away: that's Anfield.

We are, I believe, the most passionate fans in football and to an extent, the most knowledgeable. When the opposition goalkeeper comes down to the Kop they still get applauded. Now I thought that would be something that would die out, but it hasn't. It's the only ground in England where that happens. Even the Everton and Manchester United goalkeepers. They sometimes don't applaud back and they get booed. It's still one of those things that I think make the Kop special. There's also the fact that when an opposition player has a great game they'll get applauded off.

I remember when Gianfranco Zola played his last game for Chelsea and he was taken off with ten minutes to go and he got a better reception from the Kop than he got from the Chelsea fans. That's one of those things that makes the Kop that little bit special.

All those banners on European nights are typically Scouse. The thing I love about all those banners is that they are Liverpool. They are not Union Jacks or Wolverhampton Reds. They're scouse and they all have wit and humour. People go to such time and effort to make them. And it's every European night, not just the big ones, Juventus or whoever. We can be playing TNS and there will be banners and flags on the Kop. You don't see it anywhere else. When you look at other English clubs regularly playing in Europe – at Man. United, Arsenal –

you just don't see it. When opposition players come down towards the Kop and see this they must think, 'what the hell?' Flags, banners, scarves, the noise, everywhere.

I'm just so lucky to be able to go on the Kop every match. There must be people all over the world who'd give anything to be able to do that. I love it. When I'm walking down Walton Breck Road toward the Kop I just love it. It's like going to church, you're going to pay your respects. I was there, I was on the Kop. Everyone wants to be part of it. So many clubs are jealous of it. Other clubs may have their Kop but its not really the Kop.

The Kop is not bricks and mortar, it's not concrete, it's not plastic seats, I think the Kop is the people of Liverpool. It's companionship, it's passion. In recent years it has become a travelling thing. You go to away games and that's what the old Kop used to be like. They could sit with their mates and just sing. We take that everywhere with us now. It's not just confined to Anfield.

It's still the twelfth man. Some games maybe it's not as prolific as it should be but in the sixties and seventies not every match was noisy and passionate. The place could be flat even then. In those days supporters were spoilt. They took success for granted. Every season there were two or three trophies. You took a trip to Wembley for granted. You took for granted that you would beat West Ham 5–0 at Anfield. I think now the Kop becomes the twelfth man when they see the team needs it; then the Kop reacts. It can galvanise the team, it can put fear into the opposition. It's a marvellous feeling to think you are the twelfth man, that you helped the team win. You think, 'I was part of that today.' It's a very special feeling.

JOHN DOYLE
Kopite

My first period of standing on the old Kop was from about 1985 to 1991. I had a season ticket for most of this period and my main recollections are of the huge excitement for the games against Everton, Manchester United and the other big clubs. Before I got a season ticket, the memory of queuing for hours to get a child ticket for £1.80 – and sometimes not getting in as the turnstiles closed – is still fresh. Also I remember the Kop would be full at 1.30 for the big games.

The first impressions of getting through the old turnstiles was one of huge anticipation. Looking up to the Kop from inside the turnstiles made the spine tingle. When I think back to climbing the flights of stairs up to the top and looking out across the pitch over the massed heads, I still get that same feeling.

The atmosphere would build up slowly with a lot of people sitting on the concrete floor of the terraces reading their programmes, the *Anfield Review*, that were on sale inside the stadium. Slowly the atmosphere would build – songs to the players warming up and the old favourites blasting out. The chant I most loved was LIV-ERP-OOL LIVERPOOL FC and the chant of CELTIC RANGERS that always got the crowd going.

As the teams game out to warm up, Brucie G always got a few chants as did Kenny and Rushie, later John Barnes was one of the first chants. But there was some casual racism around that time and black players had to endure monkey noises from the Kop, but I only remember this being reserved for the best players, those who the Kop feared. It didn't seem to be endemic like at other clubs. My best friend was Anglo-Asian and we both always felt hugely uncomfortable about it, though it did stop after John Barnes signed. But I didn't forget that his last game for Watford was at Anfield and he received that kind of abuse.

The amount of black fans at Anfield was minimal, almost non-existent in fact. The only black or Asian fans we used to see were at Villa, Tottenham or Arsenal. Also the amount of women was small, they were usually in their mid-twenties along with their boyfriend for the match, they were always a source of interest to us.

The noise at Anfield was deafening – I particularly remember when Rush broke Dixie Dean's record of derby goals as the ball trickled over the line; the Kop almost sucking it in to the goal – the noise and the resulting crush was unbelievable.

I used to stand in the middle, a little to the right and this I always thought had the best atmosphere, it seemed that here was where many the chants started. I also remember a lot of laughing at the chants that used to start up – from celebrating Walsh's decking of Bond to the sexual habits of United players.

Another aspect was the London Bridge chant – this was always sung to London clubs and there seemed to a real dislike of London and its football followers – no doubt due to the economic and political situation of the era. I remember we used to get the 'sign on' chants and fans waving wads of cash at us too.

The Kop was pretty merciless with players they thought were not up to the job – Ablett, Walk, Whelan and Johnston all got the treatment at one point or another. The atmosphere, while not great at games against, say, Luton, still could be cranked up by a bad tackle or the antics of a player or official and would quickly get loud.

Since the New Kop was built I've generally gone about four times a year as I now live in Brighton. For the first couple of years the Kop's atmosphere seemed to die and only got going for the big games. However, the team in 1996 seemed to get the Kop going again as it was a talented young side that promised great things but didn't deliver. The games against Newcastle stand out from that era as having a good atmosphere. However, though Liverpool's success has remained moderate, and we are as far from the Premiership title as any time in last fifteen years, the atmosphere I think has started to return a little. Games that stand out for me as being right up with the past in terms of passion and noise are the Barcelona semi-final and the Chelsea semi-final – the noise that night was as loud as anything I remember. The final in Istanbul was unbelievable considering it was an open roof. However it's not consistent. The noise can be deathly quiet sometimes, especially at weekend league games. I don't think it's a coincidence that the louder nights are the midweek games under floodlights as I think that less out of town fans come and its more local fans who attend – the hardcore. The weekends seem to consist of families and affluent fans from around the country.

Another big difference is the banner culture on the Kop. When we were young, the odd flag or banner was mainly evident at finals, but I think that we've taken things to another level, with flags and banners and the Kop mosaics which are great. These are examples, I think, of fans adapting to the new space and changing the way they support the club. Being more creative if you like. They have taken control of their space by using visual aids rather than sound aids. It's just different. Perhaps it's a reflection of a more visual culture . . .

Liverpool fans seem to me to be proud of pushing boundaries, the fans trekking around Europe in the seventies and eighties getting the local sports wear and fashions are being replaced by fans intent on replicating the best of fan cultures from around the world. I hope this continues. The banners at Istanbul were amazing – and some of the Kop mosaics have been awe inspiring. The fans are finding their voice again and the lesson of 2005 is that Liverpool's twelfth man has returned – brighter and louder than before. It may push us all the way back to glory . . .

The other major difference is the huge increase in Asian and black fans and young women. This can only be positive and reflects the changing nature of the football fan. Many are from outside the city too. The fact that they identify with the club is testament to the changes John Barnes made in the city and the profile of the club I think.

People also tend to underestimate how the disasters effected the Kop, this has no doubt affected the atmosphere. I myself just didn't felt the same passion for years, but the atmosphere is returning and a new generation who were not so directly affected are now going. These young fans are creating a new culture on the Kop.

APPENDIX

Extracts from *KOP* magazine, 1967–68

Hey, Hey, We're the Kopites

MOMENTS I CAN NEVER FORGET
28 February 1968

> *Oh, to be at Anfield*
> *When it's cup time there,*
> *To be ten thousand miles away*
> *Is more than I can bear.*

... but this exile has memories of great cup-ties, great goals, great saves, at our great ground to sustain him.

I REMEMBER ... the time when Pongo Waring loomed out of a fog at the Anfield Road End and crashed the ball past Elisha Scott. I think the comments to the referee by Elisha all but dispersed that fog!

I REMEMBER ... those two superb left-foot scoring shots from Gordon Hodgson in the famous six-goal rout of the other team across the park.

I CANNOT FORGET ... a wonderful goal by Stubbins into the Kop goal one Boxing Day ... many from the mighty feet of Billy Liddell, and particularly one against Stoke, when a pass from Phil Taylor was blasted into the Anfield Road goal.

I'LL NEVER FORGET ... Ian Callaghan's long-range goal at the Kop end against Everton in 1963. Not the greatest, but one of the happiest goals I ever saw scored was by Matt Busby, against Grimsby, when we scored seven goals.

THE GREATEST SAVE I EVER SAW ... was by the fabulous Frank Swift. Alf Hanson had cut in from the left wing and shot with terrific power from such close range that it seemed a thousand to one on a goal. But big Frank caught the ball in mid-air. The Kop, indeed the whole ground, kept up their applause for Frank for several minutes. And no wonder.

Thanks for such happy memories of happy times.

TOM McNAB
Flat 4
198 Labouchere Road
Como, West Australia 6152

FEATHERED FANS (1)
3 January 1968

I think all Liverpool fans will be interested in my parrot.

His name is Roger. The reason is obvious. He can say the Christian names and surnames of every player in the current Liverpool team. He can also say 'Bill Shankly', 'We are the greatest', 'Ee-aye-addio, We won the Cup', 'We love Liverpool'.

It is funny to hear him click his beak in the way we clap for St John. If my Roger isn't unique – he is not yet three – I'd like to learn of a more remarkable supporter.

To me, Liverpool and BOTH Rogers are the greatest.

DAVID SANDLAND
2a Bennett St
Liverpool 19

NOW IS THE TIME TO SHOUT AND CHANT
19 April 1967

Your front page article 'They'll Never Walk Alone' is timely. Now is the time for everyone who really is a supporter to sing and chant as he has never done before!

Dame Luck having deserted them, the Reds now deserve all the vocal support we can give.

The concluding game of the season at home on 6 May is against Spurs. All the southern sportswriters will be here so, on this day, let us show them that when we sing 'You'll Never Walk Alone', we really mean it.

W.H. PAUL
Hampden Street
Liverpool 4

FEATHERED FANS (2)
3 May 1967

I wonder how many more Liverpudlian budgies there are in Liverpool (plenty, I bet!). Ours keeps us amused with, 'Sir Roger Hunt', 'Up the Reds', 'Ee-Aye-Addio Liverpool', 'Saint John', and one of his frequent muddle-ups is 'Saint Roger', a fact which no Liverpool supporter would ever dispute.

NORA EGERTON (Mrs)
Old Hall Estate
Kirkby

THE MARCH OF THE KOPITES
8 March 1967

It was from Crosby Boys' Secondary School that we got this effort, the work of classmates M. Reid and T. Bull in the fifth form.

They want you to sing it to the Monkees' theme song. And here are their words:

Here we come,
We're on the move,
We're the new generation,
We've got nothing to lose.

Heh! Heh! we're the Kopites,
The best crowd in the land,
We support a team called Liverpool,
And we're a happy band.

> *They call us unfriendly,*
> *They even call us fools,*
> *But we're just good supporters,*
> *Supporting Liverpool.*
>
> *We'll keep on singing,*
> *The songs are all our own,*
> *Liverpool needn't worry,*
> *They'll never walk alone.*

A BLACK DEED THAT MAKES US SEE RED
22 November 1967

KOP has received a letter which makes the saddest reading. It is authenticated with the name and address of the writer, a publican with premises near Euston Station in London.

'I have read with interest the many letters and articles in which you praise the supporters of Liverpool,' says the writer. 'I will agree that a majority of supporters who follow Liverpool to away matches are good fans and good fellows. But, sadly, I have to report that, for the second time in a year, a hospital box for the blind has been stolen from my pub counter following Liverpool's visit.

'On Saturday 4 November, half a dozen young supporters in red and white scarves were seen carrying my blind box along the Euston Road. Unfortunately, they were not apprehended. I hope you will publish this letter in the hope that all the many good supporters of Liverpool will understand how a minority can let them down.

'For obvious reasons I do not wish my name and address published, but you will understand why, when I hear the chant "We are the best supporters in the land", I cannot agree.'

GREEN, GREEN GRASS OF HOME
5 April 1967

Here's a song I heard to the tune of the Tom Jones record – Green, Green Grass of Home:

The old Kop looks the same,
As I stepped down to watch the game.
There's the old green turf that Liddell used
*   to play on.*
Now St John and Hunt and Peter Thompson
Score a goal when Shankly wants them.
It's good to see the greatest team at home.
Yes, we'll all be there to see big Rowdy,
And the team we worship proudly,
When they bring the league championship
*   back home.*

GERARD EDWARDS
Southdean Road
Liverpool 14

SORRY, EVERYONE
8 November 1967

I was involved in a recent case 'Liverpool fan fined' and I want to say I am very sorry to bring Liverpool's name down. Please believe and forgive me.

MICHAEL J. FATE
Speke
Liverpool 24

LET'S KEEP CHILDREN OUT OF THIS CROWD
8 March 1967

I go on the Kop every home game and am sick and tired of seeing young children being pulled out of the Kop half-way through the game. How they get into the Kop I don't know, but if they come in through the turnstiles they should be stopped. That way children would not get hurt, and the St John Ambulance Brigade men would have less to do.

A. EDWARDS
Church Road
Liverpool 13

SEEING RED!
20 December 1967

One day I was waiting at a bus stop, and two young boys were standing in front of me. One boy was dressed in red, the other in blue. When the bus came, the conductor allowed the boy in blue to get on, but would not let the boy in red on.

The bus was empty. Apparently that conductor was an Everton man. Surely this is not fair.

ANN McKERNAN (aged 12)
Stonedale Crescent
Liverpool 11

THANKS TO BILL AND THE BOYS
6 December 1967

In a recent issue of KOP I saw a letter from a supporter, now in Canada, who told us nothing was too much trouble for Mr Shankly and his boys.

How right he is. My daughter, Stella, was married on 20 October, and her bridegroom, Arthur Daley, is one of the famous Kopites. Unknown to anyone, I wrote to Mr Shankly, asking if he could spare time to send some form of greeting to Arthur on his wedding day, as a surprise.

Some surprise! Instead of sending a telegram, which was the most we expected, Mr Shankly turned up at my house, along with Ian Callaghan, Tony Hateley, Tommy Lawrence, Gerry Byrne, Ron Yeats and Ian St John.

I'll never forget the expression on my son-in-law's face when he saw them. Unfortunately, our only record of a wonderful day are two blurred photographs, for my niece, bless her, couldn't hold the camera steady, because she had just been introduced to Ian Callaghan.

My son-in-law has some paintings done by another Liverpool admirer, and the players all signed these.

I'd like to thank Mr Shankly, and all the lads he

brought along, for making my son-in-law's happy day so much happier.

MRS KAY JONES
58 Skipton Road
Anfield
Liverpool 4

FOR DAPHNE'S SAKE
13 March 1968

I am going to annoy Bill Shankly and please a lass from Wallasey.

She is Daphne Jane Weir, who lives at 33 Edith Road, Seacombe, Wallasey, Cheshire, and she has a story to tell which illustrates the compassion and generosity of our manager, who is reckoned to be one of soccer's sternest taskmasters. In Daphne's own words, written in a letter to us, here is her story:

'I would like to send my thanks, through KOP, to Mr Bill Shankly for his wonderful kindness.

'On Monday 19 February, a friend of mine went to Anfield to buy tickets for the Liverpool–Walsall Cup-tie. After standing for three hours she fainted, and was carried to Mr Shankly's office. When she came to, she found that the two pounds which she had for the tickets had been taken from her hand. Mr Shankly sent someone out to look for it, but as you might guess, it wasn't there. He then gave her the two pounds she had lost, gave her two ten-shilling tickets for the match, and had her driven home.

'We had a wonderful time at the match. I didn't realise football could be so exciting. My thanks to all the team for making it an evening to remember. And to that real gentleman, Bill Shankly.'

Bill will not be pleased at us for printing this true story. We have known of many incidents where he has helped fans out of trouble – and he has dared us to print them. But this time we'll risk his anger to please Daphne.

JAMES LOGAN